URGENT BUSINESS

URGENT BUSINESS

Five Myths Business Needs to Overcome
to Save Itself and the Planet

Ian Thomson and Dominic Bates

BRISTOL
UNIVERSITY
PRESS

First published in Great Britain in 2022 by

Bristol University Press
University of Bristol
1-9 Old Park Hill
Bristol
BS2 8BB
UK
t: +44 (0)117 954 5940
e: bup-info@bristol.ac.uk

Details of international sales and distribution partners are available at bristoluniversitypress.co.uk

Disclaimer: *The content of this publication has not been approved by the United Nations and does not reflect the views of the United Nations or its officials or Member States.*

British Library Cataloguing in Publication Data
A catalogue record for this book is available from the British Library

ISBN 978-1-5292-1759-9 paperback
ISBN 978-1-5292-1760-5 ePub
ISBN 978-1-5292-1761-2 ePdf

Cover design: Nicky Borowiec
Front cover image: AdobeStock_161906381

Bristol University Press uses environmentally responsible print partners.

Printed in Great Britain by CMP, Poole

Contents

Detailed Contents   vi
Acknowledgements   viii
Foreword by Paul Polman   x

Joining the Dots   1

Myth 1: A Successful Business Is a Growing and Profitable One   13
Myth 2: Only Manage What You Can Measure   36
Myth 3: Laser-Like Focus Gets Results   66
Myth 4: The Consumer Is Always Right   93
Myth 5: Irresponsible Decisions Are Made by Irresponsible Leaders   124

Do Something   154

Appendix 1: Get to Know Your Global Goals   166
Appendix 2: Connecting Purpose with the Global Goals and Systems   168
            that Underpin Them
Appendix 3: The Resilience Assessment Workbook   170
Appendix 4: Carbon Scoping   172

Further Reading   174
Glossary   178
Endnotes   181
References   190
Index   208

Detailed Contents

Acknowledgements   viii

Foreword by Paul Polman   x

Joining the Dots   **1**

Interconnectedness and the freedom to create new possibilities   1

The Sustainable Development Goals and a new 'heroic' purpose   3
for business

Busting the five business myths   5

A manifesto for responsible business   9

Do what you can when you can, but do something   10

Myth 1: A Successful Business Is a Growing and Profitable One   **13**

Values and breaking free from the profit-and-loss mindset   13

Anti-profit beliefs and the trade-off fallacy   15

The rise (and rediscovery) of the responsible business   19

Using the Global Goals to help map the purpose of a business   24

Going beyond compliance to build resilience and public trust   28

The positive multiplier effect of common goals and becoming   31
citizen scientists

Myth 2: Only Manage What You Can Measure   **36**

Invisibles, ignorance and measuring what you treasure   36

SIMPLE measures, aligned metrics and the importance of accurate   42
data

Selective reporting, materiality and embracing openness   45

Misleading metrics, alternative accounting and the rise of external   50
accountability

Accountants as scientists, radical uncertainty and the feedback loop   53

Thresholds, coveillance, market failure and accountancy in   57
a post-truth world

Myth 3: Laser-Like Focus Gets Results   **66**

Single-issue campaigns and unintended consequences   66

German bee colonies and the seduction of monocausal narratives   68

Exceptionalism, systemic resilience and cross-sector partnerships 71
Carbon literacy and the social boomerang effect 79
A circular economy and closing the loop 84
The business ecosystem and working with nature 88

Myth 4: The Consumer Is Always Right **93**
The gap between intention and behaviour and the opportunity for 93
    business to help bridge it
Misinformation, mistrust and the confusion of labelling 96
Consumer paralysis, biases, emotions and values 101
Social practice, herd mentality and business citizenship 106
Business as a social movement and engaging customers as supporters 111
Supporter-owned football clubs, the GAME system and the dangers 115
    of woke capitalism

Myth 5: Irresponsible Decisions Are Made by Irresponsible **124**
Leaders
The amplifying effect of power, initial framing and solution aversion 124
Why we lead, the poison of external motives and the new 128
    distributive models of leadership
Process-driven decision-making and the power of teams 133
Actipreneurialism, workplace culture and the value of diversity 139
    and inclusion
Managing trust, innovating and adopting a sustainable mindset 146

Do Something **154**
Creating your own business roadmap to responsibility 154
Beyond 2030 and the Global Goals 161

Appendix 1: Get to Know Your Global Goals 166
Appendix 2: Connecting Purpose with the Global Goals and Systems 168
    that Underpin Them
Appendix 3: The Resilience Assessment Workbook 170
Appendix 4: Carbon Scoping 172

Further Reading 174
Glossary 178
Endnotes 181
References 190
Index 208

Acknowledgements

This book has been inspired, enabled and shaped by many wonderful colleagues and collaborators. It stands on the shoulders of numerous giants: those pioneers in academia and business who decided to break the mould as to what business could and should do. Their efforts have laid the foundations for the next stage in the evolution of business.

This book would not be possible without the generous funding provided by Lloyds Banking Group. In partnership with Birmingham Business School and the University of Birmingham, they helped create something special: the Lloyds Banking Group Centre for Responsible Business, an interdisciplinary research centre able to embrace the many challenges of making business responsible and sustainable. It is work that we have distilled and synthesized into this book.

We would like to take this opportunity to thank Benedict Brogan, Fiona Cannon, Petra Watkinson, Rachel Vann, Ross Gardner and Geraldine Boylan from Lloyds for their enthusiastic support and help with the strategic direction of the Centre from the very beginning. We would also like to acknowledge the contribution of other grants to complement our work, including Business in the Community, the Economic and Social Research Council, the Institute for Global Innovation and Procter & Gamble Company.

From the inception of *Urgent Business*, our advisory board has enhanced – and challenged – its shape and content. Its members' insights and creativity pushed us into new spaces and further than we initially thought possible. And their experience and expertise have infused this book, undoubtedly making it all the better for their engagement. In particular, we would like to thank David Urquhart, Nicola Templeton, Tom Levitt, Jean Templeton, Andraea Dawson-Shepherd and Fred Wherry.

The many speakers, panellists, contributors and participants at our Centre's conferences, workshops and webinars have been another source of inspiration. Listening to these experts from different fields, joining in conversations and even the odd throwaway line enriched the body of knowledge that we drew on in the writing of the book. These events were expertly curated by the irrepressible Sophie Sinclair, who also created a culture of cooperation and shared value that has paid dividends. She has been ably supported by our comms experts Chloe Carpenter and Holly Brain.

We have been struck by the generosity of so many people who share our commitment to transform businesses along an equitable and sustainable trajectory, in particular, our team of associates within the Business School and organizations we have been privileged to work alongside, which include Business in the Community, World Wide Generation and West Midlands Combined Authority.

We must acknowledge our intellectual indebtedness to the Centre's incredible team of researchers, whose studies formed the baseload for this book. Professor Kiran Trehan, Dr Christoph Biehl, Professor Andy Mullineux, Dr Jennifer TyreeHageman, Dr Nana Osei Bonsu, Dr Juliet Kele, Dr Immaculate Motsi-Omoijiade, Dr Grigorios Lamprinakos, Dr Ivan Rajic, Dr Madlen Sobkowiak and Nicholas Bailey helped co-create *Urgent Business* with their ideas, discussions, research papers, writing, proofing, feedback, encouragement and support.

Finally, we would like to thank Paul Stevens and all at Bristol University Press for all their support and valuable professional advice helping us make this book as good as it possibly could be.

Cheers
Ian and Dom

Foreword

Paul Polman, former CEO of Unilever and co-author of
Net Positive: How Courageous Companies Thrive
by Giving More than They Take

There's no doubting anymore. We're in a race against time to avert a climate catastrophe that poses an existential threat to humanity. We urgently need to start living within our planetary boundaries, before we trigger irreversible tipping points that do permanent damage to our biodiversity and critical ecosystems – nature's guarantors of happy, healthy and prosperous societies.

This challenge alone should fill us with huge anxiety about the future, but we also face an immediate crisis today that should make us feel equally nauseous: hideous inequality that leaves billions behind without dignity or hope. Regrettably, the coronavirus pandemic has only exacerbated these existing disparities in wealth, with an unfolding economic emergency that could push hundreds of millions more into extreme poverty.

Capitalism, as it currently stands, is rightly seen as the author of these perverse outcomes and held up as a damaged ideology unfit for the 21st century. It's clear that we've reached a critical inflection point and must now carve a new path for the betterment of civilization: one built on sustainable, regenerative values as our engine of progress – not infinite growth.

That responsibility falls to every section of society, as we need unprecedented collective action to move at speed and scale. Governments, academia, NGOs, the scientific community and tech innovators all need to join together in deep strategic partnerships. But there is one group that can arguably make the biggest contribution – and that's businesses.

There are more and more examples of world-beating companies that enhance their performance by taking responsibility for their entire societal impact, embracing diversity and inclusion and using ESG (environmental, social and governance) metrics to strengthen their business models and strategies. While even the smallest enterprises are finding success adopting a long-term, multi-stakeholder approach that puts purpose and values at their core.

You'll find many of these inspiring companies in this book, which is unflinching in ascribing business's leading role in causing the world's most pressing problems but passionately believes in its power and ingenuity to address them just as dramatically. Yet the authors recognize that outdated and myth-bound thinking is holding businesses back from realizing their full potential on sustainability, as well as a genuine lack of knowledge and confidence about how to go about it.

Well, no more. Over the following pages, anyone interested in beginning or enhancing their sustainability journey will find the latest research-backed tools, practice and arguments you need to create a customized responsible roadmap, bring your stakeholders with you and join others in supporting the United Nations' vision for a better world by 2030 – no matter how big or small your company.

As someone who helped develop the UN's Global Goals, I know how crucial this fast-disappearing 'decade of action' is to averting an apocalyptic future that nature never intended, and humankind never anticipated. Which is why this book is so important in helping translate the Goals into practical steps every business can take now to play their part in this most vital of missions. So read on with urgency. Time may be running out, but together there's no limit to what we can achieve.

Joining the Dots

Interconnectedness and the freedom to create new possibilities

There is something simple and seductive in connecting dots. Many of us will remember spending 'dreich days' indoors as children, solving dot-to-dot puzzle books, searching for the next number in the mass of apparently randomly arranged dots. Watching a sequence of straight lines slowly reveal a hidden picture could be wondrous and satisfying. And that sense of accomplishment would grow as the number and complexity of dots increased with each page turned.

This instinctive drive to keep 'joining the dots' stays with us into adulthood – through education and on into our working lives – together with that pleasure of uncovering new insights, patterns and possibilities. But alongside it, a nagging feeling sometimes develops that things aren't quite right. That there are dots or connections missing that could help us better understand the problems we're presented with and their solutions.

Our achievements at work are often limited to meeting challenges set by others. The puzzles that accountants, for instance, are charged with completing are usually rigid and simplistic. So it's no surprise that the black-and-white pictures drawn by accounting can seem abstract, incomplete and one-dimensional, lacking any necessary depth or nuance. Yet accountants are often the only ones attempting to formally represent and connect together bits of an organization. And their monochrome reports are still hugely powerful in influencing critical decisions.

It's only in other areas of our lives – like art, activism, volunteering and academia – that many of us get the freedom to recognize and explore those missing dots that gnaw at us. These roles encourage curiosity and learning from others, which help us to imagine new ways of connecting the dots, insert new ones or change the picture entirely. It's that sense of freedom to make connections that is so important for understanding the role of business in sustainability – and this is what this book will help you

1

to do. Because joining the dots, uncovering connections, creating new patterns, possibilities and pathways lies at the very heart of responsible business transformation.

In many ways, businesses have always innovated and brought together new ideas and actions. But right now, the spider senses of business leaders around the world have been tingling for some time. Vulnerability and precariousness are growing, while perceptions of predictability and control are dissolving. Previously successful business models are failing and out of step with what the natural and social world will allow. Powerful stakeholders are increasingly challenging existing recipes for success, as evidence of their harmful impacts accumulates.

We are living in a world struggling to nourish all those who live in it, a world choking on its own waste while consuming its resources quicker than they can be replenished; a world increasingly hostile to humanity where difference or illness can lead to homelessness, exclusion, poverty, hunger or premature death. Many ecosystems, species and communities are precariously balanced on tipping points. And the risks and hazards of unfettered consumption that were recklessly cast into the future are now boomeranging back at us as we rush headlong towards them.

Given such dire circumstances, there can be no more unimaginative 'business as usual' thinking that can't see beyond deadly efficiency and incentivizing the pursuit of unsustainability. We need a new set of dots, with a vision to spot the gaps and a greater capacity to draw fresh connections that will help businesses to fulfil their responsible purpose and the essential roles assigned to them in a new, more sustainable world.

This book provides some of those dots, suggests where to find others, and demonstrates how to connect them, all the while explaining the wider value of doing so and setting out practical, positive pathways any business can follow to get started. You'll find out how, for instance, to join the dots between climate change and a company's procurement activities, connect an employee's performance to theories of behaviour, and discover how products contribute to social value.

This new model of interconnectedness reveals how business aligns or misaligns with society and nature, which helps better predict consequences (both negative and positive) and dramatically improves decision-making. There is no dichotomy between business and the rest of the world. And by relinquishing that exceptionalist mindset, companies open themselves up to many more solutions that can help fix the shared problems of sustainability. We are smarter than ever before and inventive enough to do things differently while still creating value. And with the arrival of the United Nations' (UN) Sustainable Development Goals in 2015, there is now a collective legitimacy – and urgency – for business to play its full and proper part in the complex world in which we live.

The Sustainable Development Goals and a new 'heroic' purpose for business

Every age needs a vision that helps make sense of today and shapes future thinking. The UN's Sustainable Development Goals[1] (or Global Goals) are such an aspirational rallying point for change. A blueprint of hope agreed by world leaders, they're an amazing vision of a harmonious, equitable and resilient world fit for our future.

Borrowing from business strategy and leading business practices, the Global Goals are a pragmatic statement of contributions required from governments, businesses, civil society and individual citizens. They're a game-changer in how they reimagine the purpose and role of business, providing a strategic framework to mobilize the sector's creativity and resources to secure a more sustainable world by 2030. A future where responsible businesses flourish, protecting the resources on which they depend, creating value and contributing to the resilience of our planet.

Importantly, the Global Goals have also helped define what 'doing business responsibly' actually means, translating a fuzzy concept that has been in use for years into 17 goals broken down into measurable targets that – even if imperfect – everyone can understand and agree on. As such, they provide a new consensus and vocabulary for negotiating the purpose of all organizations, including businesses, and account for what is valued, valuable and socially acceptable. All that time wasted in the past debating what sustainability or a responsible business is can now be spent doing something about them.

While business has accomplished some wonderful things for society, it has the potential to do so much more. The collective intelligence of everyone employed in business is stunning. The resources at its command and its ability to pivot them to countless different ends wherever they're needed outguns many nation states. They can channel knowledge from anywhere, invent life-changing technologies and collaborate to produce rapid solutions on a huge scale (just look at how COVID-19 vaccines were produced in months rather than decades). Business leaders, too, can inspire huge levels of commitment, dedication and effort, while their employees include the brightest and best of our youth.

So just imagine if we could take this awesome capacity and channel it under the shared direction of the Global Goals. The heroic challenges of eradicating poverty and countering climate change may not seem so far-fetched. At the very least, any decision or action by a business should help move us, even in a miniscule way, closer to the Global Goals. After all, these concepts aren't new or a passing fad; they represent fundamental values of justice, balance and equality that stretch right through human history and recognize business as deeply embedded in and dependent on the welfare of society and nature. It's only more recently that we've chosen to ignore the latter.

Medieval cathedral builders, for instance, understood that the oak beams holding up the roof would one day need replacing. So, knowing that it took at least 100 years to grow trees that could make suitable replacements, they planted seeds at the same time as construction. A few acorns to future-proof their creation and replace the oaks that were cut down – this was sustainable practice at its most elegant and straightforward.

Today, we define a sustainable business as one that contributes more widely to the resilience of the many socio-ecological systems that underpin the Global Goals – because without ensuring the long-term health and stability of all life on Earth, no human activity can thrive. To do this requires a renewed focus on the areas where a business intersects and encounters these natural systems, particularly in relation to critical thresholds of 'slow moving' systems such as global climate.

It's in these everyday relationships that we take for granted, between each other and nature, where sustainability emerges. Just because we don't appreciate peat bogs, marine plankton or tropical forests for the clean air we breathe and our 'Goldilocks' climate (neither too hot nor too cold) doesn't mean we escape our fundamental relationship to them and our mutual dependency. That's why the Global Goals are so useful: they provide a pragmatic survival guide for identifying that interconnectivity and creating a more sustainable future.

Unfortunately, there's still a widespread perception that sustainability is too complicated for most business leaders. Many companies, they say, just don't have the power or capacity to participate in such an ambitious global challenge. This book rejects that premise. From a UK social enterprise that uses its profits to help girls in India complete their schooling[2] to a corporate multinational aiming to reverse climate change through its carbon-absorbing products and factories,[3] you'll discover many inspiring examples over the following pages of companies with ambitious and often ingenious solutions to the problems raised by the Global Goals.

What prevents so many others from joining them are outdated myths that business still clings to, which entrap and limit what is deemed possible. We identify five of the most pernicious in this book, dedicating a chapter to each that challenges their contemporary relevance and reveals the enormous self-harm they encourage when enacted today. The Global Goals allow us to rewrite this mythical business narrative that seems incapable of acknowledging the damage it causes or envisioning any alternative. Once freed from these potent myths, every business can begin to unleash its sustainability potential.

Busting the five business myths

Why is it we can be so accepting of truisms, mantras and mottos, even as the case against them becomes more and more compelling? Many of them do contain useful knowledge or wisdom gleaned from the past experience of others, but, like all theories, they need an upgrade every now and again or they can become barriers to change.

There was once a process engineer at a factory, whose nickname was 'The Why Man'. In interviews conducted with his colleagues for a research paper, everyone described him as having almost mythical powers, knowing everything there was to know about the plant. Yet, when the researchers eventually met him face to face, he confessed to not actually knowing that much but was just really good at asking questions. It worried him how easy it was to expose the myths that other people thought in the workplace (including the mythical opinion they had of him!). So, by behaving like a child, he would politely keep asking 'why?' and carefully listen to the reply until he was convinced of the truth or the other person gave up. Generally, he said, five whys[4] were enough to get to the bottom of things.

We've taken that same child-like approach to challenging five of contemporary business's biggest sacred cows. Like 'The Why Man' we don't know all the answers and we don't claim to be the first to raise these questions (nor do we expect to be the last). That's why you'll find numerous 'dilemma' boxes throughout this book, where we highlight some of the more difficult and long-running business conundrums that often have no easy answers. But we'll look at the growing body of evidence for and against them, and hope to empower you to ask better questions of those who should know the answers.

Myth 1: A Successful Business Is a Growing and Profitable One

An MBA student was researching why a radical and more sustainable form of salmon ranching using lights and robot fish[5] wasn't adopted commercially. When he asked 12 business leaders who had the idea pitched to them why they turned it down, their universal reason was that it wouldn't be profitable. But digging deeper (with more 'whys'), he discovered that all of them had different definitions of profit and how it was calculated, and their theories of what made a good business had very little to do with profits or growth. Instead, they became quite philosophical about other life goals and how to achieve them through their companies.

So, while many business schools continue to teach the conventional idea that the purpose of business is to maximize profits and continuously grow, experience and research suggests nothing could be further from the truth. Most people working hard in local family businesses, cooperatives, social enterprises and even multinational corporations don't just want to make a buck; they also value fulfilling the needs and wants of others and protecting the planet for future generations.

Shouldn't a chef who only wants to make the food she loves in the same restaurant, for customers who share that love and come back time after time, be considered successful? Why would a farm entering the fifth generation of family ownership be a failure just because it doesn't always increase its yields or expand its operations? This book will challenge the narrow textbook definition of business success, explaining why profit maximization is irresponsible and growth should be a choice, and ultimately asks what the purpose of business and profits really is.

Myth 2: Only Manage What You Can Measure

As this book is being written, the world is at last recognizing our climate emergency, with nations, communities and businesses scrambling to become 'net zero' without really knowing what this entails. Climate change is often considered to be impossibly complicated to understand, written about in a special language seemingly only spoken by a secret sect of self-appointed planetary guardians. It's all buzzwords, formulas, statistics, % of GDP, and 'scope this' and 'scope that'.

But while carbon emissions may be difficult to measure, reducing them is often not that complicated, costly or difficult. The science tells us that every carbon molecule not emitted makes a difference, and that once carbon dioxide gets into the atmosphere, it will affect our climate for thousands of years. Our emissions from driving to work rather than cycling today will thicken the atmospheric blanket for millennia. It's sobering to think that the very first carbon emissions of just one of us writing this book – a one-and-a-half-mile trip home from Simpson Memorial Maternity Pavilion in their grandfather's Ford Anglia 105E – are still contributing to global warming and will be until at least 3962. In fact, right now one of us currently owes the world around 500 tonnes of carbon emissions, and unless he becomes net zero from now on, will end up with a personal carbon debt of around 800 tonnes.

So while businesses struggle to understand and measure their true carbon footprint, they cannot wait to start managing and take responsibility for their carbon debt now. Carbon emissions are already a cost and liability to business, and are predicted to grow dramatically. But like so many sustainability risks, these costs are currently obscured in conventional accounting systems. While this book will suggest new metrics and open-access reporting that better capture these risks, it will also encourage companies to take action in areas where scientific understanding is still emerging – such as environmental tipping points – because the biggest risks come from where business isn't looking, and will demand more proactive management before they can be properly measured.

Myth 3: Laser-Like Focus Gets Results

The science fiction novel *The Hitchhiker's Guide to the Galaxy* describes a delightful planet called Bethselamin, whose beauty attracted billions of holidaymakers from all over the galaxy for centuries. Tourism businesses boomed, consuming resources at alarming rates, until the planet teetered on the edge of collapse: 'Thus today the net balance between the amount you eat and the amount you excrete while on the planet is surgically removed from your body weight when you leave; so every time you go to the lavatory there, it is vitally important to get a receipt.'[6]

The author, Douglas Adams, is obviously writing for comic effect, but such a strident and simplistic strategy for sustainability by business leaders here on Earth can have unintended consequences that are similarly absurd. Research has shown that 'bag for life' schemes in the UK, for example, designed to reduce single-use plastics by customers, actually ended up increasing supermarkets' overall plastic footprint, while plastic-free alternatives are often worse for carbon emissions and consumption of natural resources.

This book will explore how business's laser-like focus and predilection for simple solutions can have this paradoxical outcome when dealing with sustainability, since they fail to take account of how complex, circular and interconnected the systems that support life on Earth are. All of today's problems have come from yesterday's solutions and – we'll argue – require the kind of collaborative, systemic response that business rarely mythologizes. Because unlike the visitors to Bethselamin, there isn't a simple transaction an individual business can settle on its way out. None of us can escape our planetary mess nor clean it up alone, no matter how focused and determined we are.

Myth 4: The Consumer Is Always Right

An exhausted customer walks into a supermarket after a long shift at work, stressing about picking up the kids in time and trying to remember how much they have to spend to fill an empty fridge. Then suddenly they morph into an all-powerful being, prowling the aisles for human rights abuses and rogue plastic, mentally calculating the social and environmental impact of each product they pluck form the shelf. As their trolley fills, their pride grows, knowing they are transforming the world into a sustainable utopia with every purchase they make.

Sounds ridiculous, doesn't it? Yet, in the minds of many experts, the ethical consumer is just a newer version of the outdated 'sovereign consumer' archetype borrowed from academic economics, imbued with the same mythical powers of wisdom and rationality, who can lead the market and compel business to change for the better. But who really has the time, power and expertise to make a difference? The tired, stressed consumer trying to optimize hundreds of purchase decisions from 60,000 product lines in 45 minutes? Or the companies and procurement professionals whose job is to put suitable products on the shelves in the first place.

While this book still advocates a vital role for consumers in responsible business, we argue it must go beyond the transactional. Companies should engage with their customers more like supporters with shared values around the Global Goals, while using their privileged position to help bring about wider social change. A new level of transparency and trust is essential for making this relationship work, as is avoiding the temptation to 'woke-wash' purely for commercial gain – because being authentic and making the right choices isn't just the responsibility of consumers.

Myth 5: Irresponsible Decisions Are Made by Irresponsible Leaders

The CEO of a paper manufacturer was once being interviewed as part of research into how well sustainable businesses were performing. He was indignant that the company was without blemish, taking proper care of its waste, local habitats and the community. Besides, he stressed, he was a responsible local councillor with a wife who sat on the local environmental network.

But two weeks later, the academic conducting the research got a bemused phone call. After following up on his own claims, the CEO had discovered numerous areas where the business was failing to recycle properly, his delivery drivers were routinely abandoning waste, and overflow from the factory was entering the local river. He confronted his senior team and they rightly pointed out all these problems had been made clear in their management reports. He apologized and asked for the researcher's help. The academic never told him that it was his wife – who also sat on the company board – who had tipped him off about what questions to ask him!

It just shows how even business leaders who are proudly committed to sustainability can unwittingly find themselves making irresponsible decisions. This book explores how a new model of inclusive leadership can help mitigate against these oversights and improve decision-making by encouraging a more systemic approach that listens to all stakeholders and employees. The latest behavioural psychology brutally exposes how the way our brains work makes it impossible for individuals to make decisions uncorrupted by bias and self-interest. So responsible leaders must become more aware of these flaws in themselves and others if they're going to properly grapple with the sustainability of their business.

A manifesto for responsible business

The science of responsible business is still in its infancy, which is why, at the end of each myth-busting chapter we summarize our observations and academic research-based theories of responsible business so they can be applied and tested by others. But we want this book to be more than an academic exercise and bring about real change. So, as well as suggesting a 'positive pathway' to bust each myth within your own organization, we've created a 15-point 'manifesto for responsible business' that encapsulates all the arguments to come.

THE RESPONSIBLE BUSINESS MANIFESTO

1. Make profits in pursuit of purpose rather than maximizing profits.
2. Choose whether to grow or not, and minimize any damage of expansion.
3. Balance the interests of all stakeholders and ecosystems, not just those of the owners.
4. Use performance metrics that accurately measure impact and align with the Global Goals.
5. Be fully transparent by using open-access reporting based on the Global Goals.
6. Use technology, including AI, to help avoid triggering unforeseen tipping points in our ecosystems.
7. Respect planetary boundaries and seek collaborative, circular solutions.
8. Work collectively to build society and nature's resilience and avoid systemic risks.

9. Understand the systemic nature of any problem to find its most effective solution.
10. Give consumers clear and trusted information to enable responsible choices.
11. Value the trust and support of the people you depend on.
12. Use your privilege to enhance society and nature.
13. Don't reward or incentivize irresponsible behaviour.
14. Create an inclusive culture that respects the dignity of your staff and stakeholders.
15. Prioritize the sustainability of the planet over your business.

Do what you can when you can, but do something

It's worth remembering that the most common outcome for a business is failure – barely half survive five years,[7] let alone blossom or flourish. They are fragile, weak entities, heavily dependent on the societies and ecosystems they evolve alongside. No business has a right to exist and they're promptly wound up once they no longer fulfil any social purpose.

Yet a business can also be omnipresent and immortal. Centuries-old corporations can redistribute resources among individuals, natural systems, institutions and public institutions across vast time and space. Many businesses leave legacies of valuable infrastructure (and sometimes terrible damage too) that continue long after the owner or the business has died.

So whether you're a small startup trying to survive or a multinational wielding its corporate might, we urgently need the heroic efforts of 'doing business' to include meeting the Global Goals by the UN's 2030 deadline. Progress has been made, but business has to be more ambitious to realize its transformational potential. While it might be unrealistic to expect any company to become immediately or completely sustainable, every business should have the courage to take small, practical steps in the right direction – which is why this book suggests a 'positive pathway' any business can follow at the end of each myth-busting chapter. Acting early on sustainability will have a greater impact than acting late, while also causing less disruption and costing less overall.

At the very least, businesses should try not to make things worse. There comes a time to stop digging, and there are many ways to make things better. If business could redirect its creativity from generating excuses for not doing things to minimizing the suffering of others, we could move from repressed guilt to pride in our work. This includes not letting perfect be the enemy of the good for fear of being called out. Just because you can't get rid of all plastics in your products or employ every homeless person doesn't mean you shouldn't reduce your packaging or help one refugee to find work.

Just imagine making a Zoom call to a dust-covered, hungry child hacking away in a mine to explain that your company board has decided to turn down the opportunity to improve their working conditions because it would only fix 10% of your supply chains. You could try convincing the child of your integrity by proudly telling them your business doesn't buy Fairtrade coffee either, because it only increases wages by 30%, which is still below the living wage level. Then finish on a positive note by saying that once there's a sure-fire global initiative to eliminate all child labour across the mining industry, you'll get right on it!

The point is that while bold ambitions are important, there is nothing wrong with moving purposefully forward in small, simple steps and picking the low-hanging fruit. A good change delayed is suffering enhanced, and those suffering won't care about claims of virtue signalling. If it seems impossible for you to imagine a zero carbon version of your business, why not focus on getting rid of slavery in your supply chain or ending workplace discrimination against gender, race, religion or disabilities? You could ensure the price you pay for goods and services is sufficient to eliminate hunger, or plant trees to promote greater biodiversity. The list of positive contributions a business can make is almost endless. Just do what you can when you can.

If business doesn't start to pivot from unsustainability towards the Global Goals, the harsh reality is that our future is bleak. In the minds of much of the public, business has already turned to the dark side. The evidence of its harmful activities is mounting, and drastic environmental tipping points have been reached.[8] Time is running out, but we have not run out of time. Nor have we run out of ideas or businesses willing to listen and daring to be different.

This book is a challenge to 'business as usual', including the mistakes of past sustainable business practice. It's not looking to blame but to understand why previous good intentions failed, presenting new and better possibilities based on the latest scientific research. It will be provocative and at times unsettling. Our journey writing this book was also disturbing as we joined the dots between our everyday production and consumption and such travesties as modern slavery, looming climate collapse, poverty and hunger. But recognizing these links also opened our eyes to the enormous influence business could have on these global issues if it chose to use its privileged position in the world to bring about more good than ill.

We'll admit now, we won't tell you precisely what a perfect sustainable version of your business should be. But with the various tools and resources provided, we can help you define it for yourself and map out the potential challenges and solutions. It won't be easy, but imagine how good it will feel working for a company that has successfully rid its procurement of child labour, eliminated the gender pay gap or cut its carbon footprint by half. Think how proud, rather than ashamed, people would be of any business that joined the international effort to help realize the Global Goals and a more sustainable world.

The stage is set for every business to repurpose itself. It's decision time. Will you continue to cling to irresponsible models, persist with outdated myths and deliberately ignore emerging facts? Or will you read on, start joining the dots and take the next steps to becoming a truly responsible business? Whatever you choose to do about sustainability, please do something. There really is no business more urgent.

A Successful Business Is a Growing and Profitable One

Values and breaking free from the profit-and-loss mindset

If we told you a company was losing a billion dollars a year, had ceased paying dividends to its shareholders years ago, and was just weeks from going bankrupt, would you think it was successful? What if, soon after shares had slumped to an all-time low of just a few dollars, it fired its CEO and cancelled 70% of its product lines? You'd probably think it was a company in terminal free-fall.

Yet the name of that company so close to collapse in 1997 was Apple Inc. And having grown into one of the world's biggest companies today, it can now boast of profits in the tens of billions, regular, healthy dividend payments and bestselling products that enjoy an almost cult-like status.

So what does this potted financial history of Apple tell you about the nature of success? Well, not very much if you just stick to the money – because it omits all of the most interesting and important ingredients, and how they're configured and catalysed to create something unique.

It says nothing about the impact of the maverick Steve Jobs, returning to the company he'd co-founded in his parents' garage. No mention is made of the obsessive drive for design and quality that led to the creation of the ground-breaking iMac, iPod and iPhone in quick succession, each one more wildly popular than the other. And it leaves out Microsoft's extraordinary

US$150 million deal with their arch rivals to end years of legal battles and secure the company's future – a deal that broke almost all the rules of competitive business, and a rare corporate example of collaborative survival.[1]

Of course, it also misses out on decades of allegations over sweatshop labour, toxic waste and tax avoidance too. But the point is, there is far more to Apple's story of success than just its admittedly spectacular finances, which is why there are so many Hollywood films, books and magazine articles wanting to tell it. Because what makes a business successful in the eyes of more than just its owners and shareholders goes beyond profitability and wealth, otherwise multinational and state oil companies would be as popularly feted as Apple.

There are many things that make a company admired and give meaning to any success story. The provenance and quality of its products, the heritage and skills involved in their manufacture, and the passion, pride and dignity of the people involved can all paint a compelling picture of a firm's positive impacts. And these often less tangible, non-financial aspects of a business that a company also deems important are sometimes referred to as its 'values'. Just like people, all companies have and are led by values – whether knowingly or not. And since values are held in common with everyone in society (unlike profits), they have a far greater reach and potential impact than their intangibility might suggest.

While making a profit and growth is part of any business, it's an incomplete measure of success and is always accompanied by other values that are equally important to its performance. Not only are these values key to determining the quality of what they do and how they do it; they can also provide a statement of purpose about what a company stands for, why it exists and what kind of world it wants to create. And it's against these non-financial commitments that a business and how it uses its profits is also held accountable.

For Apple, that purpose was first outlined in 1981 in a memo to management called 'Apple Values'. The 12-point list opened with a utopian vision of 'One person, one computer' and continued with a series of idealistic declarations, such as 'We build products we believe in' and 'Each person is important'. Of course, a primary concern for the rapidly growing company back then – which the values sought to resolve – was how to maintain a culture of high standards and quality as its workforce expanded. But there was one, more outward-looking value that still stands out today: 'We are here to make a positive difference in society, as well as make a profit.'[2]

It's a value in modern business that seemed decades ahead of its time and has only become more mainstream in recent years (although, as we'll see later, it was really a rediscovery of something that's been part of business for centuries). Today the annual reports of major corporates boast of their 'social value' alongside profits and share price, with sustainability strategies that not only aim to 'do less harm' but also positively impact society and the environment. Yet it's taken a sequence of unprecedented socio-economic crises, the latest being the COVID-19 pandemic, to show how fragilely held those sustainable values can be for some companies.

Whether it's the retail and pub chains that risked staff safety by demanding sites stay open at the start of the pandemic,[3] or the blighted aviation industry battling against planned environmental taxes to curb emissions,[4] some businesses clearly still believe that prioritizing people and the planet is too costly to their bottom line, rather than seeing them as essential to future profitability of any kind. The problem here isn't companies wanting to be profitable; it's the relentless drive to maximize profits regardless of the consequences. But with the climate emergency becoming ever greater and most countries (and many companies) committed to 'net zero' emissions by 2050, it would be astonishing if businesses abandoned sustainability measures just when they needed ramping up.

Fortunately, many companies do recognize that prioritizing short-term profits over the long-term sustainability of the planet is irresponsible and ultimately self-destructive. Yet the binary logic of profit-and-loss can still dominate how their sustainable values are framed, determining even how they're articulated (just look at the highly financialized language around carbon offsetting, impact investing and green bonds). Sustainability is too often portrayed as being in tension with profitability, rather than them being deeply interconnected and dependent on one another. Similarly, the 'social value' of a company is usually recognized in simple, transactional terms of cost and impact, rather than the complex, interactional reality[5] (which we'll explore in more detail later in the book). But if companies want to avoid their sustainable values being the first casualty of any shock to the business, it's essential they break free of this trade-off mindset and embrace a more holistic approach.

Anti-profit beliefs and the trade-off fallacy

The idea that doing good involves some kind of sacrifice is deeply ingrained in our psyche – and in business too. It's an age-old trope central to our moral and religious beliefs, which demands that we lose or deny ourselves something in order to do the right thing. And who would argue that less selfishness and a little more altruism wouldn't make the world a better place? Unfortunately, this idea is a real barrier to the whole concept of sustainable business.

In a 2017 study[6] of people's perceptions of 40 Fortune 500 firms, profit was found to be overwhelmingly negatively associated with perceived value to society. Describing them as 'anti-profit beliefs', the researchers concluded it was very difficult to persuade the public that ethical and profitable business practices do not fundamentally conflict – even if they're presented with objective social responsibility data that suggests otherwise. Put simply: people think companies can't do good *and* make money. And even if some very profitable ethical businesses know this not to be true, the same 'anti-profit beliefs' can hamper companies from being even more radical in their sustainable practices.

But sustainability isn't in a zero-sum relationship with profit. Neither is there a hostile market or mythical amoral shareholder waiting to punish any sustainable measure that doesn't deliver greater sales and instant returns. In fact, one carpet tile manufacturing company, Interface, has turned this whole 'anti-profit belief' on its head, substantially increasing sales and profits through its self-professed 'shoot for the moon' sustainable business strategy. The company's founder, the late Ray Anderson, enthusiastically called it: 'Doing well by doing good'.

Anderson was a pioneer of so-called 'modular carpets' when he started the business in 1973, and quickly became the world's largest manufacturer of them. It was 20 years later, after reading Paul Hawken's book *The Ecology of Commerce*, and having what he described as a 'spear in the chest' moment, that he decided to become a pioneer of sustainability too. He immediately committed his company to 'Mission Zero', which aimed to eliminate any negative environmental impact by 2020.

'When Ray stood up in '94 and said, "We're going to be a sustainable company", sustainability wasn't fashionable; we had no roadmap', Interface's President Nigel Stansfield told *GreenBiz* in 2016. 'It was outrageous to think that an organisation could get to a zero footprint, and we were ridiculed for it. People stood on the sideline and watched us, waiting for us to fail.'[7]

But Anderson's lofty ambition spurred a remarkable effort to transform Interface's billion-dollar operations, driving down greenhouse gas (GHG) emissions from their factories by 96% over two decades, from $1.46kg/m^2$ to just $0.12kg/m^2$, and halving the energy used to make its products. By 2019, the firm had also slashed water consumption and landfill waste by 90%, achieved 89% renewable energy use across all its sites, and took 60% of its raw materials from recycled or bio-based sources.[8]

It meant Interface felt justified in declaring that they'd accomplished their mission a year ahead of target. And while achieving a zero environmental footprint may be impossible, the firm felt they were close enough to warrant creating another 'moonshot' mission – this time called 'Climate Take Back' – aiming to give back more than they extract from the Earth and actually help reverse global warming. It sounds like pure fantasy until you learn they've already developed a 'carbon negative' carpet tile that absorbs carbon dioxide and is fully recyclable.

But what makes Interface's sustainability story even more remarkable is their financial performance over the same period of transition. From sales of $625 million in 1993, Interface's revenues had doubled to $1.2 billion in 2018 with an extraordinary gross profit margin of 40%. Far from harming the growth of the business or market competitiveness, Interface's drive for sustainability created a virtuous circle that dovetailed and spiralled with their profits.

'I always make the business case for sustainability', Ray Anderson said before his death in 2011. 'It's so compelling. Our costs are down, not up. Our products are the best they have ever been. Our people are motivated by a shared higher purpose – esprit de corps to die for. And the goodwill in the marketplace – it's just been astonishing.'[9]

Interface's inspiring story demonstrates that there needn't always be a trade-off between sustainability and profit – even for a publicly listed, behemoth multinational looking to reform decades of ingrained operations at a time when such measures were far from mainstream. Of course, there were many difficulties and setbacks for Interface along the way. An early scheme to lease carpet tiles – so Interface could own, maintain and reclaim them better – struggled because customers were initially reluctant to move a capital cost to their operating budget (but the lease model did eventually take off, as we'll see later). And the company regularly faced accusations of 'greenwashing' still unsustainable parts of the business or failing in their duty to generate maximum returns for their shareholders.[10] But Anderson encouraged experimentation and tolerance of failure[11] in pursuit of the company's purpose, and anticipated a growing zeitgeist for sustainability.

'There is no more strategic issue for a company, or any organization, than its ultimate purpose', he said in a keynote speech way back in 2005.[12] 'For those who think business exists to make a profit, I suggest they think again. Business makes a profit to exist. Surely it must exist for some higher, nobler purpose than that.'

In politics, they talk about the 'Overton window' as the range of policies that are currently acceptable to the majority of the population. Well, in today's business world, the 'Overton window' is now very much on sustainability and social value, with both public and shareholder sentiment increasingly in alignment. So there's arguably never been a more favourable time for companies to challenge 'anti-profit beliefs' and – like Interface – confidently embrace a more radically responsible agenda that moves beyond contemporary notions of corporate social responsibility (CSR).

THE GROWTH DILEMMA: IS THE IMPERATIVE TO GROW ANTITHETICAL TO SUSTAINABILITY?

It's become the norm for national governments to measure the health of their economies by referring to growth in GDP (gross domestic product, the monetary value of all finished goods and services). Without perpetual growth in business activity and/or productivity – the argument goes – successive generations will become poorer and the welfare of society would decline. This social Darwinian 'grow or die' mantra has become so pervasive and canonical in conventional business, few question whether all growth is good, even when it evidently comes at the expense of society.

While some firms expand through innovation or buying up their competitors, others do so by deliberately driving their competitors out of business or exploiting their suppliers. Such aggressive expansion strategies may not only have damaging impacts on wider society (with unemployment and poverty wages, for example), they can also harm the business by immiserating staff, stretching resources and eating away resilience (history is littered with companies bankrupted by their world-dominating ambitions). Moreover, ever-growing businesses consume more and more resources and produce more and more waste, destroying the planet's life-supporting ecosystems. As the environmental campaigner Greta Thunberg put it to the UN's climate change summit in 2020: 'We are in the beginning of a mass extinction, and all you can talk about is money and fairy tales of eternal economic growth. How dare you!'[13]

So can sustainable businesses really have their cake and eat it when it comes to growth? Certainly there are proponents of 'green growth' who are optimistic that technological advancements will allow for a less resource-heavy, cleaner economy in future – an idea that underpins green industrial policies like the Green New Deal. But followers of the 'degrowth movement' see the very premise of sustainable development as oxymoronic, arguing that encouraging capitalist growth and consumption in a finite and environmentally stressed world is inherently unsustainable. More recently, 'zero growth' economists like Tim Jackson and Kate Raworth have sought to redefine the role of business in relation to human wellbeing and planetary boundaries, where a shared prosperity is possible with slow, low or no growth at all.

The rise (and rediscovery) of the responsible business

The modern notion of CSR has its roots in the philanthropic paternalism of the 19th-century's vastly wealthy industrialists.[14] Their names – Carnegie, Tate, Peabody – still adorn the various housing schemes, libraries, galleries, civic buildings and other public amenities their donations funded to improve the lives of their workers and local communities. Businesses like Lever Brothers, Cadbury and the great textile mills of northern England famously built whole towns for their workforce, which were modern and comfortable by the standards of the day.

These companies were among the world's first commercial corporations. Previously, a corporation was granted by the state for a specific public purpose, such as building hospitals or universities. It was not-for-profit and had constitutional duties that were overseen by government. Only with Europe's rush for colonial expansion in the 17th and 18th centuries were corporations, such as the East India Company, predominantly concerned with making money. But it was the Joint Stocks Companies Act of 1844 that finally freed corporations from government control in the UK, allowing them to define their own purpose. Then, the Limited Liability Act 11 years later protected shareholders' personal assets from the consequences of their corporate behaviour.

This new freedom from either public responsibility or personal loss allowed commercial corporations to run rampant in subsequent decades. The impacts and sheer scale of their operations in a world with little public infrastructure, planning or adequate legislation was devastating. It became impossible to ignore the problems of rapid urbanization that accompanied this industrial revolution, with its squalid living conditions, malnutrition and contagious diseases. In 19th-century Manchester, the death rate for working-class children under five hit 60%, and the average life expectancy for a labourer in Victorian London was just 22.[15] For a slave in the US at this time – a descendant of the estimated 10 million Africans transported across the Atlantic to work on plantations, mines and other colonial industries in the Americas – the average life span could be as low as 18.[16]

It was these horrific social conditions – and the increasing opprobrium of the public, church and politicians – that guilted and shamed the figureheads of these businesses into their philanthropy as much as any largesse. Their workers' housing schemes and civic infrastructure programmes were on such a scale that they might be seen to morally offset the huge social damage of their operations in the eyes of their critics, as well as their own. They also had the added commercial benefit of helping attract and retain a healthy workforce. However, this responsibility didn't usually extend throughout their global supply chain, which could be oppressive, exploitative, often built on colonialism and kept largely hidden from public view.

There were, though, many 19th-century industrialists whose ethical approach to business and paternalism towards their workforce stemmed from deeper convictions. The founders of Rowntree, Cadbury, Friends Provident and several other well-known companies, for instance, were all from families with religious Quaker beliefs, which prohibits trade or investment in any business activities that harm 'god's creation' (a business principle incidentally shared by Islam throughout the centuries). And the social reformer Robert Owen, who owned a mill in New Lanark with his wife Caroline Dale, used their Scottish factory as a laboratory for testing his enthusiastic Enlightenment ideas of freedom and equality. There they pioneered the eight-hour working day, founded the world's first nursery school and created the first cooperative factory store that sold goods to workers at close to wholesale prices. Indeed, local cooperative businesses of all kinds went on to flourish during the 19th century, all founded on a common set of principles that included a 'concern for the community' in all they do.[17]

So as you can see, it's difficult to pigeonhole the values of business during this period. At the same time as some business leaders were leading the fight against slavery, there were others resisting and personally benefiting from the systematic abuse of fellow human beings. Then, as now, business encompassed a range of different values. And many companies, regardless of their size or purpose, recognized their responsibility to the communities they operated in and wanted to make positive social change. So while the idea of CSR is certainly nothing new, it became more formalized and widespread business practice in the 1970s and 1980s after the influential Committee for Economic Development in the US declared a 'social contract' between business and society.[18]

Since then, every large company has been expected to have a CSR programme of some kind, but until recently these were often peripheral operations, minimally staffed and dominated by the age-old philanthropic model of simply volunteering or donating to good causes. For some companies, it became a way of superficially greenwashing or offsetting their 'business-as-usual' activities, spending on showy side projects or tick-box exercises that did little to challenge or improve the social value of the core work of the business. At its worst, CSR was cynically used like sewage treatment to get rid of the bad smell of toxic practices.

In fact, experts in organizational behaviour have suggested that some firms have used CSR as a way of actually justifying irresponsible conduct. A 2013 study[19] of Fortune 500 companies showed that for every five positive actions a firm undertook for its stakeholders, it committed one negative action further down the line that arguably outweighed them. For example, despite all of Enron Corporation's charitable giving and employee volunteerism, it cost shareholders $11 billion when exposure of its fraudulent accounting caused its stock to tumble in 2001. While not suggesting companies always do this deliberately, the researchers did identify a pattern of thinking that social psychologists call 'moral currency'. Because humans naturally seek to maintain a moral balance between good and bad deeds, so, too, CEOs feel by investing in CSR they accrue enough 'moral credits' to offset their irresponsible actions elsewhere without fear of discrediting their overall image. It's not unlike someone eating healthily for most of the year so they can justify a blow out on their holidays. In this way, modern CSR really behaves no differently from the moral offsetting of the Victorian industrialists' philanthropy.

This financialized, transactional view of CSR was commonplace and emblematic of the oppressive profit-and-loss mindset in business. For decades it meant sustainability and responsibility to others was banished from the board room unless they could be framed in terms of a return on investment, leaving them marginalized, misused and (perhaps deliberately) neutered of their transformational potential to the business and the most pressing problems of society. It's why in recent years, faced with mounting public and stakeholder criticism, leading business figures such as Unilever's then-CEO Paul Polman have denounced CSR as no longer fit for purpose.[20]

'It's not good enough anymore to do a side activity like CSR. It has to become an integral part of the company's agenda', said Polman in 2012, two years after announcing Unilever's Sustainable Living Plan to halve the environmental impact of its products, among other commitments.[21] It's arguably the corporation's most radical act of social responsibility since their pre-merger days as Lever Brothers over a century ago, when they created the model village of Port Sunlight for their British employees (not forgetting that, at the same time, Lever Brothers' subsidiary company in the Congo was using forced labour and subjecting its workers to horrific violence for not meeting punishing quotas.[22] These contradictory and hypocritical corporate attitudes towards staff welfare in Western countries compared to other countries are still very much an issue today).

Institutional investors also played a key role in pressuring companies to integrate CSR more into their core business, rather than just using it as window-dressing or moral sewage treatment. Over recent decades, the movement for socially responsible investing (SRI) has developed extra-financial environmental, social and governance (ESG) criteria to analyse and screen companies from their portfolios, as well as using them to hold companies to account where they are shareholders. This approach has become increasingly mainstream and was consolidated by the creation of the Principles for Responsible Investment in 2006 with the support of the UN, which attracted the signatures of more than 2,450 investment managers worldwide by 2019 who look after an estimated US$80 trillion of funds.[23]

In response, many businesses have adopted these ESG metrics into their own company reporting to more explicitly demonstrate their sustainability commitments to their shareholders and other stakeholders. Paradoxically, this has ultimately led to the end for the narrow idea of shareholder primacy that economist Milton Friedman famously described as a corporation's responsibility being only 'to make as much money for their stockholders as possible'.[24] In 2019, both the World Economic Forum's 'Davos Manifesto'[25] and the Business Roundtable of leading US company CEOs declared a new model of corporate governance that respects all stakeholders – 'employees, customers, suppliers, local communities and society at large' – rather than just shareholders.

Perhaps the singling out of shareholders above all other stakeholders was always somewhat specious anyway, as fund manager Amy Domini neatly explains: 'Stockholders are ultimately human beings. Human beings have many needs and desires. We do not want the pursuit of profits for the person we are when we own a stock to damage the person we are when we breath the air.'[26] Besides which, only a tiny minority of businesses have shares that are actively traded, with just 40,000 of the estimated 300 million companies worldwide listed on the global stock exchanges.

Whether it was because of this influence of SRI or not, the more recent evolution of CSR and sustainability as integral to a company's values and everyday practices has come to be labelled 'responsible business'. Its proponents adopt a 'triple bottom line' approach to business performance, looking at people and the planet as well as profit. Only by measuring its impact on all three, they argue, can a firm account for the full cost of doing business. But these other social and environmental impacts are often unknown, ill defined or tend to be dominated by a handful of the most topical issues, such as climate change or gender equality. It means so many other equally pressing issues, such as institutional racism or biodiversity loss, are shelved by even the most responsible businesses simply because they think they are unable to account for them.

This is where the UN's creation of the Sustainable Development Goals (also known as Global Goals, as we will call them) in 2015 has helped enormously. The Global Goals are the next step on a positive pathway of change, allowing businesses to move beyond the criticisms of CSR and the limits of ESG. By clearly identifying and setting out the 17 most important global issues and translating them into goals and actions to be achieved by 2030, they've given the rather fuzzy idea of responsible business a renewed breadth and impetus. It's this 'blueprint to achieve a better and more sustainable future for all', as the UN calls it, that responsible businesses can use to align themselves and better understand and define their purpose.

THE BUSINESS MODEL DILEMMA: ARE CONVENTIONAL COMPANIES LESS CAPABLE OF BEING RESPONSIBLE?

In his satirical *Devil's Dictionary* from 1906, the American writer Ambrose Bierce famously defined a corporation as 'an ingenious device for obtaining profit without individual responsibility'. While today's corporations are increasingly stepping up their sustainability agendas, there's a wealth of other, alternative business models that may be better suited to serving the needs of all stakeholders – not just shareholders – and so align more readily with sustainability concerns.

This could be a form of cooperative ownership, like the John Lewis Partnership, that shares its profits and governance among its staff, or social enterprises,[27] like Divine Chocolate and Fair for You, which reinvest all their profits or give away at least half to community and environmental projects. There's also the community ownership model that's particularly popular for local wind power schemes and sports teams, as well as non-profit foundation-owned companies that are typically committed to philanthropic activities (although some of the biggest such companies, like IKEA, have been criticized for using their foundations to avoid tax[28]).

Some companies have gradually introduced these alternative ways of doing business as they move in a more sustainable direction or their progressive owners have left. For instance, the retailer Richer Sounds transferred ownership to its employees in 2019 after its founder, Julian Richer, stepped away from the company to encourage other businesses to be more responsible, with his Good Business Charter initiative. Others have adopted the B Corp model where they are legally required to consider the impact of their decisions on their workers, customers, suppliers, community and the environment – something that shareholders in the US had gone to court to prevent!

Yet paradoxically, because corporations are structured to deindividualize responsibility and outlive generations of owners and shareholders, they have the temporal capacity to be arguably even more responsible than many other types of business. Since corporations can still be held directly liable for crimes stretching back hundreds of years, such as slavery and colonial land appropriation, they are uniquely positioned (if they are big enough and wealthy enough) to respond to the legacy of these historic injustices that still underlie many of the sustainability issues around inequality and poverty facing the world today.

Using the Global Goals to help map the purpose of a business

In 1987, after determining that sustainable development should be defined as 'meeting the needs of the present without compromising the ability of future generations to meet their own needs', the UN spent the next few decades formulating a framework for how the world might achieve it. The ambitious 17 Global Goals they arrived at in 2015 aim to eliminate poverty and hunger at the same time as improving health and education, reducing inequality and spurring economic growth – all while tackling climate change and preserving the environment. And all by 2030.

These are huge undertakings in which governments are the primary drivers, but business can play a crucial role in all of them. It may seem easier for a business to foster better gender equality in its own workplace, for instance, rather than end hunger in another country, but many companies have a global reach through their supply chains that impact the conditions of workers in the poorest parts of the world, as well as contribute to climate change and its far-flung consequences through their carbon emissions.

Moreover, the persistent problems represented by the Global Goals have complex causes and are interdependent: poverty causes hunger, food security depends on a stable climate and healthy ecosystems, which, in turn, are affected by industrial development and consumption that are also dependent on them, and so on. So in this way, business is similarly interconnected with all these global issues and the prosperity of business, society and the environment are inextricably linked. In this context, making trade-offs that damage people and the planet to maximize profits can clearly be seen as unsustainable and ultimately self-defeating.

This is why, if responsible businesses want to help tackle these problems, they can't be picked off individually. So while it might seem overwhelming (particularly for smaller firms) to consider all 17 Global Goals, and businesses will understandably want to prioritize those most within their control, the consequences for all of them need to at least be recognized. It's another reason responsible business requires embracing a more holistic mindset, no matter how difficult or uncomfortable.

Like the 12-point 'Apple Values', the Global Goals are really a statement of 17 values that together represent a vision of the world that the UN and its supporters want to create. So if a responsible business also wants to help realize this vision, it needs to incorporate the Global Goals into its own values and purpose. There are two simple, strategic tools that can help businesses do this by reflecting on their relationship with each of the Global Goals.

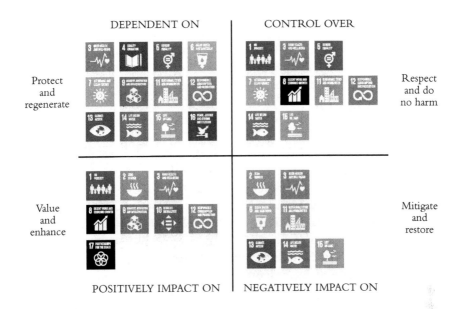

First, using a Global Goals relationship matrix, like the one above, a business can identify which Global Goals it's either dependent on, has some control over, positively benefits or negatively impacts (or potentially all four). Then it can determine how it should actively work with them. For example:

- If a business is dependent on 'life below water', it should look to protect or regenerate the marine environment.
- If a business has some control over 'good health and wellbeing', it should at least look to do no harm in this area.
- If a business contributes positively to 'no poverty', it should value and enhance those efforts.
- If a business negatively impacts on 'climate action', it should look to mitigate or reverse those impacts.
- And if a business is dependent on 'life on land', controls life on land, positively impacts on life on land and negatively impacts on life on land, this should be at the core of all its decisions!

It's worth noting that the ultimate source of any value created by a business derives from the positive contribution it makes to others and to the planet. It is these positive contributions that stakeholders will reward the business for. This might be customers buying the product, employee loyalty, reputational or brand value, reduced regulatory pressures, accessing government subsidies or avoiding sanctions or penalties. But these benefits have to be considered in relation to the negative impacts a business will have on society and nature too.

It's wrong to believe that a business won't have any negative impacts or to try hiding them, since it's highly likely evidence of harm will eventually emerge. When it does, the consequences can be much greater if the business is thought to have been concealing it. These negative impacts are where most of the future risks to the business are located, particularly if it's also dependent on the very things it harms. For instance, without access to skilled staff, capacity to innovate will be diminished. Similarly, without decent transport infrastructure, a company won't be able to deliver its goods and services. And without the consent of local communities, a company may not be able to operate its business at all.

Once the business has defined these relationships, the second step is to prioritize them in terms of its potential to make a difference. This involves positioning each of the Global Goals in one of three concentric zones relating to core business purpose, strategic importance and influence on operations (see diagram opposite).

Once categorized, businesses should consider how each Global Goal relates to others across the zones to explore in which areas any contribution would have the most potential impact overall. It's a challenging and imperfect process, but even just having these conversations helps uncover what social and environmental consequences a business is having that it doesn't know or chooses to ignore. It's a useful way of seeing all the dots, joining them up and making new connections.

Ultimately, the emerging picture can help inform the drafting of a business's purpose, values and strategy statements that would be demonstrably joined up with the UN's global strategy for a more sustainable world. The Global Goals would then provide a shared vocabulary to use in ongoing business discussions and decision-making processes. (For more about understanding the Global Goals for business and connecting them to purpose, see Appendices 1 and 2.)

Putting these new values into action across the business tends to be a gradual process, working out from the centre of the concentric zones in the purpose map. Firms start by implementing a sustainable measure in a part of their business, and then they expand it across the whole of their core operations, before rolling it out to stakeholders and throughout their wider value chain of activities. There are many organizations that are currently helping businesses to map their purpose and reorient their operations around the Global Goals, including Future-Fit, Business in the Community and the UN's own Global Compact initiative (some of whose tools and methodologies for measuring sustainability and responsible practice we'll look at in more detail later in the book).

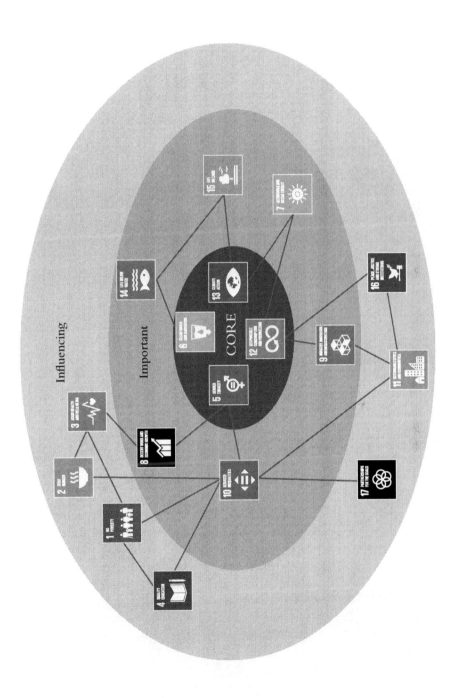

Going beyond compliance to build resilience and public trust

The idea of 'business with a purpose' or 'purpose-led' companies has become something of a buzzword recently, as more and more firms recognize that having a greater purpose beyond just profit is appealing to both their consumers and employees. But without undertaking the meticulous work of realigning their core values and actually changing the way they operate, many are risking the reputational and commercial damage of merely 'purpose-washing'.

Much like BP were pilloried for 'greenwashing' when they temporarily rebranded as 'Beyond Petroleum' in 2001 while continuing to be the world's sixth largest carbon-emitting company,[29] so today, multinationals are accused of only gesturing at their responsibilities if they don't make substantive reforms to the way they're governed or commit to real sustainability improvements. The CEO of Oxfam India, Amitabh Behar, memorably said as much in 2020 after returning from the World Economic Forum's Davos conference:

> We cannot celebrate a "social purpose" while your CEO rakes in 1,000 times more than your average employee. Or as you cherry-pick your Sustainable Development Goal to market in glossy ads. Or when you continue to run major parts of your balance sheets out of the Cayman Islands and other tax havens, or spew carbon throughout your supply chain without [an] urgent plan to reduce that to zero. Promising stakeholder capitalism while continuing to put shareholder's profit interests first will be no more than "purpose-washing".[30]

The hypocrisy that Behar is highlighting is a legacy of that hollow, transactional CSR mindset we explored earlier. If a company's social responsibility is still just an add-on or a tick-box exercise in compliance to boost its commercial appeal rather than an all-encompassing mission at the very heart of how the business operates and sees its role in the world, then it misses the point of purpose and will find its fine words continually undermined by its actions. The holistic mindset required of a truly responsible business wouldn't allow an oil company to proudly announce becoming carbon neutral by 2050 while glaringly omitting the carbon of the very fossil fuels it sells. Neither would it permit a car company to see investing in its electric vehicle division as an acceptable way of offsetting having to make EU-mandated 10% reductions in CO_2 emissions across its whole operation (both of which are real examples from recent years). If you really believe in the goal of a more sustainable world, you don't engage in sleight of hand to meet targets or ignore the real impacts of your business.

It's possible to argue that the aforementioned oil company was genuinely unaware of the need to include the carbon footprint of its products in its net zero calculations. Or that the car company's offsetting was perfectly legal and standard accounting procedure. But evidence of the negative impacts of business and who is bearing the costs of profiteering is growing, while digital technology allows new connections of harm to be exposed. Previously, businesses could 'externalize' these harmful impacts by outsourcing their responsibilities to supply chains or excluding them from their deliberations, but the capacity for deniability is diminishing as information and public awareness grows. 'We didn't know' is a weak defence when others can easily find out and society judges that you should have known anyway.

This is why the holistic approach of the Global Goals can be so effective at ensuring responsible business practice, because it helps to eliminate any genuine blindspots and identify contradictory and 'pass the parcel' behaviours. All of which leave a company vulnerable to future risks – such as historic prosecutions, reputational damage or even state takeovers – should laws be tightened or public expectations on sustainability continue to rise. You only have to look at the billions in fines Volkswagen has paid due to the 'Dieselgate' scandal over rigged car emission tests, or the continuing allegations of Nike using sweatshop and child labour many years and even decades after both issues first came to light.

Conversely, striving to do to the right thing beyond just complying with the law as it stands can help inoculate a company from these risks, while also bringing public credibility and added value. If what a business does is socially valued – not just socially mandated – then its customers and broader society will deem it and its products to be worth more. And so a business becomes more resilient as a result of its social value. Indeed, Ray Anderson credited Interface's sustainability initiative and their customers' support for it with helping the company weather the recession after the 2007–08 global financial crisis that shrunk its market by 38%.[31] And a similar shared values approach among staff, members and customers is perhaps why 80% of cooperative firms in the UK survived their first five years of trading post-recession in 2013 compared to just 41% of all other companies.[32]

As well as increasing resilience, making responsibility a key part of the identity of a business and how it operates can also help restore public trust in industries that have become mired in controversy in recent years. For instance, after the financial crisis, taxpayer bailouts and successive scandals over rate-fixing and insurance misselling, the UK banking sector went to great lengths to demonstrate its responsible credentials, introducing more diligent lending criteria, increasing its capital reserves and signing up to the UN's Principles for Responsible Banking.[33] Similarly, as commercial monopolies charged with essential public duties, privatized utilities like energy, water and telecoms have also historically struggled with public trust – their customers wary of profiteering and limited (if any) choice. In an effort to improve relations and prove their wider good intentions, many such firms are now experimenting with social contracts, which embed social value into the business model of a company.

Anglian Water, one of the nine large companies that run England's water and sewage infrastructure, became one of the first UK water companies to adopt a social contract in 2019. Like many of the UK's public utilities that were privatized after 1989, the whole water sector has faced huge criticism for customer bills increasing in real terms by 40%, while paying huge dividends to shareholders, million-pound salaries to senior staff and too little corporation tax. Critics also blame the sector for its collective lack of investment in infrastructure for the millions of litres of water lost to leaks each year and the deteriorating quality of rivers (only 14% of England's rivers met legal minimum 'good status' in 2018, down from 25% in 2009). With the industry's watchdog, Ofwat, threatening price caps and pressure mounting from the public and politicians to renationalize water, the water companies were forced to act and announced they'd work together to improve their social responsibility as part of an agreed Public Interest Commitment in 2019.

While Ofwat had encouraged the idea of social contracts within the industry for some time, Anglian Water was one of the most strident in its adoption. It changed its Articles of Association to include a statement of purpose that 'formally enshrines the public interest within the constitutional makeup of the business', underlining its commitment 'to deliver a sustainable future for the East of England'.[34] As well as consulting with the community and various stakeholders to create a statement of 'responsible business principles' against which it invites an independent body to regularly measure its performance, it also created a simpler public statement of its purpose 'to bring environmental and social prosperity to the region we serve through our commitment to Love Every Drop'.

It's too early to say yet whether these measures will materially change the public's perception of Anglian Water's social value (in 2018/19 only 57% of households agreed that 'the company cares about the community it serves'[35]), but the firm has since won another Queen's Award for Enterprise for its sustainability work.[36] And by taking a leading role on reforming the industry's sustainability and demonstrating its social value, the company has succeeded in improving its resilience to future public and political criticism and any more stringent regulation from Ofwat.

The positive multiplier effect of common goals and becoming citizen scientists

With so many companies choosing to adopt a purpose-led approach to business and incorporating sustainability into their business values, some might question why there's a need to explicitly use the Global Goals. Surely if every business aims to create a more sustainable world, it doesn't matter how it's labelled? But it's important that companies have something to measure their purposes against, otherwise there is a risk that firms will arrive at their own definitions of sustainability that may vary hugely in depth and scope.

Returning to Apple, for example, the UN's Global Sustainability Index Institute (UNGSII) has been critical of the firm's insistence on going its own way on sustainability reporting. It scored Apple zero in its 2017 *SDG Commitment Report* for the number of mentions of the Global Goals or themes in its corporate annual accounts. Apple instead produces separate, annual environmental and supplier 'Responsibility Reports' with its own standards and targets. While Apple has made impressive strides in some areas – its data centres are now 100% powered by renewables, for instance – its self-selected focus means it omits or ignores many other areas of sustainability that the Global Goals could help to illuminate. It also leaves itself open to accusations of phony or inadequate self-policing. Certainly, Apple's efforts to improve the repairability of its products and worker conditions in its supply chains have been undermined by its public lobbying to pull a 'Right to Repair' Bill in the US in 2019 and continued news reports of child labour and harsh treatment in its Chinese factories.[37]

In the end, it's too easy for companies under pressure to maintain profits – especially major corporates like Apple – to drift from their chosen sustainable values without committing to the framework of the Global Goals to guide and maintain the highest standards. As well as providing more transparency and credibility over what sustainability means to a company, the Global Goals can also make them more accountable if they're legally declared in annual reports – unlike the separate reports favoured by Apple.

As the UNGSII warns: 'The sustainability report of a company is not legally binding and is therefore of less relevance. It can turn into "greenwashing".'[38] And while companies like Shell and Volkswagen, that sit in the upper ranks of the 2019 *SDG Commitment Report*,[39] have made serious, high-profile sustainability blunders of their own in recent years, the fact they've declared their commitment to the Global Goals in their annual reports means they are more likely to be embedded in their business strategies, and their CEO and board can be held more to account by the public and shareholders. Besides, as the Global Goals have become more embedded in society, businesses have lost their power to selectively define their sustainability or continue ignoring the limits to their growth.

But another equally important reason for businesses to commit specifically to the Global Goals is the power of a shared goal that's recognized and bought into by everyone. With an agreed framework and common vocabulary, businesses, non-governmental organizations (NGOs), governments and development agencies, which have long spoken about sustainability in different and often contrary ways, can now understand each other and work together on the Global Goals. And while there is already a well-evidenced 'positive multiplier effect' for businesses that pursue a sustainability strategy, adding value to the business at the same time as wider society (just look at our earlier example of Interface), this effect is compounded again if many businesses come together and collaborate on the same shared goals. By uniting, they can extend their individual agency and reach to bring about positive social change at a systemic level, much like sector-specific lobbying groups already do to influence politicians and laws in a far more self-serving fashion.

For instance, a united front from some major international clothing retailers helped bolster the confidence of the Myanmar government to bring in a minimum wage of 3,600 kyats (about US$3) per day in 2015.[40] Having consulted with unions, government and employers to arrive at the figure, Myanmar officials faced strong opposition from some manufacturers who argued it would ruin their commercial viability, with some Chinese and South Korean firms even threatening to close their factories if it went ahead. But with the backing of their member companies – including Primark, Adidas and Marks & Spencer – the Ethical Trading Initiative and the Fair Labor Association sent a letter of international support for the minimum wage in the garment sector to the government of Myanmar, which eventually brought it into effect later that year.

This example focuses on the Global Goal of 'decent work and economic growth', but similar internationally coordinated business efforts on the goals of 'clean water and sanitation' and 'gender equality' have seen a remarkable positive multiplier effect on the Global Goals across the board, indirectly raising the floor for all sustainability issues. Gap's Women + Water strategy, for instance, not only attempts to reduce water consumption in its Indian garment factories, but also provides safe and reliable water for its predominantly female workforce, who would otherwise be part of the 200 million hours women and girls spend globally collecting water every day. This is because so many of the issues represented by the Global Goals intersect. So by targeting one, there is often an unintentional benefit for many others.

It shows the power of responsible business. Its impacts can ripple far through supply chains, influencing governments and transforming societies the world over. And while the terms of sustainability and what a sustainable world looks like will inevitably change beyond the Global Goals and 2030, the mindset of responsible business will always be essential to achieving it. As the former chair of the OECD Working Party on Responsible Business, Roel Nieuwenkamp, said in 2016: 'Responsible business conduct goes beyond auditing and stresses the importance of a continuous process of due diligence, which in addition to identifying risks requires prevention and mitigation as well as addressing negative impacts where they do occur.'[41]

That 'continuous process of due diligence' driven by a desire to make a better world for everyone is what distinguishes a truly responsible business, not just auditing or ticking boxes against sustainability targets – Global Goals or otherwise. Responsibility requires this proactive, almost scientific enquiry forever asking questions about the sustainability of the business and never accepting 'don't know' as good enough. And with this new science of responsible business, we're all venturing out of our zones of ignorance and encountering sustainability in unique and different ways. So firms need to become 'citizen scientists',[42] observing the traits of other responsible businesses and testing the theories that books like this provide against their own experiences, then feeding back evidence that can be shared with others.

Although pushing at the limits of what businesses can do in this way may feel daunting or frustrating, it can also empower them to liberate themselves from the profit-and-growth straitjacket, and reimagine their role in the world as allies in the planet's recovery rather than congenitally helpless contributors to its downfall. As we've seen throughout this chapter, the rewards for society as well as businesses that do make the effort are manifold – particularly with the current impetus and widespread support of the Global Goals.

No doubt UN Secretary-General Ban Ki-moon hoped to trigger a gold rush for responsible business at the time of their launch when he declared: 'Now is the time to mobilize the global business community as never before. The case is clear. Realizing the Sustainable Development Goals will improve the environment for doing business and building markets. Trillions of dollars in public and private funds are to be redirected towards the SDGs, creating huge opportunities for responsible companies to deliver solutions.'[43]

Given the world may already have passed the climate tipping point, with all the many environmental and social crises that could precipitate, the financial case may now be the least compelling argument for being a responsible business.

Summary: The science of responsible business

Observations to note
Responsible businesses have ...
... a codified set of values that includes social value.
... a clear purpose and ambitious vision of a more sustainable world.
... a strong sense of place or community and urgency.
... strong, committed leadership.
... the Global Goals embedded in their business strategies and annual reports.

Theories to test
Responsible profit
Profit isn't inherently irresponsible, but maximizing profits is.
- Do you know if your bonus depends on forced labour or paying poverty wages in your supply chain? (Global Goals 1 and 8)
- Are you rewarding responsible production as part of your drive to increase profit? (Global Goals 9 and 12)
- Would you be comfortable disclosing any of your activities designed to increase profit margins? (Global Goals 12 and 16)
- Are you investing any of your revenue in projects to reduce inequalities in the communities in which you operate? (Global Goals 10 and 11)
- Do you disclose your tax payments on a country-by-country basis? (Global Goals 11 and 16)

Responsible growth
Businesses can choose if and how they grow to minimize the social damage of expansion.
- Do your plans for growth improve the security of your local community? (Global Goals 11 and 12)
- Will your expansion destroy other responsible businesses rather than work with them? (Global Goals 8 and 17)
- Have you engaged with stakeholders to ensure your future plans will create more and appropriate jobs? (Global Goals 8 and 11)
- What impacts will your growth have on reducing carbon emissions? (Global Goals 12 and 13)
- Will your growth involve inclusive and responsible use of digital technology innovation? (Global Goals 9 and 16)
- Do your expansion plans include measures to mitigate or reverse historic damage to the natural environment? (Global Goals 14 and 15)

Responsible governance

Responsible businesses balance the interests of all stakeholders – employees, customers, suppliers, the community and wider society – not just those of the owners.

- Do you measure and engage with the health and wellbeing of your employees and customers? (Global Goals 3 and 12)
- How far into the future do your plans and predictions extend? (Global Goals 11, 12 and 16)
- What business-wide strategies do you have to empower women and girls? (Global Goals 5 and 10)
- What opportunities for life-long learning do you offer your employees? (Global Goals 4 and 8)
- How are you helping local communities to sustainably manage and improve their energy and water infrastructure? (Global Goals 6 and 7)

First steps to becoming a responsible business ...

Only Manage What You Can Measure

Invisibles, ignorance and measuring what you treasure

The use of SMART measures has been the norm in business for decades. First popularized in the 1980s, the specific, measurable, achievable, relevant and timely criteria for setting performance targets have their roots in the 'management by objectives' concept pioneered by the founding father of management theory, Peter Drucker. Among the many quotes from his 1954 book *The Practice of Management* that went on to become received wisdom in the business world is the famous mantra: 'what gets measured gets managed'.

But Drucker's words are often misunderstood, not least because they're usually taken out of context from the rest of the sentence that followed: 'even when it's pointless to measure and manage it, and even if it harms the purpose of the organization to do so.' Drucker wasn't just saying it's important to quantify and measure anything you hope to manage in business, which is the popular takeaway; he was also warning companies not to ignore all the important things that can't be easily measured, and about the damaging risks of measuring the wrong things too.

It's important to recognize that the formal scorecards and financial accounting that businesses use are not set in stone. They represent past choices as to what and how to measure things – past choices that may not be valid now or that are steering us in the wrong direction. Moreover, once we measure something and rank it in a league table, we wrongly tend to think we've mastered it. But big risks and mistakes come from where we're not looking. So businesses also need to manage what they aren't measuring – and that means turning on more of their other 'senses'.

In many ways business performance measures act like human senses, helping companies to understand themselves and the world around them, as well as predict consequences and correct their actions. But just as many of us think humans have only five senses (scientists estimate we actually have more than 21, including balance, pain and thirst[1]), there are many other 'senses' beyond the SMART and financial measures that businesses aren't capturing by not measuring them. For instance, although a sense of purpose, dignity and compassion are all thought essential for healthy human relationships, you'd be hard pushed to find any of them in most accounting systems. Yet it's precisely from these 'blindspots', outside a company's institutional sensory range, that risks lurk and grow while the business chooses not to look.

Which is why the Global Goals not only offer businesses a better way to measure and manage their sustainability, but also provide them with 17 new 'senses' to eliminate blindspots on a whole range of issues that are often hidden from view. So while incorporating measures around carbon emissions and diversity into business reporting has become increasingly high profile and commonplace in recent years, the Global Goals have helped bring to the fore a whole host of other unsustainable 'invisibles' that lurk behind each of the 17 aspirations and that are largely ignored by many businesses.

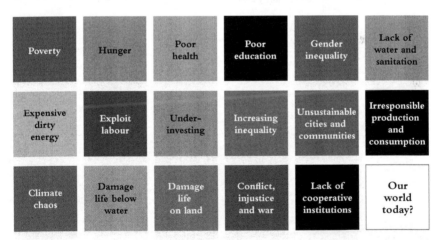

But as the Global Goals become more embedded within international trade agreements, financial markets, taxation, procurement and consumer preferences, the risks to businesses that continue to ignore them are growing. Whether it's reputational damage or the loss of competitive advantage to those companies that do address the Global Goals, what you don't know about your sustainability really can hurt you. Ignorance works both ways, however, and businesses may also be missing out on the positive impacts they are making too.

To eliminate these responsibility blindspots, there are numerous 17-dimensional (or 17D) analysis tools available – often freely – that businesses can use to get a fuller picture of their contribution to each of the Global Goals. As well as the Global Goals relationship matrix (see p 25) that helps to explore which goals a company is most dependent on overall, you can take a product-by-product approach using a simple life cycle analysis grid to assess the impacts at each stage of their manufacture and sale.

If there is a particular area of most concern or potential vulnerability, companies can employ a 'responsible radar' technique to assess their exposure. For instance, slavery, forced labour and child labour are known to be far more widespread than many business leaders would like to admit, particularly in international supply chains, with sectors such as mining, textiles, agriculture and fisheries the most embroiled. No one – be they employee, customer or shareholder – would be happy knowing they've been complicit in exploiting child cobalt miners in the Congo or trafficked fishing workers in Thailand. Many firms in these industries seem to ignore such risks to maintain a kind of culpable deniability if they're ever exposed.

However, in our world of ever-expanding and easily accessible knowledge, the protection of deniability is wearing paper-thin. And by simply downloading a forced labour map – such as the 'Products of Slavery' map from Anti-Slavery International[2] – companies can begin digging into their supply chains and identifying where they are most at risk. The first stage is to list all Tier 1 suppliers and give them a traffic light colour label depending on what sector or product they're associated: red for those most high-risk industries, amber for medium-risk and green for low-risk, including any supplier belonging to a recognized anti-slavery accreditation scheme (such as Sedex[3]). Then, after placing them on the map according to where they operate, you can see if a supplier is both a 'red' risk and located in a high-risk slavery country. Any combination other than a 'green' supplier in a low-risk country might warrant some investigation. But those suppliers that are red and in a high- or medium-risk country should be the urgent priority and subject to a second stage of evaluation: this time looking at their sub-suppliers (Tier 2) and drilling down until you are satisfied there is no slavery evident.

This 'responsible radar' process can be used to interrogate supply chains for any of the other Global Goal 'invisibles' too, with similar worldwide maps available from charities and institutions showing poverty, water scarcity, threatened biodiversity, fossil fuel dependency and education levels by country. Companies may well hit a brick wall trying to find out this sustainability information from many of their suppliers, in which case, it's worth reflecting carefully why that information isn't available and whether it's worth continuing to do business with a supplier if they aren't quick to find out. (Remember the power of 'The Why Man' and the '5 Whys' model to get to the root cause of a problem on p 5.)

Similar significant decisions will become inevitable once a company starts making a conscious effort to encroach on its areas of ignorance and take more responsibility for the full impact of its operations. The more a company knows about the Global Goals and how they impact on them, the more irresponsible not taking any mitigating action becomes. It's like a sliding scale of irresponsibility, whereby any problems can be initially excused as innocent and unintentional. But it then becomes wilful ignorance once a company is aware of certain issues but refuses to look into them or deny them when they emerge. Finally, some companies choose to double-down on their irresponsibility, knowingly causing damage and even lobbying government and the public to permit them to keep doing so.

But that's the difference between the ineffectual 'old school' social audit system associated with CSR[4] – where there is often little follow-up to correct any shortcomings identified – and the kind of continuous process of due diligence and mitigation that 17D, Global Goals-based audit systems demand today. When the eight-storey Rana Plaza building in Bangladesh collapsed in 2013, killing 1,134 people who worked in the textile factory inside, several of the international clothing brands that sourced their clothes from there had recently performed audits of the factory and ignored the serious workplace safety issues they found. That response (or lack of it) not only demonstrated how peripheral those firms' social values were relative to minimizing financial costs, but also how little sense of responsibility or inclination they felt to actually do anything about it.

A key part of the problem was lack of recognition about how fundamental social and ecological factors are to the profitability of a company. They just don't make it on to the accountants' spreadsheet, except in the crudest financial terms of their 'asset value'. (And, in the context of this tragedy, business mantras such as 'sweating your assets' are revealed as horribly inhumane.) But how profitable would a hi-tech company be without an educated workforce or a food manufacturer without healthy soil? They are utterly dependent on them.

This is why the unique accounting of Brazilian organic sugar company, Native, seems at once both delightfully novel and blindingly obvious. As well as the standard metrics, their accounting processes include measurements and key performance indicators (KPIs) for their soil, looking at its nutrients, fungi and biodiversity. As Native's CEO Leontino Balbo Jr makes clear, it stands to reason that a sugar company should be concerned with the health of the soil that sustains its crop. It's central to what he describes as an 'agroecological' approach to farming that has seen soil fertility improve, water sources regenerate, more carbon absorbed than expelled and biodiversity 'explode' in the 20 years Native has been doing it.

'All these positive changes, both in culture and in the environment as a whole, have led to a very significant increase in the degree of environmental resilience, which is characterized by the greater resistance of plants to pests, diseases and especially the harmful effects of droughts and others climatic anomalies that are already manifesting themselves', he says.[5]

Native's comprehensive environmental measurements help reinforce this natural resilience by anticipating problems with the soil and mitigating them before they lead to declining yields and wildlife. But they also help demonstrate the positive impact the company's plantations have far beyond the business, including being an important breeding ground for large cats and 45 other endangered species.[6] So rich has Native's understanding of its interconnectedness with nature become, that Balbo Jr once demanded the return of an anaconda that had been removed from their fields because he knew how vital it was to the healthy functioning of the plantation's ecosystem!

Despite this obvious interconnection, until recently most accountancy courses taught at universities and colleges have treated environmental and social impacts as 'externalities' – peripheral to the main task of monitoring financial transactions, as the term suggests. But in reality, it's money and profits that are peripheral – or at least entirely contingent – on the material welfare of people and the planet. In our current culture of profit maximization, financial measures have become the dominant objective of business, rather than following any broader purpose. Instead, companies need to decide what kind of impacts they want to have on the world, and create metrics that measure those things most valuable to them.

The Co-operative Group in the UK realized it needed to measure local community wellbeing if it was going to deliver on part of its core social purpose of 'supporting communities', which was voted a priority by its 10,000 members.[7] So the company developed the Community Wellbeing Index, a searchable online database that provides metrics about a neighbourhood based on the things they most value, such as the amount of green space, quality of education and health.[8] The results help the Co-operative identify where and what challenges are facing local communities so they can target their social programmes and encourage the public to mobilize too. They also provide the basis for numerous KPIs to monitor their impact over time.

At first glance, there are many aspects of the Global Goals that might seem as unmeasurable and intangible as community wellbeing. But a great deal of relevant data already exists, and there are many universities, institutions and new tech companies that specialize in analysing and bringing such data together – like the many universities and scientific groups that helped Native measure their soil and biodiversity, and the geo-spatial company Geolytix that helped the Co-operative with their index. What's important is that companies find ways to measure what they treasure in their business and the wider world beyond just money.

Making these 'invisibles' known and measurable is the vital first step to incorporating the Global Goals into mainstream business reporting once a company determines to stop ignoring them. Only when you name and know the issue can you start counting it.[9] And by connecting the critical parts of a business with each of the Global Goals and understanding their relationship, a company can quickly identify the knowledge gaps and information they need to monitor how responsible they are. The next step is to create meaningful performance metrics using those measurables that actually help positively address the Global Goals rather than continue to reproduce damaging behaviours.

THE FINANCIALIZATION DILEMMA: DOES MONETIZING PEOPLE AND NATURE UNDERMINE THEIR TRUE VALUE?

To encourage countries to account for social and environmental 'externalities' in the valuing of their economy (which is normally just predicated on a valuation of the country's finished goods and services, known as GDP), the UN introduced a System of Environmental-Economic Accounting (SEEA) in the 1990s. It pioneered the idea of 'natural capital' and ascribing a monetary 'asset' value to nature as a way of integrating it into the balance sheet of the economy, recognizing its value and managing it more sustainably.

But while its intentions may have been laudable, critics say it has led to a narrowly defined valuing of nature as a commodity that's owned and traded, not enjoyed in its own right. Trees, for example, are measured by their commercial timber and carbon-sequestering value, while their importance to biodiversity or recreation are also linked to market valuations that bear little relation to how people and other wildlife actually enjoy or depend on them. The political ecologist Professor Sian Sullivan says research shows this monetary valuation of nature has had a limited effect on conserving it, arguing the method is 'coherent to capital(ism), but perhaps obstructive to the system change arguably required for the sustenance of future environmental health and diversity'.[10]

The same tensions exist when companies try to monetize nature and other social externalities in their accounting. If the value of human rights or local communities is only measured by their transactional worth, they become economically determined – not socially – and the true value of them to the business, their customers, stakeholders and the wider world is undermined, reduced and ultimately misrepresented.[11] Besides, it's widely accepted in accountancy that any financial valuation is always incomplete, biased and specific to the purpose it was originally made for. So, while integrating the Global Goals into a company's financial accounts is important, it's impossible to fully capture the responsibility a company has to them if they are only measured financially and presented as a single, inadequate figure.

SIMPLE measures, aligned metrics and the importance of accurate data

The use of SMART measures that cascade down from strategic business objectives, which are themselves derived from a company's mission and values, has been the conventional way of performance managing a business for decades. But they have many inherent weaknesses that make them insufficient for tackling sustainability on their own.

Almost by definition, SMART measures are narrow, short-termist and fragmented, particularly in big business where targets are primarily concerned with financial imperatives to produce ever-increasing profits for quarterly reports and rising share prices. As a result, the same traits and priorities are encouraged in employees and the wider business culture, where silo thinking and chasing monthly sales targets for financial reward become the norm.

But greater aspiration and broader motivation are needed to seriously tackle the challenges of sustainability. So a responsible business should look to augment SMART targets with SIMPLE measures that fill in the gaps and link them more directly to their social purpose and the Global Goals, by testing if they are also:

Strategic
Interconnected
Meaningful
Purpose-driven
Long-term
Educative

The most comprehensive way of ensuring targets are always both SMART and SIMPLE from the outset is to use one of the many Global Goals-based business reporting and monitoring tools, which help companies map their social purpose and activities against the 17 Global Goals and create KPIs and measures that directly contribute to them. Examples include the World Benchmarking Alliance, Future-Fit Business Benchmark and B Impact Assessment – all of which provide a full spectrum of sustainability measures and allow their thousands of users to compile handy benchmarks across countries and sectors.

In the UK, Business in the Community's Responsible Business Tracker is used by more than 94 large and medium-sized companies across 24 sectors. Its role in sharing best practice and galvanizing the Global Goals has been recognized in the UK government's own official report into the country's progress on the Global Goals.[12] But even among these pioneering companies using the Responsible Business Tracker, a recent annual survey[13] found that:

- Only 43% mapped their business strategies against the Global Goals.
- 33% admitted having limited knowledge of the Global Goals.
- 50% hadn't reduced their GHG emissions, and only 21% had committed to going 'net zero'.
- 77% recognized the importance of maintaining a healthy ecosystem to their business, but only 18% had set targets to monitor their strategies for doing this.

An important role of these kinds of tools is to point out such gaps between a company's social purpose aspirations and its actual operations, making sure they 'walk the talk' on sustainability. PwC's annual survey of 1,000 global companies' published reports found a similar discrepancy in 2019, with 72% mentioning the Global Goals but only 14% having any specific and meaningful targets around them.[14] And without those SMART and SIMPLE targets aligned properly with the Global Goals, the cumulative effect of an organization's sustainability strategy might not be very sustainable at all, no matter how wide-ranging and ambitious it is.

For instance, despite the Scottish government drawing up a comprehensive set of sustainability indicators in its plans to create a 'Sustainable Scotland', a study in 2008 showed that they not only didn't measure progress effectively, but they also 'calculatively captured' and distorted the way sustainability could be delivered.[15] That's because the measures they chose were highly selective, representing less than a fifth of the many social and environmental impact measurements available. For instance, car use was a key indicator but not public transport, despite new train services being planned across the country. So the impacts and benefits of one but not the other were being captured, despite them both being an important part of the overall picture of sustainability.

What the study found, however, is that this was reflective of the Scottish government's political agenda at the time, which tried to integrate more market-led solutions rather than, say, increasing regulation or public spending. In this way, their measurements were calculatively capturing a subjective version of sustainability that would support their preferred strategy, rather than trying to objectively record the full range of sustainability indicators and following the science to understand what actually works best (something we'll look at in more detail later in this chapter). However, like many other governments since 2015, the Scottish government has now changed its national performance frameworks to align with the Global Goals, the impact of which is cascading through its networks of social institutions that have all developed connected or comparable SMART and SIMPLE performance metrics.[16]

Just as using SMART targets can lead a business to reward and incentivize behaviour and activities that are unsustainable, being too selective in your sustainability metrics rather than led by the Global Goals and best practice can have similar results. But even the very best sustainability strategies can be derailed by measures that are too few or inaccurate. This is why improving the data they're based on is so important. Fortunately, there are numerous tech companies specializing in niche areas of sustainability data that can not only help plug data gaps, but also employ artificial intelligence (AI) and machine learning (ML) to provide better forecasting.

One such company is digital startup Greenvest Solutions, which uses satellite data to help accelerate the adoption of renewable energy around the world – particularly in emerging countries. By applying AI technologies, the company can help identify the best sites for wind, solar and hybrid plants and provide near real-time monitoring of their operational capacity and social impacts, as well as more accurately forecasting future power generation (a notoriously difficult aspect of managing renewable energy).

The applications for this kind of AI-interpreted satellite data obviously stretch way beyond the energy sector and can be used for monitoring the social and environmental impacts of all kinds of business activity. Corporates like BP and Cargill, for example, are combining such data with drone mapping for when cloud cover hampers satellites, using them to monitor and anticipate oil pipe leaks in remote locations and illegal deforestation on palm plantations.[17]

And AI and ML more generally are helping to improve and maintain the accuracy of all reported data. Already, they can detect incorrect data and outliers using statistical analysis and plug missing data with modelling. In monitoring climate change, they're used to streamline and correct discrepancies between different global models, making more accurate predictions of GHG concentrations that will keep global temperature rises below the 2°C target threshold. AI can also draw on alternative sources of data, such as the 'Internet of Things' (any object that is connected online) and mobile phone apps (whether anonymized metadata or through active 'citizen scientist'-type initiatives), as well as be used in language processing and sentiment analytics to arrive at more nuanced interpretations and analysis of industry reports.

So whatever KPIs, indicators or metrics a responsible business is setting, it's vital they align with the Global Goals-derived purpose of the company and are based on the most accurate and granular data possible if they're to truly drive up sustainability. But equally important in that process is how the results of those measures are reported and interpreted – both internally and externally. And these can be poles apart for obvious and often cynical reasons.

Selective reporting, materiality and embracing openness

The UNGSII has been highly critical of companies' selective financial reporting, suggesting only 30–60% of the value of a business is reflected in its annual reports.[18] With some companies (especially digital ones), that figure is far higher[19] – in February 2021, only 5% of Tesla's gargantuan market valuation was contained in its financial balance sheet. So much of a firm's non-financial value – particularly on ESG matters – is missing or incomplete in annual reports, with different or a lack of standards used to measure it, making appraising and comparing performance extremely difficult. This has created a chaotic field where businesses are able to choose whether and how to report on their non-regulated, non-financial performance, which, for many of us, is the information we're most interested in. It would certainly help explain where the missing 95% of Tesla's value lies.

The UNGSII cites this selective reporting as a major contributing factor to global financial crises because it misinforms investors who then make poor investment decisions. But since the 2008 financial crash, and thanks to the concerted efforts of the socially responsible investment (SRI) movement over several decades, many new frameworks and rating agencies for ESG metrics have been introduced, including the EU's Non-Financial Reporting Directive, the UN Global Compass and the Dow Jones Sustainable Indices. Other think tanks, NGOs and political foundations, such as the World Economic Forum and International Business Council, are also currently working with the big global accounting firms to create 22 standardized ESG metrics, which will be heavily based on the Global Goals.[20]

However, many of these proposed standards have underlying interests that are not wholly aligned with the Global Goals or prioritize particular powerful groups in society. To be fair, all of the groups behind them are relatively transparent about their funders, objectives and stakeholders whose interests they're promoting. But in most cases they are self-appointed institutions trying to stake a claim in this contested arena, which is characterized by a constant and dizzying shifting of coalitions between similarly dull-named groups.

Take the Better Alignment Project, launched by Corporate Reporting Dialogue in 2019. It looked to map four different non-financial reporting standards based on recommendations from the Task Force on Climate-Related Financial Disclosures (chaired by Michael Bloomberg). The participants on the project were the Climate Disclosure Standards Board (CDSB), Financial Accounting Standards Board (FASB), Global Reporting Initiative (GRI), International Accounting Standards Board (IASB), International Integrated Reporting Council (IIRC), International Organization for Standardization (ISO) and Sustainability Accounting Standards Board (SASB). Ironically, the IASB has since launched its own proposal for a standard-setting body, and the SASB and IIRC announced their merger to form the Value Foundation.

Given all the upheaval, it's extremely difficult to predict the future trajectory of non-financial reporting. But before any business decides to adopt a new reporting standard, it's critical to undertake a review of the setting body's purpose and members, finding out who they represent and how they're funded, in order to ensure it aligns with the purpose of the business. Accounting requirements have been found to drive change in an organization towards what is reported, rather than towards purpose or vision. And profit-oriented rating agencies are interested in businesses providing them with sellable data, rather than sustainable transformation. There is nothing intrinsically wrong with that, but a dose of healthy scepticism as to their motivation or legitimacy will go a long way to making sure how and what is reported doesn't create problems later on.

While all these initiatives (however flawed) and the new norm of businesses producing annual sustainability reports have provided more scrutiny of a company's sustainability than ever before, new research shows there are still huge discrepancies between what firms voluntarily acknowledge as ESG risks in these reports and what appears in their financial accounts.[21] The study by the Lloyds Banking Group Centre for Responsible Business looked at some of the world's leading corporate sustainability reports to identify whether known threats to planetary boundaries, social stability and ecological systems informed the 'materiality assessments' as to what was included in their financial accounts.

Materiality may seem like a technical topic that only excites lawyers and auditors, but it's critical to business accountability. Something is material if it might affect the value of the company or influence a stakeholder's decisions. And materiality determines what a business should disclose to the rest of the world, regardless of financial reporting regulations. For example, if your beer requires clean and unpolluted water, then it's likely that the impact of climate change on local rainfall patterns and the effects of industrial emissions on water sources are potentially material. So a brewery may need to disclose what efforts it is taking to mitigate these negative impacts. But the study found that very few companies classified such sustainability risks as material, meaning they were effectively engaging in non-disclosure of very real threats to their business.

While standard setters, regulators and political institutions like the EU are looking to compel businesses to disclose sustainable risks they consider material, there is a lack of consensus as to how to determine what is material or to whom. However stringent the reporting protocol, the decision about what's material is left to these often self-appointed bodies to determine and not led by the concerns of the different people and stakeholders using the company reports for their decision-making. But a new generation of more comprehensive and transparent online reporting platforms allows the material concerns of the user to be addressed more easily.

The G17Eco platform by World Wide Generation is one of the leading examples.[22] It aims to measure and align all companies and reporting protocols to the Global Goals, providing a one-stop shop to compare progress, see how it links to national and international targets, and search for specific issues that are most material to the user. It's an extraordinarily ambitious project that is built using 'open architecture' to allow as many different partners as possible to plug in and use the system, which employs data bots and distributed ledger technology to integrate their different measurements.

But what makes G17Eco so powerful for users is the ability to map, measure and monitor any sustainability issues that are most material to them. The Global Goals provide a stable, authoritative and inclusive set of risks understood by all, and together with an open reporting platform like G17Eco, the balance of power is shifted as to what is chosen to be disclosed, in what format and to whom. Companies can no longer hide their sustainability by being selective or using non-standard measures, and the public can get a full picture of a company's non-financial risks, even if they aren't materially acknowledged in their financial accounts.

While this openness might feel threatening to a company, exposing it to reputational risk should it fall short on some of the Global Goals, it's far less risky than ignoring or remaining unaware of those sustainability issues and being vulnerable to future damage. Take the tobacco industry, for instance, which, for decades, denied the damaging health impacts of smoking and tried to suppress scientific research that proved it. That strategy may have prevented a loss in sales in the short term, but in the long term it's left big tobacco companies facing vast compensation claims today for the cost of caring for smoking-related illness and deaths – including US$9 billion a year to US state governments *forever* since a legal settlement in 1998.[23] While this was a sustainability impact that was known and relatively easily measured, these companies chose to hide rather than mitigate it at huge expense and with great cynicism. In hindsight, it seems individual managers were trying to push forward in time the recognition of the liability as it was inevitable that others would eventually find out. Not only was this irresponsible, but a really bad business decision too.

Imagine, then, the potential damage of all those issues that are currently unknown, knowingly or not. This is where the biggest risks to any company lie, and the Global Goals provide a comprehensive roadmap for where to look for them. And just because some of the goals may be more qualitative in nature or seem more difficult to measure (although new and better metrics are being developed all the time), it doesn't mean they aren't important or even vital to include. Ask Robert McNamara.

The former US Secretary of Defense gave his name to the 'McNamara fallacy' (also known as the 'quantitative fallacy') after trying to draw up metrics to measure the progress of the Vietnam War.[24] Enemy body count and other easily quantifiable indicators were included, but the feelings of the Vietnamese people were omitted as being too difficult to measure. So, while US deaths tracked well below those of the North Vietnamese during the campaign, McNamara's metrics couldn't capture the growing Vietnamese resistance on the ground and the impending defeat of the US.

Like the sliding scale of irresponsibility we mentioned earlier, the social scientist Daniel Yankelovich neatly describes the self-defeating path a McNamara-like aversion to more nuanced factors leads:

> The first step is to measure whatever can be easily measured. This is OK as far as it goes. The second step is to disregard that which can't be easily measured or to give it an arbitrary quantitative value. This is artificial and misleading. The third step is to presume that what can't be measured easily really isn't important. This is blindness. The fourth

step is to say that what can't be easily measured really doesn't exist. This is suicide.[25]

With expectations now so high around companies addressing the Global Goals and the tools and metrics available to do it becoming increasingly more accurate, pretending these sustainability issues aren't important or don't exist is suicidal for businesses too. So companies shouldn't be afraid of embracing Global Goals-based reporting or ashamed of what it might discover – in the same way they wouldn't avoid or omit recording losses and liabilities in their financial accounts. Besides, a full-spectrum sustainability report, like that produced by pasta maker Andriani, can be an excellent way of showing a company's commitment to a more sustainable world and how it is already contributing, not just where it's failing.[26]

The Italian firm has fully adopted a GRI standard approach since 2018, publishing a sustainability report that breaks down its impacts against six areas of accountability: financial, employees, products, suppliers, the community, and the environment. It doesn't have detailed, year-on-year targets for every Global Goal, but it does show Andriani's commitment to all of the UN's Agenda 2030 long-term targets – as well as more ambitious ones of their own, such as becoming carbon neutral by 2025 – and provides metrics to track their progress towards them. Any suspicions of box-ticking or playing 'buzzword bingo' with the Global Goals are belied by links to substantive sustainability activities being undertaken, such as a new energy-efficient office building and on-site electricity generation.

But more than that, the report takes the time to show the wider social and environmental context for everything Andriani is doing, talking through the methodology and demonstrating the company's understanding of the issues involved with making a more sustainable world. In this way, the report is a tool for educating others about the importance of the Global Goals. The company accountants behind it don't limit themselves to proudly telling the story of their employer's success over the course of a year; they're also explaining its values and wider purpose to encourage others to think and do the same.

The benefit of a business having its Global Goals-based purpose so well integrated into its accounting and performance management in this way is that it can be far more engaging than conventional annual or quarterly accounts. Not many external (or perhaps even internal) stakeholders will be that moved by how they're helping a company's profits or share price to soar, but seeing how they're contributing to the global fight against climate change or empowering women and girls living in developing countries is far more powerful.

This is what the UK social enterprise Wildhearts attempts to convey to its clients and suppliers.[27] Each invoice it sends carries a calculation of how much the money they're paying will contribute to its environmental and social initiatives, which includes providing sanitary pads to girls in India and South Africa so they can finish their schooling and microloans for women in sub-Saharan Africa. And the reason Wildhearts supplies stationery and document services to some of the world's biggest corporates is largely because it helps them meet their own Global Goals targets by using their largely recycled or reusable products and collaborating on their social initiatives. (This idea of businesses helping customers to realize their own sustainable values is encapsulated by the Good Life Goals, which we'll look at in more depth in Myth 4.)

Purpose has become the driving force for Wildhearts' business model, eclipsing other considerations in its offer to future clients and how it accounts for itself. Its impact report is a virtuous assemblage of non-financial metrics, concerned more with the lives it has helped improve than the revenues of its business supplies operation. Of course, as a social enterprise, Wildhearts has chosen to take such a non-profit-centric approach to business. But it demonstrates the enormous potential for all companies to engage, trade and collaborate with each other and their stakeholders by using purpose rather than money as its primary measure of success.

Misleading metrics, alternative accounting and the rise of external accountability

Accounting is, in essence, a dividing practice. It simplifies things and decides if they're profitable or non-profitable, up or down, positive or negative, dividing the results again and again. These scores can then be ranked internally, to see which department or product is most profitable or costly, and externally, to compare a company's share price or GHG emissions, for example.

This works well on a single dimension but becomes much more complicated with 17. How do you divide and rank a firm along the 17 dimensions of the Global Goals? A company might perform well on 10 Global Goals but awfully on the other 7, or fail to give any information about any of them at all. Even if a business does all of the right things described so far – capturing all its Global Goals impacts, setting meaningful targets based on the most accurate data, and reporting its progress in an open and comprehensive way – it's still entirely possible to draw misleading conclusions that could jeopardize sustainable decision-making. Why? Because of the way accounts can be analysed and misinterpreted by people with varying levels of literacy when it comes to sustainability.

For example, one common metric for procurement decisions is to rank companies by their total carbon emissions divided by their revenues.[28] On the surface, this 'carbon intensity' ratio would appear to make perfect sense, equating emissions with trading activity. But do emissions really vary by sales in such a linear way? Just because a well-established fossil fuel company makes vast revenues doesn't make its equally vast carbon footprint more sustainable than that of a solar energy company with smaller revenues and the carbon debt of building new production facilities. Besides which, fossil fuel companies *still* don't include the carbon stored in their products as part of their GHG emissions calculations. Obviously the issue is much more complicated than the carbon intensity ratio suggests (as we'll explore further in the next chapter), but recent research has shown that inappropriate carbon accounting methods like this result in investments that are actually adding to the climate crisis.[29]

Unfortunately, simplistic and misleading metrics are everywhere in business analyses. That's because company reports are replete with so-called 'vanity metrics', which are there more to make the business look good to others – to make them attractive to invest in and do business with – than help anyone understand its performance in a meaningful way.[30] Running totals and cumulative sales graphs are the classic example, since they can only improve and have no context or timescale to judge if things are getting better or worse. When was the last time you saw a graph in a corporate report that didn't have a rising trend from left to right? But even monthly sales and customer acquisition numbers don't tell you about the acquisition costs, security of supply or lifetime value of a customer, which would reveal far more about the long-term sustainability of the business.

Because they're so non-specific, vanity metrics tell you nothing about their cause or potential non-financial consequences. That's why any sudden spike in sales or other unexpected positive results should be treated with initial scepticism and investigated as seriously as declining or negative ones. They can be red flags for a litany of unsustainable business practices, such as selling below cost, bribery, corruption, inferior products, misselling, using forced labour and illegal pollution.

Conversely, some sustainability metrics can be so overly complex as to be rendered indecipherable and ultimately just as meaningless. For example, the water companies in England and Wales have been reporting their GHG emissions in compliance with regulations for years and are recognized as exemplars for sustainability reporting, ranking among the most sustainable businesses in the UK. Yet an academic study of the metrics they use for emissions showed them to be inconsistent, incomplete and incomparable – both between companies and over time. In some cases the different formulas they used had margins of error of more than 50%, which made it all but impossible to determine if a company's climate change impacts were really decreasing or not over time.[31]

Critics would say this obfuscation and confusion is deliberate on the part of the water companies to prevent too much interrogation by customers, capital markets and other stakeholders. On the other hand, the companies' supporters would argue that they are providing more non-regulated, non-financial climate change information than many others. Either way, why wouldn't a business choose measures and metrics that give them as much leeway as possible to selectively paint themselves in the most positive light? Because whether a metric is overly simplistic or complex in its presentation is arguably by design. Both presume and rely on a prima facie acceptance of their significance and veracity, with the primary aim of creating a favourable impression of a business's performance. That they even-handedly inform and help someone wanting a true appraisal in order to hold the company to account is of secondary importance.

That's why open reporting platforms like G17Eco are so potentially revolutionary. They neutralize this company-centric bias and democratize the accounting process, allowing more scrutiny and accountability by external stakeholders beyond just shareholders, such as local communities and campaign groups. And because data is collected across all 17 of the Global Goals, stakeholders can ultimately create their own sustainability reports and decide what is material to them. At its most radical, this approach can help stakeholders create alternative accounting systems, which companies could then be obliged to participate in and integrate into their own accountability practices.

One of the most interesting examples is in the Niger Delta, where the persistent problem of oil spills since the 1990s, caused largely by the activities of the petrochemical multinational Shell, required a new approach by local regulators. The data used by Nigerian authorities to sanction Shell for environmental and social damages was scant and often supplied by the corporate's own monitoring programmes, making it hugely partial and selective. Shell consequently got away with under-reporting spills and avoiding the costs of clean-up for years.

So a coalition of NGOs developed a web-based 'counter-account', which allowed those affected by these oil spills to record when, where and what was being spilled, including images, videos and first-person testimonies of their suffering. This counter-account was highly effective and led to a partnership with the authorities to enable government agencies, oil companies, civil society groups and communities to all engage and share critical information. Now fully integrated into government regulation and rebranded as the Oil Spill Monitor (OSM), it provides open access to detailed accounts of the cause, timing, location, quantity and remediation of every single oil spill in the Niger Delta. Most importantly, it gives everyone affected a chance to give their accounts of the impacts, including local people whose voices would normally go unheard and whose lives have been blighted by disease caused by polluted farmland, fish, drinking water and air.[32]

By capturing all the stakeholders in the region, not only did OSM equip the Nigerian authorities with a more complete range of data to hold Shell to account, but it also allowed local communities and NGOs to audit, verify and challenge the authorities and their official accounts, too. Undercover filming by Amnesty International found the Nigerian authorities' oil spill investigation teams to be under the control of Shell, bribing locals to lie about pipe leakages being caused by oil thieves' sabotage. Shell eventually paid £55 million in compensation in 2015 for deliberately minimizing its oil spill assessments after losing a court case led by the human rights charity. And in 2021, a Dutch court found Shell Nigeria liable for damage caused by oil leaks and ordered them to pay compensation to farmers and install equipment to prevent future damage, ruling that they had a duty of care to the communities wherever they operated.

What the OSM illustrates so vividly is how powerful accounting can be in the way it helps represent events that have happened and leads to material changes in the present. All those various stakeholders in the Niger Delta helped to construct an account of the past that could be used to influence future decision-making and governance at a distance – whether Shell's management at their headquarters in The Hague or the high court judges in London and the Netherlands who heard Amnesty International's court case. Far from being dull and inert documents, accounts can bring to life the past actions of a company, the specific impacts it has had and the people who were there to see them. As such, they're an essential tool for NGOs to lobby governments, shareholders to protest against company executives at AGMs and communities to engage with businesses on issues that are often many miles and many years away.

Accountants as scientists, radical uncertainty and the feedback loop

We've seen how the best sustainability reports require company accountants to be more than just collators of numbers and engage in more storytelling around the non-financial impacts of the business. But while accounting has always involved an element of artistry in its use of judgement and presentation, it is fundamentally an evidence-based practice with many similarities to scientific methods.

Accountants observe and gather evidence of a business's activities. They measure, quantify and analyse according to established methods that are informed by widely agreed theories. This disciplined, methodical work is what gives the profession its legitimacy and power. And the rules-based rigour of traditional financial accounting means accountants can be jailed for fraud if they intentionally overstate revenue, fail to record expenses or misstate assets and liabilities. But a similar rigour has yet to be established in the kind of non-financial accounting that characterizes sustainability reporting. So Enron levels of misrepresentation in some corporate sustainability reports continue to go on unsanctioned. Indeed, the fact that Enron was publicly praised for the quality of its CSR reports and environmental performance at one time is a lesson for everyone.

Like all modern sciences, accounting idealistically assumes that if you quantify and mathematically model all of life on Earth accurately enough, it's possible to formulate universal laws that provide certainty and produce outcomes that are both predictable and comparable. But the latest sustainability science is starting to reject those ideas. It acknowledges the inherent uncertainty, complexity and non-linear dynamics of the Earth's living systems, such as its ecology, atmospheric chemistry and meteorology. No matter how comprehensive and advanced the quantifying and modelling by scientists, these systems are impossible to predict.

This is why many researchers in these fields are now building this uncertainty into their measurements and evaluations, using ranges, probabilities, qualified estimates and scenarios that are less definitive and more candid about their unpredictability. It would require quite some cultural shift in the world of company accounting for accountants and stakeholders to understand and accommodate such flexible and uncertain measurements in their sustainability reports, but it would provide a truer, fairer representation of their business and its impacts if they did.

For now, it seems banks, insurers and even institutions like the UN are determined to press on with financializing externalities so that all environmental risks can be 'priced in', modelled and managed by the allocation of capital.[33] This financialization of nature proffers the tempting notion that if, for example, whales are ascribed a monetary value for their contributions to fisheries, tourism and carbon sequestering (the International Monetary Fund [IMF] has actually come up with an estimate of US$2 million for each whale), then banks and businesses will be more inclined to preserve them.[34] Even allowing for the moral dangers of this commodification (see p 41), it's an approach that persists with the flawed idea of nature's certainty and predictability that is fast becoming an outdated and even dangerous assumption.

Indeed, researchers at the UCL Institute for Innovation and Public Purpose now argue that there is 'radical uncertainty' when it comes to the environmental breakdown we are currently seeing.[35] Nature is so complex and interconnected that it's impossible to predict or even imagine what it will do next. Vast forest fires, floods and extreme droughts thought to be once-in-a-century events are happening all around the world with alarming frequency. Therefore it can't be considered as a 'conventional market failure' that can be calculated, say the researchers, because 'the relevant information that markets require to reorient capital may never be known in full'.[36] As the former US Secretary of Defense, the late Donald Rumsfeld, famously once put it, there will always be 'unknown unknowns: the ones we don't know we don't know'.

So the UCL researchers advocate taking more of a 'precautionary principle' approach, being wary of any innovations that may pose a risk to the environment while the scientific evidence of their effects remain unclear. This is well established in the fields of health or environmental protection, but less so in the world of finance and business (despite accountants' similar and long-held concept of prudence). After the 2008 global financial crisis, when the limitations of financial modelling and forecasting based on prior data were brutally exposed, new regulatory measures for financial institutions such as stress-testing and minimum capital reserves were introduced. But that same precautionary approach has yet to be taken towards non-financial risks, even though regulating for a transition away from high-emissions activities and products would clearly mitigate against further climate-related crises and the financial crises they would likely precipitate.

So what is the role of a responsible accountant in this chaotic and unpredictable world if they can no longer adequately measure or forecast their company's impacts? Certainly, they must continue to be committed to the scientific gathering, measuring and analysis of evidence as best they can. But a new flexibility in measurements, caution in forecasting and self-awareness of the dangers of rigidly sticking to conventional models is needed to prevent becoming blinded by methodological certainty, in the same way banks and credit-rating agencies did with subprime mortgages before the 2008 financial crisis. Accountants still have a duty to take decisions and strive for perfect knowledge, even if the latter is impossible. But just making do with discredited models and techniques is no longer defensible.

More broadly, accountants should see themselves as vital feedback loops that can help improve the workings of the business. By setting meaningful and strategic targets and monitoring their outcomes, accounting constantly informs and helps managers to adjust their strategy in order to improve efficiencies and productivity. Without those corrective feedback loops – or were the feedback to be dysfunctional – the business would soon go into decline. Beyond the performance of the business, accountants can also provide effective feedback loops from wider society and the external environment on which the business depends. To do this, they need to have some understanding of how various socio-ecological systems work and the relationships that keep them stable. Primarily, this means knowing what the most important 'slow variables' are and how they feed back and interact.[37]

For example, nutrients are a critical slow variable for clearwater lakes. The phosphorous and nitrogen runoff from nearby urban and agricultural development is absorbed by plants growing on the lake's floor, so the plants effectively have a dampening feedback on nutrient pollution. But if the amount of nutrients exceeds the absorbing capacity of the plants, it can lead to algae blooms that have a reinforcing feedback on nutrient pollution by blocking sunlight to the lake floor, killing the plants and making even more nutrients available. Eventually the whole lake ecosystem becomes overwhelmed by algae, destabilizing its regime of carefully balanced relationships, and it finally collapses.

Of course, it's impossible for an accountant to have such detailed knowledge of every slow variable and socio-ecological system! But if their business is particularly dependent on the kind of local freshwater sources in this example or impacts on them, they should know what levels of nutrient pollution risk that tipping point of overwhelming the environment's natural dampening feedback so they can, in turn, feed back to the business that it needs to take mitigating action.

These tipping points or thresholds exist all through our society and environment, whether it's an average global temperature that would trigger unstoppable climate collapse, an infection rate that will lead to runaway levels of disease or unsustainable debt levels that will cause the financial markets to fail. It may be difficult to perceive and quantify exactly what these undesirable tipping points are, and accountants must rely on external experts to do so, but there's no doubting their catastrophic impacts for business if they're ignored. At the very least, it's the scientific and professional duty of accountants to try to make visible these wider socio-ecological connections, risks and dependencies for the business in their reporting, no matter how necessarily imprecise, uncertain or incomplete they may be.

THE STATISTICS DILEMMA: IS THE WAY WE ANALYSE ACCOUNTING DATA FLAWED?

The phrase 'lies, damned lies, and statistics' has been around for more than a century. And while people's perennial scepticism over numbers may have soured into cynicism in recent years thanks to their deliberate misuse by politicians and business, much of their power to deceive lies in our own innate inability to interpret statistics properly. The statistician Hans Rosling called it our 'dramatic instinct' because of our emotional propensity to crowd out the more unremarkable truth, identifying ten of them in his book *Factfulness*.[38] But there are five that are most relevant to accounting and interpreting accounts:

- *The size instinct:* We assume a number is big without putting it into context to check its proportions. It's one of the reasons 'vanity metrics' are so popular and effective. But it also encourages blindspots by distracting from data of real concern or leads to misconstruing the significance of smaller numbers.

- *The negativity instinct:* We instinctively pay more attention to bad figures rather than good ones. But 'good' figures can be caused by many unsustainable factors and 'bad' figures can provide valuable context so shouldn't be left out. Indeed, the more precautionary, prudent approach of sustainable accounting means it will inevitably focus more on risks anyway.

- *The gap instinct:* Accountants routinely divide things into good/bad, profit/loss, increasing/decreasing, assets/liabilities. But the reality is much more nuanced and the gap between things less polarized. False dividing practices can lead to critical misunderstandings, misleading trend analysis and oversimplistic theories, so how things are categorized needs to be more considered.

- *The blame instinct:* We tend to oversimplify the world in our analyses of business performance, looking for obvious culprits and heroes for bad and good outcomes. But this prevents us looking for alternative explanations and avoids looking at structural issues in particular. Research shows that when accounts are used to attribute blame, they get more creative and manipulative. In other words, the blame instinct can create an incentive for false accounting.

- *The destiny instinct:* We assume that certain things are constant and predictable when everything is really in a constant state of change, even if it may be at a very slow rate. This was particularly evident in early discussions around climate change, where talk of tipping points and apocalyptic weather events were once considered fanciful. So it's important to measure slow changes, being aware of their cumulative impact over time, and avoid short-term trend analysis.

Thresholds, coveillance, market failure and accountancy in a post-truth world

There is no doubt that over the last decade there has been a gathering consensus among businesses on the need for sustainability and the responsible principles behind the Global Goals, if not always the goals themselves. Initiatives like decarbonizing and anti-slavery commitments are rarely disputed and part of everyday business practice today in companies large and small. The broader problem now is not agreeing on what the sustainability issues are, but how severe and what the thresholds for action should be – particularly when it comes to the environment.

While some businesses are taking a far more precautionary approach to environmental risks, minimizing their impacts and looking to restore rather than further damage ecosystems, others are continuing to push their exploitative activities beyond environmental limits while investing more heavily in mitigation and offsetting schemes instead. Yet both groups can reasonably claim to be working towards the same sustainability targets – it's their measurements and understanding of environmental limits and thresholds that are different. Regulating for these at international, national and local levels would seem to be an obvious way to standardize them for all companies to follow and respond in a more consistent way.

But the urgency for action is such that we can't wait for this level of certainty and political consensus before acting. Sadly, regulations and laws tend to lag behind scientific proof. And scientific proof lags behind emerging evidence of harm. However, we do have models that can predict impacts and offer the chance to act before causing irreparable harm to critical socio-ecological systems. These are similar to the models used by governments during the COVID-19 crisis, where interventions were based on modelled predictions of the outbreak rather than waiting for the death toll to mount and the virus to overwhelm the healthcare system before acting. But because these models are incomplete and constantly evolving, we need to accept that sometimes what was the right thing to do one moment may suddenly become insufficient.

For example, currently the net zero carbon targets in the Global Goals are set for 2050 based on an average global temperature rise of no more than 2°C. But already the science has changed, with climate scientists predicting catastrophic sea level rises unless average temperatures are kept below 1.5°C. Unfortunately, with our current targets, the Intergovernmental Panel on Climate Change (IPCC) estimates we'll sail past 1.5°C by 2040.[39] And NASA warns that even this 1.5°C figure belies the fact that it's an average temperature rise that is not equally distributed around the world (another example of the potentially misleading nature of statistics). Its satellite mapping shows the greatest temperature increases are in the Arctic and mid-latitude regions, where average temperatures have already risen more than 2°C.[40]

These kind of moving sustainability thresholds are going to be our new normal, and businesses need to prepare for this. Luckily, successful businesses have experience of acting on leading indicators, models, forecasts and incomplete data. Business decisions have always involved a combination of known facts, trends, experience, intuition and imagined futures. Budgeting and targets are predictions based on models, and investment decisions are based on imagined outcomes measured against different scenarios. While everyone wants as much certainty as possible, we all accept that the future is essentially unknowable. This is why the better your ability to imagine or predict the future, the better your decisions will be. Learning about how different systems will behave will pay back considerably, protecting investments and future-proofing businesses.

Unfortunately, many people's understanding of the sustainability of socio-ecological systems is skewed by self-interest and incorrect assumptions. Many governments (including the UK's) still take a 'goods and services' approach to nature, determining fishing quotas, for example, on the basis of sustainable, commercial exploitation of certain species rather than what's best for the whole of the marine ecosystem. And forests, too, may be sustainably logged for commercial timber, given their capacity to recover over the next 300 years. But this takes no account of the impacts on people's enjoyment of the forest or the cultural importance of it remaining intact and undamaged by industry.[41]

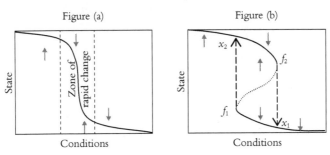

Source: Haines-Young et al (2006)

Furthermore, these incomplete models of sustainability wrongly assume that a socio-ecological system will respond in a balanced and predictable way, restoring itself if we simply leave it alone. Even when their condition passes a point of rapid decline (see Figure a), we often mistakenly assume our human impacts will ultimately be reversed in a similar, incremental fashion over time. But the truth is that the resilience of any system can be damaged by humans beyond repair, and resilience behaves in a far more complicated and non-linear fashion (see Figure b).

Once a system passes a certain threshold (represented by the dotted arrows in Figure b), even the smallest disturbance may quickly push it beyond a tipping point (f_2) where it catastrophically 'flips' to a far worse and possibly irreversible state (x_1). That's why f_2 should really be considered the 'point of no return'. Even if all pressures on the system are removed, it is incredibly difficult, if not impossible, for it to recover and flip back in equally dramatic fashion $(f_1$ to $x_2)$, which is why so much of the UK's overgrazed uplands have never naturally reverted to their original forest cover even decades after farming has ceased.

Predictive models that incorporate the reality of tipping points can help mitigate and reduce the possibilities of catastrophic collapses happening in the same way that the predicted realities of COVID-19 helped politicians to justify lockdown, collaborative action and mass mobilization of resources for treatment and vaccination. The various modelled scenarios of collapsing education systems, health systems, economic systems, transportation systems and supply chains if coronavirus was left to spread unchecked were accepted as evidence in this decision-making, despite ongoing debates over their accuracy. What was important was that this evidence was considered robust enough to be trusted and powerful enough to trigger necessary action, so that the harm the models predicted never came true.

Similarly, while many regulatory authorities, NGOs and businesses are locked in subjective debates about the environmental limits of the oceans, forests and other ecosystems to determine how much damage is considered both socially acceptable and environmentally sustainable, the objective existence of catastrophic thresholds remains indisputable. But we don't quite know where those 'points of no return' lie. And in practice, even the most knowledgeable scientists admit that it is difficult to identify a threshold before it is crossed.[42] But the important thing is to be aware that they do exist. And any accounting system that doesn't contain some limits or thresholds will only create future problems and perpetuate risks.

Given this struggle for governments and even the Global Goals to keep up with the changing science and be specific about thresholds, legally binding and advisory sustainability targets can only ever be a part of the solution. Businesses and their accountants will also need to proactively follow and respond to the latest science themselves without waiting for any external regulation or protocols. Better still, businesses can help inform the latest science by using their own impact monitoring and data from across their operations to feed into wider sustainability research projects. This could be a combination of collaborative research with scientists (such as the Brazilian sugar company Native did with its soil measurements), 'citizen science'-type initiatives involving companies' customers agreeing to collect or share useful data, or finding new, alternative data sources, such as drone mapping and the Internet of Things.

What's important is that this information is collected and shared ethically and universally, for the purposes of improving sustainability measurements and scientific understanding, not commercial gain. At its most ambitious, it could be an attempt to harness the somewhat dystopian direction of our mass surveillance society as a potential means for improving threshold knowledge and mutual accountability. Call it 'coveillance', if you like, where those being monitored are willing participants in a collaborative effort to avert a global ecological catastrophe.

Indeed, new distributed ledger technologies, such as blockchain, are already helping major companies to capture, store and share sustainability data about the life cycle of their raw materials and resources. The cosmetics company Estée Lauder uses blockchain to trace vanilla products across its whole supply chain. From the smallholder farms in Madagascar where the vanilla is grown to Estée Lauder's factories via local and international suppliers, information is gathered at each stage using QR codes that allow full transparency and traceability of the product and environmental and ethical standards to be interrogated.[43]

It's this accumulation of data with each transaction or activity that makes blockchain so powerful. Normally, this chain of knowledge is broken with each sale of a product and the data destroyed in conventional accounting ledgers. But blockchain has the potential to attach details of all of the various impacts of a component or raw material throughout its journey, tracking it everywhere it goes and gathering more and more data about its life. So accountants working for electric vehicle manufacturers, who have often found it notoriously difficult to evidence things like environmental pollution, biodiversity impact, health and safety issues, forced child labour and human rights abuses in their mined raw materials, can now use blockchain to provide full visibility of the provenance of precious metals like cobalt that are essential to making batteries.

Whether businesses take this proactive approach or just follow the regulations and guidelines set by external authorities, company accountants certainly can't leave their sustainability measures to be led or determined by the market, which is failing in plain sight. Accounting in publicly listed companies has long had a symbiotic and somewhat parasitical relationship with finance, whereby accounts are seen merely as a tool for plugging into the markets. The evidence they provide is primarily modelled on investors' narrow criteria, which, for the most part, are concerned with hitting SMART-based financial targets and the occasional handful of ESG measures. So the company ends up being evaluated using a very partial picture of its future sustainability, which accountants are then more motivated to focus on and improve rather than scrutinize and manage all areas of the business. The result is that the markets have proved far better at serving the financial interests of companies and investors than coming anywhere close to addressing the world's most fundamental sustainability problems.

Take decarbonization, for example, which has been a well-known sustainability priority for businesses since the UN introduced the first GHG reduction targets in 1992. The market-led solutions were to have carbon intensity ratios and mandatory disclosure of carbon-based assets that would allow investors to allocate capital to those companies with the lowest carbon footprints. In this way, the issue of carbon would be 'priced in' to their valuations and encourage businesses to decarbonize to increase their market value.

As well as the obvious flaws of intensity ratios that we explored earlier, this trust that the 'wisdom of the markets' would eventually win through has been an abject failure. After 30 years, there are still a handful of highly valued oil corporations whose carbon assets alone would comfortably take the Earth past its 2°C global warming target if they were burned.[44] The evidence has been in their accounts for years, but the supposed 'rational efficiency' of the market has failed to identify and help eliminate these unsustainable carbon risks in their valuations, which could have incentivized the companies to leave their oil, gas and coal in the ground.

Despite demonstrating how making risks visible simply isn't enough to move the so-called 'invisible hand' of the markets to resolve real-world sustainability issues, responsible investors do play a vital role in influencing companies to at least account for their sustainability more stringently and comprehensively. In 2020, Ceres Investor Network and Climate Action 100+, that together represent investors with more than US$47 trillion in assets, demanded hundreds of the world's largest corporates disclose details of all their government lobbying and introduced a benchmark tracker to identify where their engagement and business models are not in line with net zero carbon commitments.[45] The Institutional Investors Group on Climate Change has also promised to align its members' US$1.3 trillion of investments with the Paris Agreement on climate change.

Not only are companies facing more rigorous sustainability demands from investors, but also from their various trade associations and third party certification schemes. The World Business Council for Sustainable Development (WBCSD), for example, recently tightened up its membership criteria from just having any kind of plan to improve sustainability to requiring science-based strategies to reach net zero GHG emissions by 2050, as well as due diligence commitments on human rights in their procurement procedures and more rigorous ESG disclosures.[46] Similarly, the TCO Certified scheme, that initially became famous for approving the power-saving credentials of computer monitors, has dramatically expanded its sustainability criteria for IT equipment over the decades so that it now includes stricter requirements on things like recycling and supply chain responsibility.[47]

From all directions, a growing sense of urgency is compelling companies to be more ambitious and committed in their sustainability targets or risk being ostracized and facing financial losses, legal penalties and public censure. As the CEO of WBCSD, Peter Bakker, has said to his members, ambitions now need to be turned into concrete actions if we're to bring about the transformations needed to prevent climate and environmental collapse. 'The bottom line is that if we don't radically change in the next decade, there is no point in optimism, because we will run out of time', he said.[48]

So accountants have to think big, think differently and set targets that lead to the Global Goals and even surpass them. Many businesses, as with several mentioned here, are aiming for net zero GHG emissions well before 2050, for example. Others have commitments to use 100% recycled or reusable materials, abolish plastics, use fully renewable energy, be gender-balanced at management level and actively enhance and enrich biodiversity through tree planting and stewardship schemes – all before the end of the decade.

Of course, the great advantage of being so ambitious is that the company will be adopting a more precautionary approach by default and is therefore less likely to be caught out by any future changes in the science or fall foul of unknown ecological thresholds. The business will also be more likely to stay ahead of market and stakeholder demands on sustainability and be more alert to future innovations and scientific developments. In short, a company that's both ambitious and committed on issues of sustainability is a more risk-averse and resilient one.

This doesn't mean that accountants should litter their reporting with metrics that are completely unrealistic or hollow. A series of incremental and marginal gains across a comprehensive sustainability strategy can have a remarkable multiplier effect when done together in much the same way as small changes do within a threshold dynamic, potentially leading to a tipping point and a desirable 'flip' in the overall sustainability of a company. But those incremental, annual metrics should be part of more unrepentantly ambitious, longer term goals whose progress they are conspicuously tracked against.

All of this might sound a little uncomfortable to a profession that requires a certain amount of dispassion and restraint. But accountants have a leading role in making sustainability issues visible, determining how they're measured and framing the way a company responds. And their accounts are powerfully performative (in the original, non-pejorative sense of the word), in that they have the power to invoke real-world measures and commitments that bring about material changes by simply articulating and contextualizing the problems of sustainability.

In a post-truth world, where whoever has the deepest pockets gets to tell their story loudest, accountants can be the heroic standard-bearers of scientific evidence and statistics that help properly inform and guide business and the wider world towards a more sustainable future. Certainly, if management by objectives is going to work to that end, it's the accountants who will have to take on the challenge of setting them. And to do this, they have to regain their legitimacy as fact checkers, providers and predictors for the Global Goals.

Summary: The science of responsible business

Observations to note
Responsible businesses …

… augment SMART targets with SIMPLE measures.

… embrace open-platform, Global Goals-based reporting and monitoring tools.

… recognize the intrinsic value of society and nature, not just their financial worth.

… use the most accurate data from a range of specialist external sources.

… avoid selective reporting and 'vanity metrics'.

… include sustainability materiality in their financial accounts.

… follow the latest science and incorporate it into their risk management.

… are flexible, cautious and wary of precision and certainty in forecasting.

… have longer term sustainability targets more ambitious than the Global Goals.

Theories to test
Purpose-led metrics

Only metrics that are based on accurate data and aligned with the Global Goals will improve a business's sustainability.

- What percentage of your supply chain expenditure is free from slave labour? (Global Goals 8 and 12)
- Do you have any metrics on the impacts of your business on biodiversity? (Global Goals 14 and 15)
- How much do you invest in collaboration with universities, institutions and specialist organizations to plug the gaps in your sustainability data? (Global Goals 9 and 17)
- How many Global Goals have you chosen not to account for in your corporate scorecards or KPIs? (All Global Goals)

Open reporting

Open-platform, Global Goals-based reporting is the only way to make a business truly accountable to its stakeholders.

- Do you publicly share the gender and ethnicity pay gaps in your business? (Global Goals 5, 10 and 16)
- What sustainability benchmarking schemes do you use and contribute to? (Global Goals 9 and 17)
- Could your customers use your public disclosures to make responsible purchase decisions? (Global Goals 4 and 12)

- How do you engage with stakeholders, including local, national and international bodies, to determine what information is material to them? (Global Goals 16 and 17)

Precautionary principle accounting

Responsible businesses allow for radical uncertainty in their environmental risk management to avoid triggering unforeseen tipping points.

- Are your business's GHG emissions targets aligned with the latest climate change science? (Global Goals 12 and 13)
- How aware are you of the impacts of water scarcity for your business? (Global Goals 6 and 15)
- What mechanisms for feedback from local communities do you have? (Global Goals 11 and 17)
- Could your targets for profitability and growth be less aggressive to allow more time to assess their impacts? (Global Goals 11 and 12)

First steps to responsible accountability ...

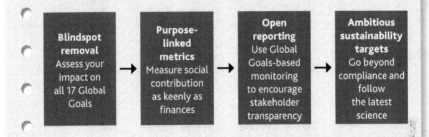

Blindspot removal	Purpose-linked metrics	Open reporting	Ambitious sustainability targets
Assess your impact on all 17 Global Goals	Measure social contribution as keenly as finances	Use Global Goals-based monitoring to encourage stakeholder transparency	Go beyond compliance and follow the latest science

MYTH 3

Laser-Like Focus Gets Results

Single-issue campaigns and unintended consequences

Much to the dismay of legions of scientists and campaigners over the years, it can be almost impossible to anticipate when a certain issue will finally break into the public consciousness. For plastic pollution, that moment came at the end of 2017 with the airing of the final episode of the BBC's *Blue Planet II* wildlife documentary series.

Millions around the world watched in distress at the carcass of a baby albatross killed by a plastic toothpick and a pilot whale carrying her dead calf for days, poisoned by the plastic-derived toxins in her milk. The response from the public was immediate: online searches for 'dangers of plastics in the ocean' increased by 100% and 'plastic recycling' by 50%.[1] Suddenly calls for plastic-free flushable wet wipes and cotton buds that had been ignored for decades were top of the news agenda and fast-tracked by previously disinterested manufacturers.[2]

These single-use plastics make up about half of the estimated 300 million tonnes of plastic waste produced worldwide each year – 10 million tonnes of which ends up in the sea.[3] Plastic bags make up a significant part of it, killing 100,000 marine animals each year, including leatherback turtles – one in three of which have been found with plastic bags in their stomachs.[4] With 1 million binned every minute after less than 15 minutes of use, plastic bags had already been targeted by the UK's government in 2015, with a levy introduced for larger supermarkets to encourage more people to reuse and consume less of them. So when many of those supermarkets later chose to remove all single-use plastic bags and make those they sold thicker and longer lasting 'bags for life', surely it would only help to cement the desired changes to customer behaviour?

On the face of it, it did. The number of single-use plastic bags sold fell dramatically, from 7.6 billion in 2014 to 1.75 billion in 2018.[5] But paradoxically, that same year the total plastic packaging footprint of UK supermarkets actually grew by 17,000 tonnes to 903,000 tonnes. Not only had supermarkets failed to address the increase in throwaway plastic packaging across all its other product lines, they had exacerbated the problem with a 26% surge in sales of their heavier plastic 'bags for life' to 1.5 billion.[6]

The fact that customers often still chose to buy new 'bags for life' each time they shopped rather than reuse them as intended can't necessarily be blamed on the supermarkets. But their focus on just one aspect of their overall plastic consumption was at fault. After all, it's plastic waste that's the issue, not what form it takes. But even those campaigning for a total ban of all single-use plastics are guilty of being overly simplistic in ignoring the environmental impacts of alternatives, which are often far more resource intensive. A paper bag, for example, requires 43 times as much land, water and CO_2 emissions to produce than a single-use plastic bag, while a cotton bag can be up to 20,000 times more resource-heavy and have substantial social and environmental impacts unless produced organically.[7]

Even though well intentioned, this is a classic example of linear thinking and unintended consequences that stem from dealing with the symptoms rather than the root cause of a problem. Painkillers might alleviate the symptoms of coronavirus, but they do nothing to stop its spread. What both the misguided supermarkets and environmentalists were failing to recognize is the complex interconnectivity of the plastics problem and its social and environmental knock-on effects elsewhere. Such single-issue, single-solution campaigns can potentially transfer the problem somewhere else or to someone else, in a global game of pass the parcel, although this game is rigged, with the parcel usually ending up with those least able to deal with it. So while the simplicity and focus of such interventions can be an effective way to communicate a problem to a wider audience and influence their behaviour, such campaigns can also preclude a proper understanding of the topic, omitting or ignoring the full range of causes and precipitating solutions that may make things worse.

This same paradoxical phenomenon can also occur when a business tries to address a specific Global Goal without considering its impacts on the other 16. Like a Rubik's Cube with 17 sides, as you twist one row to solve one problem, all the other faces change their configuration – sometimes for the better, sometimes for the worse. A grocery company, for instance, may look to tackle poverty in its supply chain by paying more to its sub-Saharan suppliers. That extra money could inadvertently worsen food scarcity by driving up its cost for everyone in the country as more agricultural produce is exported for more cash rather than sold domestically.[8]

More broadly, perhaps the domination of the whole sustainability agenda by a handful of totemic, single-issue campaigns that have become panacea-like in their importance has hampered a more holistic, multidimensional understanding of sustainability. For example, the 2°C global warming limit and net zero emissions target have been crucial tools to bring the wider problem of climate change to the attention of policy-makers, businesses and the public. But these simplistic measures have had unintended consequences of their own. Some scientists have blamed the 2°C limit for creating a lack of urgency, when more and more research suggests that even a 1.5°C change in global temperatures could have disastrous consequences for the world's most vulnerable people and ecosystems.[9] And while cutting carbon emissions hogs the news headlines and sits at the heart of many businesses' sustainability strategies, the arguably even more damaging impacts of water use, biodiversity loss and poverty struggle to get an equal hearing.

What underpins all these things is a human propensity for simplicity – what the statistician Hans Rosling calls 'the single perspective instinct'. 'We find simple ideas very attractive', he says in his book *Factfulness*. 'All problems have a single cause – something we must be completely against. Or all problems have a single solution – something we must always be for. Everything is simple. There's just one small issue. We completely misunderstand the world.'[10]

While the idea that any of the sustainability problems covered by the Global Goals have one single cause or solution might seem hugely attractive to anyone looking for an obvious way to tackle them, it fundamentally misunderstands the world's messy interconnectedness. That's why when the UK's National Health Service was first set up in 1948, it included provisions for public housing, since homelessness and poor homes were identified as massive drivers of poor health. So if we want to avoid any 'bag for life'-type unintended consequences that might exacerbate the problem or distract us from useful and effective measures elsewhere, we need to embrace this complexity and think through the problem and any solutions more holistically and systemically. That way, any partial solutions for sustainability, such as reducing single-use plastic bags, won't end up creating new problems elsewhere, and businesses can responsibly harness people's inherent bias towards simplicity to encourage positive social change.

German bee colonies and the seduction of monocausal narratives

If something so small and seemingly simple as plastic bags proves so challenging under closer examination, imagine how complicated it gets dealing with the mysterious collapse of bee colonies and its threat to our whole natural ecosystem. Pollinators worldwide have been in steep decline in recent decades, with periodic, unexplained collapses in honey bee colonies of particular concern for food security and the US$265 billion dollars of fruit and vegetable crops that depend on them for pollination.[11]

In Germany, one study in 2017 recorded a 75% decline in the total biomass of flying insects in protected areas over the last three decades, and currently half of the country's 557 or so species of bee are at risk of extinction.[12] But it was the unusually high winter losses experienced by honey beekeepers over the winter of 2002/03 that sparked the German Bee Monitoring Project (DeBiMo) – the largest bee monitoring project in the world – and a national effort to understand and deal with the problem. Around 30% of the German honey bee population was reported dead in spring 2003, with some beekeepers reporting 80–100% of their hives wiped out.[13]

Quite quickly, the discussion for what was to blame became dominated by the varroa mite. These parasites attach to the body of a bee and suck away vital tissues. As well as weakening the individual bee, it was thought that the more mite-infected bees there were in a colony, the more likely it would collapse over the winter hibernation period – a theory given some weight by DeBiMo's 2011 study,[14] which found 15.8 out of 100 bees had the varroa mite in colonies that collapsed, whereas only 3.6 out of every 100 bees had it in surviving colonies. But later studies also found viruses, such as acute bee paralysis virus and deformed wing virus, as well as varroa mites, in collapsed colonies, and quickly concluded that these diseases were carried by the mites. So the advice continued to be that fighting the mite was the best way of preventing winter losses of hives.

More recent research suggests this monocausal 'varroa mite narrative' is too simplistic and completely neglects other factors – known and unknown to DeBiMo – that could be the cause of bee colony losses or act as a catalyst.[15] The previous research had been limited by its narrow parameters and the correlation it found had been misinterpreted as causality.[16] So because a greater overall number of mites and viruses were found in collapsed bee colonies, the two former things were assumed to cause the latter. Moreover, it didn't explain the increasing deaths of bees during the summer, which DeBiMo admitted hadn't been robustly analysed.

One explanation for DeBiMo's continued focus on the varroa mite as the culprit might well lie in its funding. Before it became fully government funded in 2010, DeBiMo received 50% of its budget from corporates, including the world's leading pesticide manufacturers: Bayer AG and Syngenta.[17] For decades, pesticides have been identified as a key stressor affecting both wild and cultured pollinators – in particular, those belonging to a class of chemicals known as 'neonicotinoids'. Numerous studies have shown that bees that come into contact with these pesticides on plants and soil have their ability to find their way back to the hive impaired and are more susceptible to viruses as they weaken their immune system. Concerns about neonicotinoids in Europe culminated in an EU-wide ban on such products in 2013, which Bayer AG and Syngenta have since sought to overturn in the courts.[18]

A number of critics have noted the unreasonable focus on varroa mites in German bee research. Could it be DeBiMo and other pollinator initiatives funded by the big chemical companies, such as FitBee and Operation Pollinator, are designed to distract from the role of pesticides, in much the same way the scientists nicknamed the 'merchants of doubt' were used to protect the tobacco and oil industry in the past?[19] That's what Walter Haefeker, president of the European Professional Beekeeper Association, thinks, and he argues that the chemical companies have deliberately 'shaped' the German research landscape through their funding to concentrate on a monocausal narrative that suits their interests. Pitched against this are a loose coalition of independent research institutions and professional beekeepers who argue that varroa mites, disease and pesticides are part of a multicausal effect chain that can't be easily observed and certainly extends way beyond the confines of individual hives.

In fact, the new research suggests two additional contributing factors are the decline in beekeepers and (perhaps more unexpectedly) the rise in renewable energy. While the number of beekeepers in Germany has actually gone up since 2006, most of these are hobbyists with very few hives. Semi-professional beekeepers with more than 20 colonies have declined since 1951, reducing beehive numbers by almost three-quarters to around 600,000. Whereas renewable energy has impacted bees because of the increasing demand for land for use in the biomass and solar industry, Germany has set itself ambitious targets for both as major parts of its renewable energy strategy, which has encouraged the widespread ploughing of biodiverse and bee-friendly grassland to grow monocultural corn and rapeseed to make biofuels and biogas, as well as the development of farmland and forestry into solar plants.

As we can see, not only are the reasons for Germany's bee decline much more complex than any monocausal narrative allows; the solutions collide with other important Global Goals efforts around clean energy, food security, healthy ecosystems and climate change. In other words, it's complicated – as are most things in life. Which is why responsible businesses need to embrace that complexity, be open to new information and willing to adapt their sustainability strategies accordingly. Bringing on board experts and critical friends who can help businesses constantly re-evaluate and check their assumptions will be crucial. But ultimately, no action will be perfect: all will likely have consequences that are both positive and undesirable. The important thing is to act while also being aware of those tensions within the systems that businesses operate – be they ecological, financial or socio-political.

The motives for doing otherwise would certainly be less responsible, and may even be dishonest. The monocausal narratives around bee decline encouraged by the chemical giants in Germany were at best a kind of confirmation bias, and at worst the cynical protection of vested interests. Without thinking systemically and adopting a more holistic point of view that looks beyond only self-interest, we are all susceptible to these reductionist narratives and Machiavellian behaviours. Part of the seduction of simple solutions is their straightforwardness and the reassuring sense of control they seem to offer. But they rarely deal fully with the messy reality of the problem – with its many overlapping and circular relationships – or the multiple roles we play in it. Fortunately, there are some novel ways to manage this complexity inspired by doughnuts, smog and the latest systems theory.

Exceptionalism, systemic resilience and cross-sector partnerships

We are currently consuming the Earth's resources at a rate well beyond what it can sustainably replenish,[20] while we throw away more and more waste each year – with business responsible for the large majority – and recycle less than half of it.[21] So why do so many businesses continue to operate in such a linear and self-destructive 'make-take-waste' way? One obvious reason is that governments and their laws still permit and encourage such behaviour. But even with more effective regulation, it's likely businesses would continue to unsustainably consume the planet and themselves so long as they view themselves as somehow separate from society and the environment.

This business exceptionalism isn't just a failure of understanding on the part of business leaders, but a systemic failure inherent in the highly financialized market economy within which they operate. All systems are prone to what system theorists call 'operational closure', which is like a person who stops being sensitive to what's going on around them and only takes their cues from their own internal logic and desires. The usual sensory feedback loops that previously helped moderate and balance their thoughts and behaviours, to prevent them, for example, from overindulging or hurting others, are shut off or ignored in favour of a more primitive, selfish instinct.

For our finance-driven economic system, that instinct and internal logic is to maximize profits. And as shown by the perennial boom-and-bust cycle of modern economies, the system routinely falls into operational closure, ignoring the world around it and overheating as it chases gains before collapsing again. The global financial crisis of 2008 demonstrated the disastrous chain of consequences when the financial markets become increasingly abstracted and disconnected from other systems, such as housing, politics and social inequality. The bubble burst when it finally intersected with the outside world, triggering systemic collapses around the globe. All of which proved that Wall Street wasn't disconnected from the rest of the world. Rather, it was intimately connected, but just chose to ignore it for a while – and seems to be ignoring it again.

This instinctive pursuit of profit that dominates the current global economic system might explain why profit and business are so often perceived as being more important than people and the planet. It is now an almost universally accepted idea that the health of the economy and business sector is the most important priority for government and the public (more so than human health in the case of encouraging people back to work during the COVID-19 pandemic). But more recent academic thinking sees the world as a complex socio-ecological system, where the health of society (people) and the natural world (planet) are the most important and decisive factors, on which all human activity is dependent – including profit-pursuing business.

This idea is most powerfully illustrated by the 'Doughnut Economics' model that was developed by Oxford economist Kate Raworth for Oxfam in 2012.[22] It depicts a sustainable economy as like a ring doughnut, existing between a social foundation and an ecological ceiling, whereby the needs of people at the centre of the doughnut have to be serviced without overshooting the Earth's resources that surround and sustain them. In this context, all business activity operates in constant tension between social need and ecological capacity.

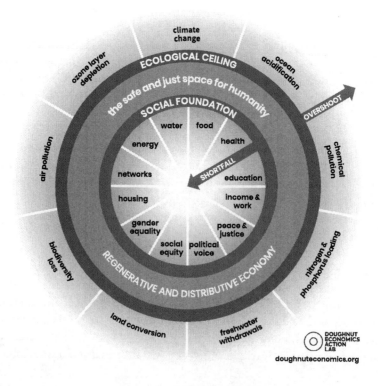

doughnuteconomics.org

It might seem blindingly obvious that business and profit are materially rooted in and systemically dependent on people and the planet, but this socio-ecological framing helps debunk the prevailing order that business is somehow separate or more important. And even if you're one of the many responsible businesses that are already well aware of this fact, the latest thinking in this field (called 'complex adaptive systems theory', or CAS) takes this reframing further and fundamentally challenges what a business's strategic approach to sustainability should be.

CAS theory suggests this socio-ecological system is made up of an interconnected web of different systems – be they natural, social, cultural or economic – that relate to each other in complex, non-linear and dynamic ways.[23] So complicated and cumulative are these relationships that it becomes almost impossible to scientifically prove the impacts of any one part on the overall socio-ecological system. Thus when a systemic disaster strikes, it's easy for individuals to pass responsibility, claiming 'it wasn't me' because other people were to blame too.

A vivid example of this phenomenon was the 1952 Great Smog of London, where nobody and everybody was partially responsible for the death of up to 12,000 people. While the weather that December was cold, it wasn't unusually so. People responded the way they normally did in winter by putting a bit more coal on the fire and burning the fire for a bit longer in the day. Darker, colder days put extra demand on the electricity systems as well, which at the time were generated from coal. And most of the factories in London were largely powered by coal generators, too. Traffic levels had grown alongside the population of London, with more steam locomotives, diesel lorries and buses than ever before after the closure of the electric tram system.

But when this noxious mix was combined with some unusual weather patterns, the level of air pollution turned lethal. Suddenly there was no wind to disperse the air pollution and a heavy fog acted to trap the air pollution at nose-level of London's unsuspecting population. This stagnant weather continued for a few days, allowing the pollutants to accumulate to the point where people couldn't see or breathe. But Londoners, who were used to smog, initially didn't change their behaviour, continuing to expose themselves to this toxic air. Death wasn't instant, coming about through respiratory infections over the following weeks and months that took a major toll on the very young, very old, those with underlying conditions and those in poorer living conditions.

So who was to blame for all those deaths? The citizens burning coal? The coal producers? The factories? Those running the transport system? The people who went out in the pea-souper? The landlords who provided poorly ventilated houses? The government for not locking down the communities? The planning authorities that had known about London's air pollution problem since at least 1661?[24] The weather system? The butterflies half a world away whose beating wings may have shifted the anticyclone over London? The list is endless, but no one can identify the source of the soot that tipped a normal set of behaviours into catastrophe or know exactly where this tipping point lay. What we can see is that each individual soot emission reduced the level of resilience of the complex adaptive system that is London, until the system collapsed so dramatically and tragically.

The solution wasn't to hunt down and punish individual culprits, but rather to look for ways that re-established London's resilience in order to reduce the risk of this concurrence of different events from ever happening again. This included systems-level reforms, such as the Clean Air Act of 1956, changes to the powers of local authorities and revised planning regulations. The Great Smog of London was a critical learning event for many other cities and nations that had the opportunity to understand the systemic complexity of air pollution and act in advance. While many did, many others chose to ignore it, resulting in massive deaths from human-induced air pollutants combined with predictable weather patterns that continue in some countries even today. London itself failed to learn and act quickly enough, leading to another lethal smog event in 1962 – no doubt due to the significant controversy over the science, risks and who pays for solving the problem in 1952 (in much the same way as what happened during the recent COVID-19 crisis).

However, CAS theorists suggest that the flipside of this systemic complexity and volatility is that the effects of any individual can also be remarkably powerful too – which should be hugely encouraging to responsible businesses doubtful of what impact their individual efforts can make. Who knows how many catastrophic ecological tipping points have been narrowly avoided by the responsible actions of just one person? Equally, how many social and economic recoveries have been sparked by the influence and investment of one business? The most important thing is for businesses to try to understand how these various systems operate and interact so they can recognize what impacts they have (or could have) on the resilience of society and the natural world.

That's why CAS theorists argue that sustainability needs to be subtly reframed as supporting socio-ecological resilience – or 'resilience-based stewardship', as they call it. In practice, this would encourage responsible businesses to look beyond the impacts of just their operations and take an active role in the preservation and enhancement of the wider social and ecological systems their operations are dependent on. So rather than Unilever just looking to improve the sustainability of the palm oil it sources from somewhere like Borneo, it has worked with other national and international groups, governments and agencies to prevent the wider degradation of regional and global ecosystems and alleviate the underlying social issues that damage the longer term resilience of Borneo. (It's interesting to consider if Unilever not buying palm oil from Borneo at all would actually help or hinder the country's sustainability, such is the complexity of systemic dependencies.)

Such cross-sector partnerships with NGOs and public sector bodies – whose expertise and core mission are about socio-ecological systems – can provide the knowledge and skills to help businesses 'close the loop' between their operations and the wider systems they depend on and need to protect. These collective activities might be harder for companies like Unilever to direct and measure than their own Sustainable Living Plans, but there can be no effective strategy for business resilience that doesn't also support the resilience of wider society and the environment.

In fact, recent research found that most corporate sustainability strategies actually sought to optimize their existing, destructive business practices rather than challenge them, which has led to a 'systemic failure' to properly invest in any transformative innovation that might move them away from such damaging behaviour.[25] So any business wanting to take a systemic approach to tackling sustainability needs to break out of the limitations of its own internal logic and open itself up to the disruptive logic and ideas of wider socio-ecological resilience. Only then will business stop inadvertently sowing the seeds of its own destruction through the sociopathic destruction of others.

An ambitious example of such an approach is Keystone Dialogues, which set up a Seafood Business for Ocean Stewardship (SeaBOS) initiative in 2016 to try to transform global seafood production in a more sustainable way that would protect the long-term health of the oceans.[26] It hopes to simultaneously addresses seven of the Global Goals, including life below water (Global Goal 14), decent work and economic growth (Global Goal 8) and responsible production and consumption (Global Goal 12). The idea is to connect 'keystone actors' in the global seafood system – marine scientists, seafood companies, fisheries and aquaculture – to collaborate on tackling problems such as forced labour, marine plastics and overfishing through creating and lobbying for systemic measures, like supranational regulation and traceability technologies.

Keystone Dialogues' working hypothesis is that a small minority of powerful actors can influence a majority of smaller actors and precipitate change on a global, systemic scale.[27] Much like the CAS theory of individuals' potential power within a complex system, Keystone Dialogues is looking to harness the power of organizations' individual and collective agency through collaboration to improve the socio-ecological resilience of the world's oceans. So far, 10 of the world's largest seafood companies participating in SeaBOS have agreed to advance sustainable practices within their global supply chains, including adopting new tracing technology successfully trialled by SeaBOS to combat illegal fishing and slave labour.

As the name suggests, at the heart of socio-ecological resilience initiatives like SeaBOS is the concept of stewardship. That intergenerational responsibility to maintain the health of society and the planet for decades and centuries to come is incumbent on everyone, and is a particular challenge for business where a culture of short-termism and quarterly profit-making is so prevalent. But while many businesses readily engage with systems-wide initiatives to deal with specific social issues and environmental protection more generally, many avoid engaging in politics beyond simply lobbying for or against legislative changes that impact their commercial interests. Yet a country's governance has a huge bearing on social and environmental issues, and ignoring it is failing to truly engage with the problems structurally and holistically.

As researchers into responsible investment have pointed out, authoritarian and corrupt political regimes are unlikely to prioritize environmental measures to combat climate change or champion greater social equality.[28] Yet business and investors continue to pour money into projects in these countries without challenging their adverse political conditions, while commercially exploiting their draconian labour laws and weak environmental standards. Even in more established democratic countries, unequal and unstable societies have given rise to more reactionary politicians and precipitated more social unrest, which has, for example, seen the US briefly withdraw from the Paris Agreement on climate change and the ascendance of far-right groups across Europe. But businesses seldom critique government policies beyond those that impact their profitability in the short term, seemingly wary of publicly engaging in party politics, and normally avoid making any overtly political statements. Yet this reticence sits rather at odds with some businesses' fondness for lobbying and convoluted corporate devices to hide political donations.

However, during the Black Lives Matter protests in 2020 following the murder of George Floyd by police in Minneapolis, businesses worldwide joined in a day of antiracist protest on so-called 'Blackout Tuesday'. Ice cream manufacturer Ben & Jerry's went so far as to issue a list of demands to the US government that aimed to 'dismantle white supremacy'.[29] 'Silence is compliance' was the contention put by black activists to the whole of society, which strikes at the heart of the dilemma for businesses that don't find their voice on systemic issues of racism, inequality and corruption. From a systems point of view, any component that is neutral still enables the same systemic outcomes. So for any business committed to a more sustainable world, it needs to challenge the governing systems that enable these outcomes.

This doesn't mean all firms should become political activists, but it does require businesses to be proactive in enabling the kind of society they want to see. At the most basic level, that means proudly paying tax – rather than unethically avoiding it – to help governments invest in the physical and social infrastructure they provide. It also means being the change you want to see in the world, as Mahatma Gandhi famously once said. So a business becomes a microcosm of a fairer, more sustainable world by enacting the Global Goals within the workplace – providing decent, well-paid work and gender equality, for example – and using its procurement power to encourage those sustainable practices throughout its supply chains too.

Beyond that, rather than passively waiting for government policy and laws to steer them, responsible companies should seek out and act on the latest scientific findings on climate change and the environment before any enforcements around it emerge. They could even lead on lobbying for those laws in the same way corporates have traditionally lobbied government to cut back regulation – just as the We Mean Business coalition of companies and investors in the US is doing on policies to accelerate the transition to a low carbon economy.[30] Similarly with other social problems, businesses can be actively open and receptive to the work of specialist organizations advocating for different causes and back their campaigns for government action, while applying those organizations' expertise and insights to their own relevant operations. For example, Refugee Councils around the world not only lobby governments to protect the welfare of this vulnerable group, but also provide guidance for businesses to create training schemes and employment for refugees.[31]

Whatever the issue, it's about business taking an ongoing and active stance on society's welfare based on science and knowledge, not regulation and compliance. Of course, no company has the capacity to do that on its own. It requires those cross-sector partnerships to close the loop and provide the feedback that stimulates change within the firm, which can then agitate for wider, systemic change without. From simply promoting an outside campaign and bringing in specialists to help tackle workplace prejudice, to committing to the wider Global Goals agenda across all operations and joining external organizations in lobbying for government change, businesses can enable the processes and arguments that will help eliminate the dysfunctional elements of our socio-ecological system and build its resilience instead.

As well as providing a more holistic and systemic approach to sustainability, resilience-building offers a better strategy for a business's long-term profitability and sustainable growth too. We know the mortality rate for businesses is very high – barely half survive more than five years and less than a quarter more than 15 – suggesting most companies lack resilience. But innovating and investing in any of the 17 Global Goals will help build overall resilience and produce returns far beyond their initial targets. As the former IBM executive and sustainability expert Bob Willard explains, the

Global Goals 'define the end state for a resilient and sustainable environment that supports a resilient and just society, that fosters a resilient and inclusive economy. There is $12 trillion in potential economic growth linked to achieving the [Global Goals]. It's in the self-interest of companies to contribute to them.'[32]

What Willard describes is both the 'social boomerang effect' and multiplier effect that investing in socio-ecological resilience has on the resilience of business, whereby any contribution by the business is returned many times over in the long run. Lessening inequality and poverty, for example, increases the potential market and consumer base for a business's products. While better education makes for a more productive workforce, and cheaper and cleaner energy increases profitability. The interconnectedness of each of the Global Goals means they all contribute to the overall resilience of society to the mutual benefit of everyone – including businesses. So despite the sometimes daunting complexity of tackling any systemic problem, the rewards are often systemic, complex and many too.

THE SYSTEM TRAPS DILEMMA: ARE THE GLOBAL GOALS TOO EASY TO MISUSE AND TOO HARD TO DO?

Because the Global Goals offer such a broad, systemic approach to sustainability, they are open to misuse by business. Whether deliberately or not, they can be cherry-picked, selectively interpreted, subject to confirmation bias or used to promote self-interest. For instance, contrary to encouraging companies to take more responsibility, the interconnectedness of the 17 Goals can allow businesses to pass the buck for certain issues on to others, blaming them for their own inaction (much like the responsibility of 'nobody and everybody' in the Great Smog of London example). They also open up the opportunity of profiteering from sustainability issues, disincentivizing the need to actually resolve them – an accusation often levelled at carbon-trading schemes, for example.

No doubt the PR value alone makes it worthwhile for many businesses to adopt the Global Goals. For others, the opportunity to strategically lobby and shape policy around their delivery may also be an incentive. But the Global Goals are intended to be disruptive, not used to maintain the status quo or as a fig leaf for unsustainable, business-as-usual activities. And while choosing to focus on a few goals as an individual business makes sense, the problem is addressing them and their impacts in isolation. That's because the Global

Goals' systemic approach – and the full picture of sustainability – breaks down if they are not viewed as a whole.

Any systems-wide change, such as is envisioned in the Global Goals, can be difficult and subject to resistance and relapses. These 'system traps' are like black holes that keep pulling businesses back to their old destructive logic and routines. But a responsible business can build its resilience to these external and internal traps by always looking up and down its value chain – whether it's suppliers below or the political landscape above – and asking, how does each system disturb or influence its organizational behaviour?

The aim is not to simplify or control the complexity of everything around the business, but to map out and understand how these systems operate and interact. That way, a business is more able to identify vulnerabilities and points of leverage where it can intervene in the system and escape potential traps. By undertaking such a systemic approach, a business is less likely to adopt a false or simplistic strategy for sustainability and focus on the resilience-based stewardship the Global Goals require. (Read more about resilience and doing a resilience assessment of your business in Appendix 3.)

Carbon literacy and the social boomerang effect

Imagine if every raw material, product or service a business bought came with its own balloon full of GHGs as well as a price tag. Every process, use of energy, resource consumed, days stored or distance transported involved in acquiring and transforming them into goods further inflates their balloons as more GHGs are produced, which are all attached to the final product. Then the customer inherits these balloons with the purchase of the final product and through use, consumption or disposal, further inflates them again.

Just as with costs, businesses need to know the size of the 'carbon balloons' of anything they buy and do and how much bigger they will inflate before they are sold on. Climate change won't be solved by passing on these balloons, with whoever is holding it when the music stops subject to all the liabilities. While it's true that a business may be able to deny any legal responsibility for that balloon after sale, it may be more difficult to deny moral responsibility or avoid reputational damage. And in the future, smaller carbon balloons will be a source of value as carbon emissions increasingly become monetized and unacceptable.

With demands also growing for full carbon accountability from customers, investors, regulators, tax authorities and other stakeholders, it's now essential for businesses to be carbon literate. And no matter how daunting accounting for all those carbon balloons across a business may seem and trying to reduce or not inflate them further, it becomes much easier when you think about it at a transactional level. In 2016, the French multinational Capgemini became the first IT services company to embrace carbon emission reduction targets ratified by the UN-backed Science Based Targets Initiative, aligning them with international efforts to avoid future global temperatures increasing by more than 2°C. It aimed to slash carbon emissions per employee by 40% by 2030, but managed to achieve 38% by 2019. Key to Capgemini's accelerated success was its 'end-to-end' approach, considering the sustainability of every aspect of its value chain: from investing in a new, energy-efficient data centre constructed from reused materials to working with its clients further downstream to reduce carbon emissions by 10 million tonnes.[33]

Like Capgemini, businesses need to recognize how every decision they make throughout their value chain drives carbon emissions up or down – what you buy, who you buy from, how you ship it, what you invest in, how you heat your buildings, how energy efficient you are, how much you waste, how you design, make, sell and ship your product, how your employees get to work, how you store your product, how you move things round, how you finance your operations, how and where you sell your product and what people do with your product. Carbon emissions are the consequences of these decisions, and carbon reduction is much easier done at a granular level.

For example, in procurement decisions it's important to think about what inflates the carbon balloon of anything you are planning to buy or sell. Think about what has had to be done to transform that 'thing' from its origins somewhere on or within the planet to the 'thing' that turns up at your warehouse, office or shop floor. Distance and mode of transport, energy used in processing and raw materials used in intermediate production are all carbon balloon-inflators. And different suppliers and materials have carbon balloons of different sizes, too. A farmer who uses solar panels for irrigation pumps, for example, will have a lower carbon balloon than one who uses diesel pumps. But that advantage may be lost if their produce is then airfreighted to the other side of the world. Materials delivered in returnable containers will come with a smaller carbon balloon than if packaged in single-use plastic and require less work to unwrap, store or dispose of.

But across all their operations, there are lots of simple actions businesses can take that will minimize how much they inflate their carbon balloons, from reducing waste and insulating buildings to video conferencing and facilitating staff active travel. Together they all improve a business's carbon efficiency, increasing their value to other carbon balloon-wary businesses and consumers, as well as to everyone else on the planet for generations to come – because scientists tell us carbon dioxide will affect our climate for at least a thousand years after it's emitted, and every atom of carbon not making it into the atmosphere makes a difference.

Businesses can go much further than improving their carbon efficiency, however. Imagine if by innovative design a product could be used by customers without any further inflation of the carbon balloon – such as electricity produced by wind power, for example. Or perhaps the product can have multiple useful lives, meeting numerous customers' needs without the unnecessary costs and carbon impacts of ripping more virgin materials out of the earth. Old electric car batteries, for instance, can be reused as storage in domestic solar power systems. New technologies can also replace products with a service that fulfils the same customer need in a low or zero carbon way, as with the digital transformation of music consumption. Some more radical products actually absorb carbon during their life cycle, such as US carpet tile manufacturer Interface's carbon-absorbing carpet tiles.[34] Even just collaborating with other companies, sharing expertise and resources to co-create innovative solutions can unleash value in ways that are unimaginable within a single business.

In this way, it's easy to see how investing in carbon literacy and developing low carbon instincts is likely to pay back very quickly for a company, particularly given increasing expectations that businesses show how they plan to go 'net zero' in the near future. But to achieve this goal will be impossible unless a company knows the magnitude and sources of its carbon emissions. So simple carbon calculations should be integrated into a business's decision-making, such as emissions per mile for alternative shipping methods, the embedded carbon in potential raw materials and the carbon debt incurred by replacing any technology or infrastructure even if it is cleaner to run. (For more about how to comprehensively calculate carbon emissions using the gold standard Greenhouse Gas Protocol methodology, see Appendix 4.)

Businesses have to be careful about what 'net zero' carbon means, however. In most cases net zero refers to the most common definition used by governments signed up to the Paris Agreement, which says any emissions from the business must be balanced out by the emissions removed from the atmosphere through carbon capture or offsetting schemes, such as storing emissions underground or planting trees. But for other businesses, net zero is a self-defined aspiration that can exclude the carbon balloons of their raw materials, assets, business investments and technology. In either case, it normally excludes any carbon emitted after a product is sold and being used by the consumer. And it certainly won't include any carbon emissions made prior to the business signing up to the pledge.

So it's important businesses are clear about what net zero means when they say it, because powerful stakeholders will start to demand answers as to what carbon balloons businesses are referring to, what time frame they are zeroing to, and to what extent they are paying off their historic carbon debts, whose emissions will still be swirling around the planet for the next millennia or so. What they won't want to see is businesses finding 'smart' ways to get around confronting this global risk, employing creative compliance techniques as they continue the global game of carbon pass the parcel.

Reducing carbon emissions and liability	Reducing carbon emissions, future and past
Historical Offset Zero Emissions	Historical Offset and Projected Emissions
Increasing carbon emissions and liability	**Stabilizing carbon emissions and liability**
Partial Annual Zero Emissions	Total Annual Zero Emissions

The diagram above outlines four different net zero strategies and their likely impact on climate systems: partial annual zero emissions from now (PAZE); total annual zero emissions from now (TAZE); historic offset zero emissions (HOZE); and historic offset and projected emissions (HOPE). If all businesses choose a TAZE strategy, which follows a common definition of net zero and is better than PAZE, this will only stabilize the bad situation the planet is currently in, not solve it or reduce GHG levels in the atmosphere. Actually making things better will require HOZE or HOPE strategies that take into account past emissions and even offset for estimated future emissions in the case of the latter.

None of this should be seen as knocking net zero as an ambition or aspiration, which is essential for addressing catastrophic climate change. But for many carbon-concerned businesses, net zero will be far too low a barrier. Most should have no problem being fully accountable for their historic carbon emissions and those associated with the entire life cycle of their products (what's called 'full-scope' carbon accounting). Not only is it the responsible thing to do, it will also future-proof the business against the likely introduction of carbon rationing and more stringent attitudes about what's socially acceptable. Narrowly defined net zero benchmarks won't be enough to differentiate a responsible business making real reductions to the cumulative carbon in our atmosphere from those just passing the buck.

Having understood more about what carbon emissions are and how to measure and mitigate them most effectively across the business, it's vital companies also understand the social context of decarbonization, because reducing carbon emissions isn't just about avoiding climate collapse in the near future, but tackling social inequality now.

While air pollution and climate change affect the health and environment of everyone, they impact the poorest most severely. The majority of the 8 million deaths each year from air pollution are in poorer countries, which also have the least resources to cope with extreme weather events. Moreover, notwithstanding that the vast majority of the 40% increase in atmospheric carbon dioxide since the 18th century is as a result of more affluent Western countries' mass industrialization, the world's richest 10% are still responsible for more than half of all carbon emissions through consumption today, while the poorest 50% are behind just 10%. The impacts of those emissions are not only felt unequally across countries with differing GDPs, but across different income groups within a country, too.[35]

Much of this disparity comes about through an 'out of sight, out of mind' attitude to waste. GHGs are, of course largely invisible and their source impossible to prove. But other waste material, like plastic packaging, is much more difficult to ignore or disown. Before a ban on plastic waste imports in 2018, China was the world's main dumping ground for the Global North's plastic waste, where it caused life-threatening human diseases from the toxic air and waterways polluted by burning and landfill. Now that waste is flooding into poorer Southeast Asian countries like Malaysia and the Philippines, where it's having similarly damaging effects on people and the environment.[36]

The trouble is that there is no such thing as throwing 'away' – all waste has to go somewhere. And while Southeast Asia might be far enough out of sight for the Global North not to worry about, the interconnectedness of life and its many systems – ecological, financial and socio-political – means we can never fully escape it (even if we might avoid the worst of its impacts). Wherever it's dumped, plastic degrades into microplastics in the soil and the oceans, entering the global food chain and blowing in the wind to end up as some of the 74,000 plastic particles (at least) humans are estimated to ingest every year.[37] Even in somewhere as far away and remote as space, the accumulation of junk since the first satellite launched in 1957 now threatens the future of our entire global telecomms satellite infrastructure on which we're so dependent.[38] Waste always seems to catch up with us in the end.

This phenomenon is another example of the 'social boomerang effect' in business. Companies play pass the parcel with their climate change risks by exporting their waste and outsourcing their carbon emissions, but eventually the impacts of those risks return to bite the business, whether directly or indirectly. While domestic recycling and circular production methods might be more onerous and expensive in the short term, it's the most responsible and logical thing to do. Any solution that doesn't tackle a problem holistically, at a systemic level, only passes the problem somewhere else along the chain.

A circular economy and closing the loop

For a responsible business, there are numerous benefits to abandoning any linear 'make-take-waste' processes in their operations and reimagining their products as part of a circular value chain. With no waste, just the indefinite reusing and recycling of resources, the financial savings and reduced environmental impacts are potentially enormous. Such a 'closed-loop' process encompasses every stage of a product's life cycle, from raw material extraction and energy use during manufacture to sales and distribution and after-sale use, looking to eliminate waste and pollution at every stage.

More and more businesses are turning to circular economies like this, not just because they are more sustainable and share the same regenerative characteristics as natural ecosystems, but because they are cost-effective. Waste costs, and costs a lot. It's just that this cost is usually hidden in accounts or temporarily externalized by ignoring or outsourcing it, where it lurks in the shadows to bounce back on the business. But with circular solutions, a business needs to know where costly waste and pollution is at every stage of a product's life cycle. Owning every part of the value chain certainly helps, and many of the world's largest corporations – such as Samsung and Sony – have taken this approach for the financial benefits of economies of scale, as well as to control quality and ensure security of supply. But for the vast majority of smaller businesses, closing the loop requires working with others at different stages of the process – sometimes at very local levels and in very different ways.

The UK waste management company, Viridor, has had considerable success adopting such a collaborative model in a pilot project to deal with the issue of black plastic waste, which routinely gets missed by optical sorting machines and is difficult to reuse. Having developed a machine that could identify black plastics in regular mixed waste at one of its plants in Rochester, Viridor worked with its reprocessing plant in Lancashire to turn it into plastic flakes and pellets that can then be reused. They then brought on board a food packaging manufacturer to make use of the reprocessed plastic and secured the commitment of high-street supermarkets to use this packaging in their products, creating a circular economy for black plastic that prevented 120 tonnes of it going into landfill each month.[39]

One of the simplest things a business can do to start transitioning to this more circular approach is to stop thinking about its products in a 'sell and forget' way and take more responsibility for them post-sale. Of course, the customer is normally responsible for the use and disposal of anything they buy, but the manufacturer and seller of any product should also be concerned about how easy their products are to repair and recycle, and play an active role in encouraging both. This can either be through directly providing repair shops and recycling points themselves, or indirectly by working with broader government initiatives that aim to achieve the same outcomes.

One of the best ways some companies have found of locking in such post-sale responsibility is to switch to a leasing model where most appropriate, replacing ownership of a thing with the provision of a benefit. Interface credit such a paradigm shift for not only giving them the greatest control over the life cycle of their carpet tiles, but for opening up all kinds of other opportunities throughout their value chain. For instance, leasing out their carpet tiles instantly increased the available reusable material for them to make new recycled tiles and cut the cost of sourcing these materials externally. It also allowed the firm to manage their carbon footprint more effectively, and legitimized offsetting the carbon absorbed by their latest 'carbon negative' carpet tiles. Interface realized that customers valued the aesthetics and functionality of a carpet, not the sense of ownership. What appeared to be a simple conceptual shift, from making and selling carpets to a long-term contract to provide floor covering, revolutionized its business.

Similarly, but in a more incremental way, the UK media company Sky TV has begun introducing a 'service model' of its set-top box that the company retains ownership of so it can better repair the product, as well as more easily recover and reuse the materials once it's reached its consumer end-of-life. Its ability to do this starts at the R&D stage, where Sky TV works with its recycling partners to make sure the design of its products incorporates the easiest materials and components to recycle, as well as being mindful of other sustainability concerns – such as minimizing the energy consumption of their 'always on' technology.[40]

While both these examples are commendable attempts at circularity in an individual company, what about being more ambitious and extending the approach across a country's entire sector? This is something the UK's electric vehicle (EV) industry is grappling with when it comes to its use of batteries. With road transport responsible for nearly a quarter of the UK's GHG emissions, encouraging the widespread adoption of EVs is a vital part of the country's drive to go net zero by 2050. Experts estimate around 36 million EVs will be on UK roads by 2040, and there are already concerns about what to do with the future stockpile of millions of used lithium-ion batteries (LIBs) that power them.[41] Once the capacity of LIBs falls below 80%, they become no good for EVs, yet they still have many potential second-life applications – as energy storage in housing or the national grid, for example – and many of their raw materials can be recycled in the longer term. But setting up the circular economy for this reuse and recycling in the UK is proving hugely challenging, with no recycling facilities for LIBs in the country.

Recent research that spoke to 30 key stakeholders working within the EV sector – from manufacturers like Jaguar Land Rover and Honda to fleet operators and policy-makers – revealed two main reasons for this.[42] First, there was a lack of knowledge and knowledge-sharing on the issue within the industry, with EV retailers unaware that used LIBs could be recycled or reused. One car manufacturer admitted it 'didn't have a clue' what would happen to their batteries after they'd finished using them. Second, many complained of a lack of government support, which needed to do more to legally enforce and financially stimulate both supply and demand for second-life applications, including standardizing LIBs to make them easier to repurpose or break down and recover raw materials en masse. One interviewee said there was currently 'no strategy and collaboration amongst stakeholders vis-à-vis end-of-first-life applications, both nationally and EU levels'.

Certainly, the EU's Circular Economy Action Plan, which will legislate to make all products easier to repurpose and less wasteful, may well help in this regard. But most significant will be the billions of public money already being invested in a new Battery Industrialization Centre in Warwickshire, which could form the hub of a large-scale and advanced battery ecosystem in the UK for the very first time.[43] Without this circularity operating at the heart of the EV industry, one of the key green technologies the UK hopes will mitigate air pollution, environmental degradation and global climate change may unintentionally exacerbate all three of them.

What this case illustrates is how important government intervention can be in building the infrastructure and encouraging the cross-sector partnerships that are so essential for a circular economy on a larger, more macro scale. Like many of the challenges behind the Global Goals that require disrupting and changing a whole system, you ideally need the buy-in and involvement of all the stakeholders within that system. But as Viridor and Sky TV demonstrate, it is possible for businesses to forge these partnerships and create smaller circular economies on their own initiative – particularly if those involved share the same Global Goals-based purpose.

But one of the world's most remarkable circular economies needed neither ideological nor government intervention. The Kalundborg Eco-Industrial Park in Denmark began life in 1959 as a single power station. Then, over successive decades, an oil refinery, pharmaceutical company and plasterboard manufacturer moved in and began to share resources. The refinery supplied excess gas to the plasterboard manufacturer, which also received gypsum from the power plant's chimney scrubbers, that, in turn, received effluent water for its boilers from the refinery – and so on and so on, in what's described as 'industrial symbiosis'. This exchange of waste materials, energy, water and information between these plants has prevented millions of tonnes of natural resources from being extracted and transported, saved the companies an estimated US$15 million a year and sustained a network of local businesses and farms that also benefit from some of their industrial by-products.[44]

Astonishingly, none of this symbiosis was pre-planned. Instead, each link in the system was negotiated as an independent business deal between firms purely on the basis of saving money. In fact, many attempts to imitate Kalundborg's success at eco-industrial parks elsewhere in the world using government planning and incentivization to force such circular relationships have failed.[45] Those parks that allowed self-organization and organic development were far more likely to succeed. As in natural ecosystems, businesses are drawn to surplus resources, particularly when they are free to use. Just as the dung beetle cleans up ecosystems for its own benefit, perhaps when it comes to creating more circular industrial ecologies, even individual businesses driven purely by financial self-interest can be a powerful exponent for sustainability.

And that shouldn't be entirely surprising, because in a world where we're rapidly reaching the limits of our planet's natural resources, many companies' best opportunities for growth will be from optimizing the long-term value within their business ecosystems (like Interface selling the same raw materials hundreds of time rather than just once). And this means harnessing the circular potential of their waste, recycling and reusing materials and selling or exchanging any surplus with other businesses to save costs and diversify revenue streams. In a sustainable world, growth can no longer be contingent on increasing resource extraction and consumption, but should rely instead on innovation and circular economy strategies that release untapped value.

THE LOCALISM DILEMMA: ARE YOUR SUSTAINABLE SOLUTIONS ADAPTABLE ENOUGH?

There's no doubt that some simple solutions have universal application – such as washing your hands to prevent disease transmission. But their effectiveness is still dependent on how well it's tailored to local circumstances and needs. Solutions that work in one context may fail or even make things worse in another. That's why the World Health Organization has had to adapt its handwashing advice for those people living where soap and water are scarce to include using ash or mud instead.[46]

For businesses, the pressure to follow the herd on certain popular issues and be seen to 'do the right thing' might be preventing them from picking more appropriate solutions. For instance, fast food chain McDonald's switching their plastic straws to paper ones in the UK in 2019 seemed like it was rightfully responding to long-time customer demands to cut single-use plastics. But not only did the new straws not work well, quickly getting soggy, they couldn't be conventionally recycled – unlike the plastic ones.[47]

The best way to avoid these sustainability missteps is to take a bottom-up (as well as systemic) approach to any proposed solution, consulting communities on their specific needs and constantly assessing and tweaking to make sure the initiative is still having the desired outcome. The Global Living Wage Initiative, for example, obviously doesn't just set one hourly rate and apply it worldwide. It calculates a figure based on research into the living standards and needs of a particular country, including the costs of a locally agreed basket of goods. Then it regularly reviews these assessments to ensure the wage is still sufficient to cover workers' basic costs of living.[48]

With the Global Goals, too, businesses should tailor their activities to meet their specific Global Goal deficits and priorities (which can be identified through the purpose-mapping exercise on p 25), taking into account their capacity to tackle them and the needs of all their stakeholders. So having a net zero strategy or diversity and inclusion policy might not be very plausible or useful to a microbusiness or small-scale farmer, but switching to renewable energy and investing in more efficient technologies is and could have many knock-on benefits for employees and the local community. Although the Global Goals represent an ideal world to strive towards, none of it is sustainable if the strategies for achieving it aren't effective or constantly adapted to the local reality of each business and their specific needs.

The business ecosystem and working with nature

Isn't it amazing that when nature is left to its own devices, it creates an ecosystem that is so beautiful and diverse? Just think of the abundant life and verdure of a tropical rainforest or the eye-popping colours and intricate patterns of a thriving coral reef – what a contrast to the monocultural wastelands, eyesore development and pollution produced by businesses let loose on nature. But why can't doing business produce or at least maintain such beautiful ecosystems where life can thrive too?

Perhaps one of the world's most environmentally friendly businesses today is one practised in the depths of the Peruvian jungle. The latex farmers there have been harvesting white sap from the bark of shiringa trees for generations, which is exported around the world to make anything from surgical gloves to carpet backing. But unlike the destructive, monocultural rubber forests elsewhere in the world, the Peruvian cooperative of natural rubber producers – called ECOMUSA – uses traditional, sustainable techniques and values harmony with nature to leave the forest largely untouched by its activities.[49] The forest is its factory and the farmers defend any trees from being cut down, which, it argues, would degrade the natural balance that sustains its valuable rubber trees. This is working with nature in its purest form, protecting its resilience to sustainably extract resources at minimal cost to both the business and the environment. It's also an ethos that can work just as effectively on a more industrial scale.

Anglian Water in the UK, for instance, created a whole new wetland in Ingoldisthorpe, Norfolk, in keeping with the region's ecology to act as a natural water treatment plant. While their conventional waterworks produced waste water that was legally safe, it was impacting on the delicate health of the local river – one of only 200 chalk rivers in the world. So, in partnership with Norfolk Rivers Trust, the company made four interconnected lakes that it planted with thousands of wetland plants, which naturally filter millions of litres of water from the waterworks before entering the river. As well as saving Anglian Water huge sums in energy, carbon filtration and chemical treatments, the site has become a biodiversity hotspot, attracting amphibians, birds and bats. It also improves the sustainability of water supply in a region that is particularly vulnerable to climate change, forming part of a cross-sector initiative the firm is leading on to restore fenland more widely and manage Norfolk's water resources in the longer term.[50]

Even for the vast majority of industries that don't manage and sell natural resources but do manufacture them into products, there are numerous ways to work with nature to minimize local ecological impact. Many modern factories and business parks are built with eco-friendly features such as rainwater harvesting, solar panels, bioclimatic-designed buildings that passively heat and cool, green spaces and living roofs that attract a host of local wildlife. Even megafactories, like Toyota UK's 58,000-acre car plant outside Derby, become recolonized by plants and animals over time. Twelve years after it was built in 1992, the Japanese firm partnered with the Derbyshire Wildlife Trust to create an on-site nature reserve and a Biodiversity Action Plan centred around its three man-made balancing lakes that collect rainwater from the site and prevent downstream flooding of the nearby brook. By 2007 the reserve was recognized as a 'Site of Biological Importance' and is now an integral part of a wider wetland management scheme along the Trent Valley looking to reintroduce ospreys in the area.[51]

So an industrial site needn't be moribund of wildlife, and can even become an important part of the local ecosystem. By working with the natural adaptive cycles of nature, businesses can help accelerate its renewal locally and build its resilience more widely. But what if a business's ecological role went even deeper, informing every part of its operations so that it provides the same benefits as a high-performing ecosystem? This is the premise of 'biomimicry' that uses nature's designs and processes to solve human problems. The idea stretches back to Leonardo da Vinci's 'flying machine' that he based on the structure of bats' wings, but has been popularized more recently by the scientist and natural history writer Janine Benyus, who sees it as the key to unlocking sustainability.

'Life's technologies tend to be elegant', she says. 'They sip energy, they shave material use, they really avoid toxins – they're all the things we're looking for these days.' Benyus describes biomimicry as like 'tapping into an R&D lab that you could never afford and that has been going on for 3.8 billion years', and argues that 'when the forest and the city are functionally indistinguishable, then we know we've reached sustainability'.[52]

It's a concept that Interface is pioneering with its ambition to create a 'factory as a forest'. Working with Benyus's consultancy firm, Biomimicry 3.8, Interface has reimagined its factory at LaGrange in Georgia as behaving like a high-performing forest that provides an array of ecosystem services, such as recycling nutrients, carbon sequestration and water storage. So Interface has devised a range of ecological performance standards based on a healthy, local forest ecosystem, which it will use to measure the factory's contribution to the soil, atmosphere, biodiversity, water and carbon levels. The metrics have helped drive innovations, like creating carpet tiles that sequester carbon, returning more fresh water to the water table than used in manufacturing, and reducing levels of water runoff from the site. It has also encouraged the factory to reach out to nearby businesses and act as a 'pollinator' of best environmental practice locally as well as in its own factories worldwide, transforming the business ecosystem further afield.[53]

The metaphor of an ecosystem and using the natural sciences to understand how to work more sustainably compels businesses to reidentify themselves in intriguing ways. What ecological role does a company play in this business ecosystem, for instance? Is it an extractor, concentrator, recycler or disperser of nutrients? Does it pollinate and create new life, or help consume and break down waste material? Is it large enough to act like a keystone species that impacts the health of the whole ecosystem? Or is it one of the many smaller organisms that performs essential routine tasks?

More and more scientists are recognizing how important biodiversity is to maintaining a stable and healthily performing ecosystem because of the unique abilities each ecological community has to respond to a disturbance.[54] This 'response diversity', as it's called, is equally important for the resilience and high performance of a business ecosystem. Yet how much does the current profit-maximization culture encourage a diverse range of businesses and business models? Is our business ecosystem becoming overwhelmed by a eutrophication of nutrient-hungry corporates that are choking the oxygen from other smaller firms? Is the exponential growth demanded by so many companies causing desertification of the business ecosystem to the detriment of everyone?

Using ecological taxonomy to characterize business like this is a useful way of flipping the ideological framing that business runs the world when we really know that nature does. But it also foregrounds the fact that business *is* a part of nature, just as much as it's a part of society – inseparable from the ecological systems on which it depends and impacts on so greatly.

Yet although business is subservient to this overarching socio-ecological system, it does have enormous power to organize and manipulate society and environmental resources – for good or ill. Despite some people's demonization of business, it's quite feasible to imagine a world without it not as some undisturbed natural Eden, but as a more heterogeneously organized society depleting the world's resources just as aggressively.

Either way, with the global population and levels of individual consumption rising rapidly, business undoubtedly plays a vital role in managing these socio-ecological stressors on our planet. At their most innovative and sustainable, businesses could be our best opportunity to marshal the world's resources to the benefit of the most people while safeguarding the planet's long-term future. But this means truly working with society and the environment to enable the kind of systemic interventions that will not only prevent climate collapse, but also restore and rebuild society and the environment's resilience for generations to come.

Summary: The science of responsible business

Observations to note
Responsible businesses ...
... have a net zero strategy with full-scope carbon emissions reporting.
... make society and nature integral to their business resilience strategies.
... have a circular value chain and make products that are easy to repair or recycle.
... forge numerous cross-sectoral partnerships.
... use their voice to challenge systemic social problems.
... respond to the latest research and emerging knowledge from stakeholders without waiting for policy or laws.
... look at least one system level up and down when solution-finding.
... adapt any sustainability initiatives to meet local needs.

Theories to test
Closed-loop working
A sustainable business is circular and must collaborate with others to close the loop.
- What percentage of your products do you recover, reuse or recycle? (Global Goals 12 and 15)
- Are you actively engaged in collaborations that enable repairing, recycling, sharing or selling of your waste materials? (Global Goals 8 and 9)
- How much responsibility do you take for the sustainable use and disposal of your products after they're sold? (Global Goals 11 and 12)

- Do you lobby your industry and/or government for better access to clean and affordable energy? (Global Goals 7, 13 and 17)

Resilience-based stewardship

Sustainable businesses help build the resilience of society and nature to avoid systemic risks.

- How would you define your approach to net zero emissions: PAZE, TAZE, HOZE or HOPE? (Global Goals 13 and 15)
- Is your company paying its fair share of taxes wherever you operate? (Global Goals 10 and 11)
- Do you pay your staff according to the principles of the Global Living Wage and communicate this commitment to your suppliers? (Global Goals 1, 2 and 3)
- What measures do you take to restore and enhance the ecosystems you impact on? (Global Goals 14 and 15)

Systemic agency

Understanding the systemic nature of a problem will help identify where and how a business can intervene most effectively.

- When was the last time you proactively responded to the latest academic research before there was a change to regulations? (Global Goals 9, 16 and 17)
- What elements of your business are perceived by staff and peers as innovative or best practice in relation to any of the Global Goals? (Global Goals 9 and 17)
- How do you customize your interventions to take account of local circumstances or values? (Global Goals 11 and 16)
- Do you issue ethnic pay gap reports and contribute to wider inclusivity schemes? (Global Goals 10 and 16)

First steps to responsible production ...

Product life cycle responsibility	Net zero strategy	Social resilience-building	Partnership working
Own your products' impacts, from raw materials to disposal	Measure and mitigate carbon emissions across entire value chain	Pay fair taxes and wages and help enhance the natural environment	Work with others to tackle big, systemic issues

The Consumer Is Always Right

The gap between intention and behaviour and the opportunity for business to help bridge it

The rise of the ethical consumer over the last few decades has been credited as a major driver of businesses transitioning to more sustainable products and practices in recent years. From an exponential rise in veganism leading to more meat-free alternatives in supermarkets to boycotts of single-use plastics by both retailers and shoppers, the propensity for ethical consumers and responsible businesses to symbiotically shape each other for the better is a powerful combination. But research has shown that despite these mutually good intentions, many sustainability-conscious consumers are still struggling to make good choices.

In their seminal, decade-long study, 'The myth of the ethical consumer', published in 2001, researchers Marylyn Carrigan and Ahmad Attalla found limited evidence of consumers choosing the most socially responsible product available to them beyond certain niche products – despite having said it was important to them in surveys. In structured experiments, they found that when an 'ethical' product required sacrificing some aspect of functionality compared to its regular counterpart, almost everyone bar the most committed activists ditched ethics. Similarly, with Fairtrade alternatives offered at the same price, only 1% opted to purchase them unprompted – but remarkably that jumped to 70% after the individual was prompted and was told their choice would be made public.[1]

Not only does this study show that sustainable consumption is complicated even for shoppers sympathetic to the cause; it also demonstrates that the context of someone's purchase often seems to matter more than the actual 'ethicality' of the product. In other words, it's more important for some people to be perceived as ethical consumers than actually being one. But given the billions spent on promoting almost everything else about a product except its sustainability credentials and the generations of past conditioning to shop in a way that rarely took into account the social and environmental costs of a product, perhaps this shouldn't be a surprise.

While it may be dispiriting to learn so many people are saying one thing in public and doing quite another in private, this 'intention–behaviour gap' does present an opportunity for responsible businesses to help bridge, because, according to a 2018 survey of 1,000 US and UK consumers by the sustainability consultancy firm Futerra, 88% want the brands they buy to help them be more ethical in their daily life, although 43% think they're making it harder for them to do.

'Too much of the cause-related-marketing, sustainability or CSR activities of brands promote what the company is doing, rather than helping the consumer to make their own difference', explains Solitaire Townsend, who co-founded Futerra, and argues consumers want a business to not only talk about its values but also help them to live theirs. 'This isn't only a problem for business brands. Governments and even many NGOs take for themselves the role of "actor/hero/change-maker" and relegate the public to mere "audience/beneficiary/cheerleader". Perhaps this is why today, consumers feel that companies are actually making it harder for them to make a difference in the world.'[2]

To more clearly understand the role of consumers in the Global Goals, Townsend helped launch the UN-backed Goodlife Goals – a reframing of the Global Goals for individuals and what they can do to help.[3] From 'love where you live' (Global Goal 11) to 'treat everyone equally' (Global Goal 5), they're an excellent way of personalizing the goals and making them more active and accessible – for companies as well as people. If businesses are going to make it easier for their consumers to fulfil their Goodlife Goals, they need to consider whether their products are helping them in their efforts. This doesn't just mean making sure products are sustainably produced, eschewing such flagship issues as slave labour, environmentally damaging raw materials or excessive and non-recyclable packaging; it also means labelling clearly and honestly and avoiding exclusionary price markups to help everyone make ethical choices more easily when shopping.

It's all too easy to blame consumers for being lazy, fickle or hypocritical when it comes to making poor choices, but many are rightly sceptical of some companies' dubious ethical claims or are bamboozled by confusing

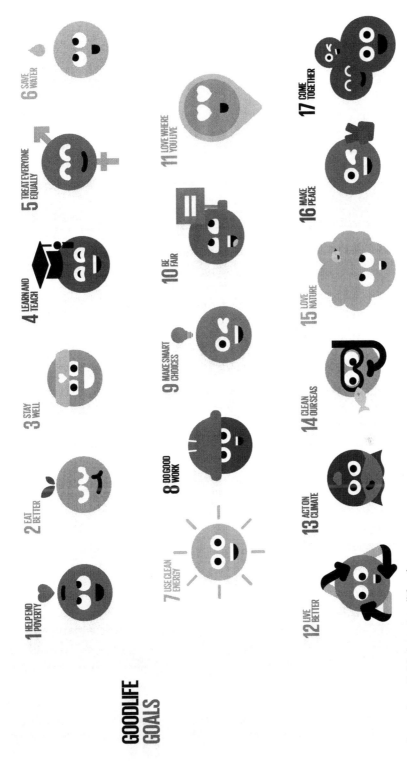

Source: https://sdghub.com/goodlifegoals

or deliberately misleading labelling. They're also up against incredibly sophisticated and manipulative marketing, where packaging, placement on a shelf, special offers and pricing are all proven ways to increase sales of products, however unsustainable they might be. In fact, a recent study found that product marketing deploys a lot of the same subterfuge performed by stage magicians to dupe consumers, exploiting language ambiguities, providing illusions of control and using sensory misdirection![4] Even for the most shrewd and well-informed consumers, there's the risk of being paralysed by the Aristotlean paradox of 'the more you know, the more you realize you don't know' when it comes to sustainability and the burden of realizing no choice is entirely sustainable.[5]

So given this distorted playing field, where even committed ethical shoppers struggle to buy sustainably, the challenge is what responsible businesses can do to help improve the situation for consumers – because there's no point in companies spending all their energy and resources on more sustainable goods and services if people aren't buying them. A product that doesn't sell is unsustainable by definition (also known as waste).

Misinformation, mistrust and the confusion of labelling

One area where businesses can have a greater influence on steering consumers towards more sustainable choices is labelling. Food shoppers in the UK are now well used to the traffic light label on packaging detailing the fat, sugar and salt content as either low (green), medium (amber) or high (red). In tests, it proved to be easier to spot and interpret than the raw Guideline Daily Amount figures, and so could help people make more informed and healthier choices.[6]

Given the UK's burgeoning obesity problem and the fact traffic light labelling is still voluntary, it's difficult to determine how successful the scheme has been since its introduction in 2013, but research looking at its potential impacts for food shoppers in Canada found that traffic light labelling could reduce intake of calories by 5% and saturated fat by 14%.[7] So could the same approach work for influencing consumers on other sustainability issues, such as a product's carbon footprint?

That's what researchers in France set out to examine in 2019. Setting up an experimental grocery store with 300 products, each either had single or multiple traffic light labels for GHGs or stated the number of kilometres a car would need to drive to produce the equivalent level of emissions. Some had no special labelling at all. Examining the shopping baskets of the 275 people who took part revealed a marked change in their previous choices, with significant numbers of products swapped out for lower GHG items.[8] Interestingly, the impacts were similar regardless of the format of the GHG labels. Another study in a Belgian supermarket showed shoppers increased the eco-friendliness of their purchases by 5.3% after introducing a comprehensive eco-label on goods.[9]

If sustainability labelling of any kind has shown some positive effect, what specific features of a label have been proven to work best? One study in China found that products with carbon calculators, showing the percentage of the price going towards carbon offsetting schemes, were less effective than a more ostentatious environmental label.[10] Another in the US found that the more the label showed the personal impacts of sustainability, the more favourably the product's ethical credentials were viewed.[11] Even the country-of-origin and its environmental reputation has been found to be a strong influencing factor in how credible consumers found a product's sustainability to be, as well as more obviously the reputation and transparency of the company that makes the product – including its executives.[12]

But whether a label is about making information more easily comparable and available to ethical consumers or about highlighting a product's more sustainable credentials above the fray of less ethical competition, trust is essential to any label's effectiveness. Researchers have found that sponsorship or third party certification schemes are not only an important way of ensuring consumer confidence in any eco-labels, but the source of those endorsements is also key. While labelling schemes run by governments and environmental NGOs were most trusted by consumers, those developed by business organizations were deemed untrustworthy, unless audited by credible third parties.[13] The best examples have proven highly effective at reducing buyers' anxiety, offering comfort and reassurance at the time of purchase, particularly with controversial products such as farmed salmon.[14]

A well-established and reputable scheme, such as Fairtrade or organic accreditation, not only helps with consumer understanding of what the label represents; it can also boost sales and the price people are willing to pay. An experiment in one chain of US grocery stores found sales of their most popular own-brand coffee increased by 10% when carrying the Fairtrade label and were unaffected by an 8% increase in price. By comparison, a similar price hike on their 'unfairly traded' coffee saw sales collapse by 30%.[15] Numerous other studies from around the world have confirmed that people in general are willing to pay this price premium for products that are labelled as being more sustainable and environmentally friendly.[16] In fact, the price point itself can become a measure of a product's sustainability for some more suspicious consumers, who are convinced nothing can be more sustainable without being more expensive – even if the cost of production is similar or even less.[17]

Yet even the most rigorous and reputable of certification schemes can sometimes fail for unanticipated reasons. Palm oil is one such example. Following distressing media coverage of orangutans left homeless by vast rainforest-clearing for palm plantations in Malaysia and Indonesia, consumer groups and governments demanded manufacturers specifically highlight any use of palm oil on their labelling (rather than hiding it as 'generic vegetable oils') so consumers could avoid it. But environmental groups like WWF (World Wide Fund for Nature) that once spearheaded these campaigns against the industry are now encouraging people not to boycott palm oil, recognizing that it's a far more efficient, less land-hungry and environmentally damaging crop than the soya, rapeseed or fossil fuel oils it replaces. 'We knew a boycott wasn't the right solution', explained Adam Harrison, senior policy officer for food and agriculture at WWF in 2015. 'The trick is to cut the link between palm oil and the unacceptable impacts rather than cut it out.'[18]

So WWF helped set up the Roundtable for Sustainable Palm Oil (RSPO) in 2004 with producers, manufacturers and NGOs among its nearly 5,000 members today, including big corporates like Nestlé and Mondelez International. It sets standards to ensure all RSPO-certified palm oil is traceable back to the mill and the smallholder farms they buy from to eliminate palm grown on illegally deforested farms.

Unfortunately, despite the huge financial and reputational investment made by WWF in the scheme, many businesses have been reluctant to use the RSPO label even if their products did contain certified sustainable palm oil – particularly on food items. The whole issue of palm oil has become so toxic in the mind of consumers that any use of it – regardless of its sustainability – is shunned, and many companies (such as UK supermarket Iceland[19]) have pledged to remove palm oil from their products altogether, to avoid being associated with any controversy. It's another example of how resorting to blunt, overly simplistic solutions to complex problems – often driven by an overriding desire to boost or protect a brand's reputation – can just increase damage elsewhere.

Of course, certification schemes can also lose the confidence of consumers if they fail to maintain the standards they espouse. The internationally used Forest Stewardship Council (FSC) label, that's meant to guarantee wood is sourced from responsibly managed forests, was brought into disrepute after an investigation into IKEA furniture in 2020 found timber from illegally logged forests in the Ukraine.[20] IKEA, which aims to have all its wood from sustainable sources,[21] blamed the FSC for not thoroughly auditing the Ukrainian timber strictly enough, and the FSC subsequently admitted that illegal timber in Ukraine could 'likely' pass its compliance tests.

Another drawback of these various eco-labels and certification schemes is that their sheer number can be confusing. One international study in 2014 found the public's understanding of sustainability was narrow and limited (particularly around carbon footprints) and largely only pertained to the environmental rather than social impact of a product. Only a handful of the most well-known and self-explanatory labels, like Rainforest Alliance and Animal Welfare, even registered with the participants, and very few referred to even these when considering which products to purchase.[22]

Other studies have shown that while eco-labels are less effective or trusted by consumers already highly committed to the cause, they are persuasive for conscientious consumers who are less involved. Similarly, consumers who were more well informed about the sustainability of a certain product, such as fish, tended to ignore any new eco-labelling and looked for specifics most important to them, like whether the fish was caught wild or farmed.[23] When asked which of the many eco-labels on food products were most important to them, US consumers put locally sourced and Fairtrade top, while shoppers in Belgium valued free range and animal welfare certification most.[24]

With people becoming increasingly more literate about sustainability and the range of ethical products and eco-labelling growing ever wider, conscientious consumers are likely to face even more shopping confusion in future. This is why a new generation of digital platforms has emerged to cater for these time-pressed, information-seekers that aims to help shoppers compare the sustainability credentials of different products.

One of the most popular is the Giki app.[25] Launched in 2018, it allows users to scan the barcodes of any supermarket product using their smartphone to see if it qualifies for any of Giki's 15 sustainability badges, which cover everything from animal testing to chemicals of concern – including a 'hero product' badge for those that are the most sustainable and healthy. The registered social enterprise claims that the app has helped 80% of its users change their consumption habits and make more sustainable choices, and is now expanding into a website that can help individuals and companies calculate and improve their sustainability score.

Giki works by pulling in and analysing huge amounts of data on each product, using complex modelling to align the different metrics with their simplified badge system.[26] Other apps are turning to crowdsourcing and information provided by their users to rate the sustainability of products and businesses. The Find Green app, for instance, maps sustainable businesses that are submitted and scored by its users for their environmental footprint.[27]

With more and more ethical consumers relying on these digital sources to inform their buying choices, it's becoming ever more important for sustainably minded companies to be transparent with their data, share their sustainability credentials and make sure they engage with and are included on these platforms. They'll also make it easier to expose price-gouging (that is, those sustainable or healthy goods with excessive premiums to cash in on the prestige market) and misleading or overstated claims of sustainability – both of which breach consumer trust. For a responsible business, that trust is vital, so its pricing and marketing needs to be just as ethical as its products.

Eventually, digital platforms will offer the potential for any citizen with access to the internet to curate a full life cycle account of a business's raw materials, labour conditions, processes and waste. Already, blockchain technology is revolutionizing transparency and traceability, helping create a tamper-proof, digital record of things such as conflict minerals, EV components and GHGs (despite blockchain's own problems with energy consumption and associated emissions). How would consumer trust in your business fare if the Global Goals' impacts of your entire value chain were subject to such full disclosure and public scrutiny?

THE CONSUMPTION DILEMMA: WHAT LEVEL OF CONSUMPTION IS SUSTAINABLE?

According to Global Footprint Network, our demand for the Earth's resources exceeds what it can sustainably replenish by 60%. This means that our current levels of consumption require 1.6 Earths to sustain, and that's set to increase 25% by 2030. If everyone was to match the US's level of consumption, we'd need closer to five planets' worth of resources.[28]

So it's clear that any sustainable future for our planet requires us to curb our consumption by at least 60% and more as the global population continues to increase. What might that look like on an individual basis? Well, even if everyone shared the same per capita environmental footprint as Kyrgyzstan, where people earn an average of just over US$4 a day, we'd still overshoot the Earth's biocapacity by 1.4%. Hence, while a drastic reduction in individual consumption is key, it needs to be matched by business innovations that consume less and reuse or recycle more (currently just 8.6% of the 100 billion tonnes of natural resources extracted annually are recycled[29]) – with government regulations to encourage and enforce such measures.

It also illustrates that *how much* people buy is arguably even more important than *what* they buy. So companies concerned about the sustainability of their products should be equally concerned about their overconsumption. It might sound totally heretical to regular business thinking, but any advertising should emphasize responsible consumption and disposal of a product rather than just a hard sell – perhaps avoiding advertising altogether if it encourages overconsumption or the product is unhealthy. In some cases, it may be that a product is intrinsically antithetical to the Global Goals, and any refining of its footprint is just perpetuating the problem rather than solving it. In which case, proactively withdrawing the product and eliminating its consumption altogether may well be the best option, avoiding the risk of future legal cases, fines, imprisonment or liquidation.

Fortunately, there is an emerging trend of businesses, scientists, NGOs and governments working together to produce useful guidance on sustainable consumption. The EAT-Lancet Commission, for instance, has produced a report that offers a solution on how to feed a future population of 10 billion people within our planetary boundaries, right down to individual recipes.[30] Our consumption knowledge gaps are being filled and there is now evidence and future modelling that can and should be integrated into business strategies.

Consumer paralysis, biases, emotions and values

While a well-informed consumer – both in terms of the availability and veracity of a product's sustainability credentials – is vital for enabling and influencing more responsible consumption, there's growing evidence that too much information can have the opposite effect.

In a 2017 study called 'It's not easy living a sustainable lifestyle', researchers interviewed numerous individuals who were highly knowledgeable and engaged with living more sustainably but reported often failing to live up to their principles – quite deliberately and often. From purchasing farmed smoked salmon to ordering mass-produced Chinese clothing, these conscientious consumers were wracked by feelings of tension, hopelessness and paralysis over their knowingly unsustainable choices, yet made them anyway. The researchers labelled this behaviour the 'self-inflicted sustainable consumption paradox', whereby the more expert someone becomes on sustainability, the more difficult it is to choose any product, since ultimately nothing is truly sustainable or free from negative social and environmental impacts.[31]

What this study reveals is that even if the most committed ethical consumers are furnished with the best sustainability information, they will still make less sustainable choices – maybe even the worst possible ones. That's because humans aren't rational and reflective processors of information; we're impulsive, self-interested, whimsical and prone to social conformity. Moreover, because we have been socialized in irresponsible consumption, consuming responsibly is undoubtedly harder work and we all have limited physical and cognitive resources to apply to the task. So we rely on quicker, non-cognitive and more emotional decision-making far more often than we'd like to admit.

This is what Nobel Laureate Daniel Kahneman popularized as System 1 and System 2 thinking. System 1 is fast, automatic and intuitive, and most connected with emotional responses, while the slower, analytical System 2 is dominated more by reason.[32] These two distinctive ways the mind processes information – emotional and rational – and how they interact are at the heart of a growing strand of behavioural science that continues to surprise and confound with its findings.

This is why so much business practice around customer profiling is usually wrong, because it's often predicated on the myth of the 'sovereign consumer', who makes rational, cognitive choices that always align with their preferences and values. Unfortunately for businesses pitching their products, people are much less consistent and predictable in reality than in textbooks, Excel spreadsheets or old lab experiments. Or, to put it another way, humans are human. And given what we've already discussed, it should come as no surprise that purchasing decisions aren't monocausal and depend on a complex array of different factors when that decision is made.

One important factor is the many biases that affect human decision-making, which businesses need to invest in understanding and work with responsibly (that is, not just cynically exploit). Some of these biases come from the way our brain is preconfigured and deeper neural processes that we don't yet fully comprehend. Physiologically speaking, thinking is a resource-hungry human function that takes up time, calories, chemicals and nutrients. So our brain has evolved mental shortcuts (or 'heuristics', as psychologists call them) that are quicker and less energy-intensive, which are the basis of our emotional, System 1 thinking. These mental shortcuts have their primordial origins back when time wasn't money but about life or death. So they generally point us in the right direction more often than not, and provide useful rules to follow in most situations. If we hear a loud noise and see crowds running in one direction, for instance, it's generally better to follow the herd and ask why later. But they also lead us to create mental models based on past experiences, making us more likely to observe things that confirm these models and ignore anything that contradicts them – known as 'confirmation bias'.

As you can see from the list below, there are numerous types of mental bias, all giving us the illusion of control and cause and effect. Our brain works with stereotypes, instincts and stories, often filling in the gaps automatically rather than by conscious reasoning, factual analysis or weighing up the costs and benefits. It's just so much easier to use System 1 rather than System 2 thinking. The problem is that System 1 generalizes far too much so can get things badly wrong. If everyone is running to the same emergency exit, your chances of survival may be better heading for an alternative exit. There is wisdom in the crowd, as there may be in having some biases, but not in every situation.

Examples of mental biases[33]

Confirmation bias – ignoring confounding evidence
Emotional bias – convinced by emotional stories
Familiarity bias – that worked fine before
Contagion or lemming bias – but everyone else is ...
Social conformity bias – want to be in your gang
Survivorship bias – doesn't take into account failure

No idea what is going on bias – hit and hope
Urgency bias – crises need fast action
I'm in control bias – creates false causal connections
Negativity bias – focus on downside risk
Loss aversion bias – prefer to avoid a loss than make a profit
Stereotyping bias – they are all the same
Substitution bias – when asked a hard question, we answer a different, simpler one
Blame bias – looking for someone else to blame
Justification bias – look for a reason after action not before
Single cause bias – always one driver of events
Silver bullet bias – always one solution
Status quo bias – aversion to change

Just to be clear, these biases aren't a result of problematic individuals; rather, they're our default conditions. This is how we think and how others will react to what we say and do. So it's worth reflecting on whether businesses encourage customers to use System 1 thinking when buying their products and not just the slow, rational cost–benefit analysis of System 2. Does a business's marketing, point of sale, packaging and pricing only appeal to the myth of the rational economic consumer? Or does it use any mental biases to trigger an emotional and instinctive lifting of the product off the shelf and into the customer's basket? For example, compare the information a business demands of its supplier when making a procurement decision (which will no doubt be led by System 2 rationality) and the information provided to the customer. Is it the same or has the business chosen not to disclose something to the customer that would be unacceptable to the business as a buyer?

Ultimately, a business needs to knowledgeably and responsibly engage with both the rational and emotional thinking of a consumer to really empower them to make more sustainable choices – because when it comes to purchase decision-making, it's the *feeling* of power at that moment that often has more impact than any new information imparted.[34] A raft of fascinating new research known as 'self-validation theory' has found that the more powerful people are made to feel, the more confident they are about acting on their pre-existing thoughts – and vice versa.[35] So while adequate labelling and communication may be enough to influence consumers who feel less sure of themselves about sustainability, for those most confident and knowledgeable, such information may not be enough to counter their habitual choices and biases. Paradoxically, then, it may be the most experienced ethical consumers who are hardest to reach for responsible businesses with any new or improved products – particularly those who are already convinced that no product is truly sustainable anyway, and who prefer to make minimal or long-lasting purchases.

For this most wary cohort, the whole activity of ethical consumerism can be tainted by negative feelings of anxiety and fatalism that undermine its perceived value and their likelihood of engaging with it at all (what psychologists call 'task-related affect'). That's because the tenor of different emotions has been found to have a similar self-validating effect on people's thoughts as power.[36] So, if after thinking about something you experience unpleasant emotions, like anger or disgust, researchers have found this tends to invalidate those thoughts immediately preceding it − even if they are logically unrelated − because the emotion is misattributed to them. In the same way, pleasant emotions, like awe and surprise, can have the opposite effect and so validate any preceding thoughts.

Given this, it would seem important for businesses to try to create generally pleasant emotions around ethical shopping where possible, and encourage positive associations, even though the nature of the issues sustainability is trying to address can often be depressing. Fortunately, the 'warm glow' of positive emotions experienced by consumers making choices that chime with their personal values is well documented and a powerful driver for responsible consumption. Yet interestingly, for those shoppers yet to consider ethical purchases, researchers have found that negative emotions can also be a useful tool to invalidate any preconceived prejudices and open them up to alternatives. This is because the more pleasant the emotions, the more confident people feel in their thoughts, and so the less receptive they become to new information. If you are in a good mood, you are more likely to go with the flow and be persuaded by special offers or make habitual choices, letting System 1 thinking take control. If you are a bit grumpy (for whatever reason), you are more sceptical and likely to look closer at the label or terms or conditions, triggering System 2 thinking. Emotions, it would seem, are complicated!

Reading all that, a responsible business might suspect different emotional marketing strategies are required depending on how engaged with responsible consumption its intended audience is. But simply priming people with an emotion that is generally congruent with the values of the product has proven to work very effectively in the charity sector.[37] One study showed evoking feelings of compassion raised the most donations when the charitable cause was to do with caring for others − whether it be environmental, animal or human welfare issues − whereas gratitude prompted more donations to charities concerned with fairness and equality, like LGBTQ rights and social justice issues.[38]

On the face of it, this might seem blindingly obvious. But the counterpoint is that emotions that appeal to consumers' more self-interested values − such as financial reward or their public image − can make them less amenable to issues of sustainability. In fact, the 'Basic Human Values' model that social psychologist Shalom H. Schwartz developed in the 1990s (shown with annotations opposite) charts this antagonistic relationship between

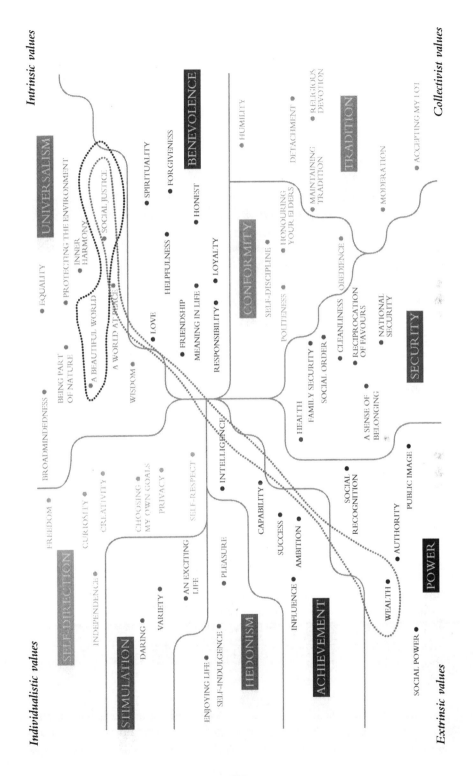

'intrinsic' and 'extrinsic' values. From surveys of more than 25,000 people in 44 countries, Schwartz identified 56 human values that are related to 10 different goal-driven motivations (the labels in capital letters) common to all cultures.[39] Those motivations can themselves be roughly divided between those that are focused on external approval and rewards and so are extrinsic (these sit towards the bottom left of the chart), and those based on more inherently rewarding pursuits and so are intrinsic (which sit towards the top right of the chart). They can also be broadly split between individualistic and collectivist values (moving from the top left to the bottom right of the chart).

Many researchers using this model have described a 'see-saw' and 'bleed-over' effect when drawing people's attention to a specific value. For instance, engaging the 'wealth' value through prompting concern about financial loss or reward tended to suppress the 'social justice' value, which sits on the opposite side of the chart to it, while prompting the value of 'a world of beauty' through evoking feelings of awe and wonder tended to also enhance concern about 'social justice' that sits adjacent to it in the chart. So again, there's this congruence and antagonism between emotions and the values they engage that responsible businesses should be mindful of when communicating with their customers about the sustainability of their products.[40]

Taking these values and emotions together with System 1 and 2 thinking and our many mental biases, it's clear that everybody has their own unique 'rationality' for decision-making that's far more complex and open to contradiction than the simplistic psychological model of the 'sovereign consumer'. But thankfully, as well as behavioural science providing businesses with new insights to better understand the vagaries inside consumers' heads, there are also sociologists connecting these theories to material things outside the consumer that can be more straightforwardly changed to encourage sustainable behaviour.

Social practice, herd mentality and business citizenship

In recent years, researchers have acknowledged that there's been an over-emphasis on the individual and their internal psychology when it comes to consumer analysis, which tends to overlook the vast influence of external society and culture. Sociologists have long argued that behaviour is often less about cognitive choice and more about habit, routine and social conventions.

Daily showering, the buying of petrol and weekly food shopping are as much about passively following society's cultural norms of cleanliness, car use and supermarkets as they are about active, individual decision-making. As we've seen, while behavioural psychologists continue to demonstrate how little people deliberate on their values when they act, this socoiologists' theory of behaviour as 'social practice' suggests people's values are also a product of their habits.[41]

Consider the cultural factors around the issue of food waste in the UK, where a fifth of food purchased is binned, unused.[42] Despite the vast majority of people being appalled at the idea of wasting food, researchers found patterns of consumption – such as shopping for food weekly rather than daily, supermarkets' buy-one-get-one-free offers and parents cooking extra meals for their kids in case they refused to eat what's first offered – meant people often bought more food than they needed or could eat before it perished.

Rather than a rational reflection of people's values, this ingrained behaviour, researchers suggest, is the result of people's material circumstances, such as the increase in suburban living where supermarkets dominate, and longer working hours that leave less time and energy to research and shop sustainably. Moreover, purchasing food often forms part of a routine social practice, like grabbing lunch every day with work colleagues or visiting a monthly farmers' market with friends, which has more bearing on sustainable choices than any cognitive decision-making. As well as being limited to the options available in that specific locality at that time, the social influence of others involved in that practice is also key: whether it's a household agreeing a week's meals that they all like or buying brands that are trusted or familiar from childhood.[43]

So it's easy to see how conventions and force of habit can dictate people's choices, both practically and emotionally, as much as their sustainable values. And that's not even considering the economic barriers to buying sustainably, where often the most ethical products are more expensive or perceived as a luxury. Yet this example is just looking at food waste, which is largely undisputed as being a problem. Imagine how much more difficult it is to influence people on other consumer values, such as having a car or air travel, where opinion is far more divided![44]

But for responsible businesses, this multitude of externalities that shape people's behaviour can actually provide an alternative means of intervention beyond just personal education and converting people's values, which circumnavigates consumers' intention–behaviour gap altogether. As Alan Warde explains in his book *Consumption: A Sociological Analysis*, because our actions are for the most part 'rapid responses to cues provided in the external environment, conjured up from habits and intuitions about the nature of the situation in which we find ourselves', the focus for changing people's behaviour should be on 'altering the environment of action rather than changing people's minds'.[45]

In practice, this means using simple, environmental 'nudges' to trigger people's System 1 thinking that will make the desired outcome more likely. For example, snack shops in Holland that placed fruit and healthy foods by the checkouts, where they were most visible to consumers, caused a marked uptick in their sales.[46] Could similarly purposive design in other commercial and public spaces encourage more sustainable behaviour too? Peer pressure (or 'social proof heuristics', as behaviourists like to call it) is also remarkably effective at influencing behaviour. So rather than trying to persuade people through rational argument, simply using the power of normative behaviour and informing them of what most other people do can often get better results. The British government's tax department, for instance, found sending letters that said most people pay their taxes on time increased payment rates significantly.[47] Such government messaging has also worked for reducing littering and encouraging energy conservation.

Another effective nudging strategy is to make doing the right thing fun and rewarding, rather than highlighting or punishing the wrong behaviour. Volkswagen's The Fun Theory project has come up with numerous 'gamification' ideas that do just that, including musical stairs to lure people away from escalators and be more active, and bottle banks that react like arcade games to encourage more recycling.[48] One of their most successful was a clever twist on the speed camera that rewarded drivers for *not* speeding, sending them a lottery ticket to win a share of the fines paid by those drivers who were caught speeding. In just three days of trialling the camera on a Stockholm street, the average vehicle speed dropped from 32km/h to 25km/h.[49]

What belies the nudging power of many of these environmental cues and appeals to social norms is people's susceptibility to herd mentality, especially when overwhelmed or exhausted by consumer choice and information. They also demonstrate how sustainable consumption is determined socially and collectively and not by the whims of the individual consumer alone. Even if we do have an innate desire to play and seek reward, gamification is still a response to a game set by others.

In recent decades, disproportionate emphasis has been placed on individuals' 'purchase power' to affect positive societal change. For ethical consumers, every pound spent represents more than just the immediate purchase they're making; it's also an investment in the kind of values they want to see in the world. There have been many instances of consumers forcing firms and even governments to reform their practices through targeted spending and boycotting products. Nike has faced pressure from what's been dubbed 'political consumerism' or 'brand activism'[50] to address labour issues in its supply chains, while consumer lobbying of Walmart to adopt better workforce equality and LGBT rights led to the corporation vocally opposing a proposed anti-LGBT law in its home state of Arkansas in 2015 and persuading the governor not to sign it. Similarly, buycotts can have a double-whammy impact, defunding less responsible firms and directing consumer spending towards more sustainable companies.[51]

But more and more people are becoming disillusioned with this idea of purchase power as awareness has increased of the scale of public behaviour change and structural reforms needed to create a more sustainable world. Consumers are just one link in an enormous economic chain, whereas businesses, governments and authorities are far less numerous and make many more transactions. And those transactions occur at much more critical intersections between different systems, where positive change can ripple across the whole value chain. For instance, eliminating carbon emissions from mining at source benefits every future user of those mined materials, reducing the 'carbon balloon' passed on to thousands, if not millions, of others. This is much more effective (and cheaper) than cleaning up or mitigating the pollution once it's gone wild. So it stands to reason that any behaviour changes at these more powerful and connected levels will have a far greater impact than an individual's spending.

The problem, Warde argues, is the continuing emphasis on individual choice based on the bogus idea of consumer sovereignty. 'After all, how much choice do individuals have if the range of products offered are mostly terrible sustainability-wise?' he says. 'The social context for your choices are largely beyond your control, making them restricted, constrained and intermittent.'[52] Indeed, the citizens of Lagos may know buying plastic sachets of water for 6 cents is a poor choice for the environment, but only 10 per cent have piped water to their homes, and it can't always be relied on for drinking. With an average wage of around US$3 a day, how can you blame the two-thirds of this megacity for drinking sachet water? What other choices do businesses and local authorities give them?

Perhaps, then, production and its relationship to consumption should be the focus of any effective drive towards responsible consumption. Ultimately, business has the power to make all consumer choices sustainable if it chooses or is compelled to, taking the responsibility off the shoulders – and out of the pockets – of the public. So it might be more worthwhile for individuals to pursue sustainability as citizens rather than consumers, championing the policies, causes and politicians that would push firms to be more sustainable rather than agonizing over which product to buy.[53] Trying to find these strategic inflection points is critical. These are parts of the system where small interventions can leverage massive positive change for minimal effort. The elephant in the room is regulation and whether business will invite the kind of government intervention that would make this possible.

But we needn't wait for government action. Responsible businesses and many consumers are already united in their shared Global Goals. It's why the 12th goal is both 'responsible consumption *and* production'. The two are so closely interlinked that there can't be one without the other. In this respect, the roles of business/consumer/citizen/producer collapse into each other. Businesses, like consumers, can assume the role of a responsible citizen, obeying the law, paying taxes and taking an active role in the public sphere, while also making products and services that support their sustainable values and using their purchasing power to buycott producers that share their values. Within this business model, the consumer becomes an ally in a shared cause, working side by side for positive social change. Consumer demand in this context is just another expression of these shared values and the relationship between business and consumer fundamentally changes from an extractive transaction to one of belonging to a coalition of supporters or even activists for wider reform.

Recent experiences with #MeToo and #BlackLivesMatter demonstrated that business's silence, inaction or neutrality is no longer considered an adequate response to social injustices. Complying with problematic laws and outmoded regulations is no longer an excuse, and businesses are being called out for legal but socially unacceptable behaviour. In the case of tobacco, leaded petrol and animal testing of cosmetics, public opinion and civil society groups have led the regulatory agenda. Given the exponential growth of social media, it's likely that future calls for reforms will increasingly come from online activism as well.

THE REGULATION DILEMMA: IS RESPONSIBLE BUSINESS POSSIBLE WITHOUT STATE INTERVENTION?

The issues involved with sustainability are so interconnected and urgent, it would seem absurd to suggest leaving them just to business and consumers to resolve. It's possible to make a sizeable dent in climate change through increased production, sale and use of electric vehicles (EVs), but can we really entrust it to the market to deliver? Given the sophisticated, centralized and highly politicized fossil fuel vehicle ecosystem, with its subsidized infrastructure and technology that has evolved over decades, how can we expect EVs to compete against such unfair odds?[54]

Besides, there are too many systemic problems with EVs that individual producers and buyers can't solve on their own and may even exacerbate, because while EVs emit no GHGs when driven, producing the electricity to power them may still contribute to climate change.[55] The manufacture and scrappage of EVs creates a different set of problems, such as pollution and worker exploitation (even slavery) in the extraction of raw materials.[56] And EVs won't reduce traffic congestion and the stress, noise pollution, accidents and economic waste created. In fact, more people might be inclined to drive EVs if they feel they are less polluting and cheaper to run than petrol cars.[57]

These problems can't be solved through the actions of individual producers and buyers, no matter how responsibly they behave. Neither producers nor buyers can directly influence how electricity is generated. Consumers can't directly affect how cars are made and disposed of, and car manufacturers tend to be guided more by profit than what's best for society and the environment. Congestion is an unavoidable consequence of driving any type of car, and is a prime example of how the pursuit of individual interest, even if done responsibly, can lead to undesirable outcomes overall.

What are needed are *collective* solutions. And for problems of this magnitude, only governments have the size, capacity and power to tackle them. Regulation of utilities could steer them towards renewables. Stricter regulation of production and recycling could be introduced, with a legal requirement for car companies to investigate their supply chains for instances of slave labour. And congestion could be alleviated by increasing public transport alternatives to the car.

All of these initiatives fall well beyond the remit of any business or consumer but are essential for closing the loop on a circular economy for EVs, enabling all stakeholders to better play their part in tackling society-wide problems. Crucially, they also accelerate the sustainability of production and consumption for all businesses, and deal with any impacts at a systemic level. In this context, responsible businesses should welcome any government intervention that makes sustainability more joined-up and effective, including increased regulation.

Business as a social movement and engaging customers as supporters

Over the years, many businesses have used their products and marketing to encourage people to change their behaviour for the good of society.[58] From Procter & Gamble's Ariel laundry detergent campaign to 'Turn to 30' and reduce energy consumption when using washing machines,[59] to Colgate toothpaste's #EveryDropCounts campaign to stop people running the tap when brushing their teeth and save water,[60] firms start with influencing how consumers use their products to encourage a sustainable attitude more widely.

In this way, companies are treating consumers as potential supporters of their social purpose too, trying to convert people's values as well as product sales. Alan Warde compares this to business operating more like a social movement, whose aim is to change values as well as inform. 'The tenor of the campaigning messages of movements is often one of persuading people to exercise their moral consciences and thereupon to behave better', he says,[61] which could easily describe TV broadcaster Sky's Ocean Rescue campaign 'Inspiring people to make everyday changes to #PassOnPlastic' and reduce plastic pollution, for example.[62]

It's this added moral or ethical dimension to responsible businesses that reframes their conventional, transactional relationship with consumers into something more akin to an activist's commitment to a cause. If a company has a strong social purpose and meaningful sustainability targets in addition to making profits, it needs to actively recruit consumers to its cause, not just take their money and ask them to 'like' a clever tweet.

To do that, the dynamic of the relationship can't be too hierarchical or just one way. Instead, the consumer must get involved by sharing the campaign's message with friends and family and becoming an advocate for the cause in their own communities – with funding even provided by some companies to do it. This consumer involvement goes beyond just campaigns, however. Companies of all sizes are turning to crowdsourcing to help drive their sustainability: whether it's Unilever's Foundry platform that invites consumers and outside experts to come up with innovative ideas to help improve the sustainability of its operations,[63] or UK supermarket Waitrose's customer voting scheme to decide which community projects each store donates to.

Given the value from really engaging consumers in a common cause, it's not surprising that some of the leaders in this field are cooperatives and social enterprises, where consultations with members and social purpose are integral to all they do. But one relatively recent cooperative stands out for the extraordinary extent to which its customers lead the company. C'est qui le patron?! (CQLP) was initially set up in France in 2016 to help farmers receive a fairer price for their milk than offered by the big supermarket chains that dictated the market. Founder Nicolas Chabanne suspected people would gladly pay a few cents more to help the welfare of farmers, their animals and the natural environment. And he was right: CQLP quickly became the fourth biggest milk brand in France.[64]

But Chabanne didn't just rely on his hunch. He sent questionnaires to thousands of potential consumers asking them about every aspect of the product before launch: from how much they'd be prepared to pay and the quality of life they expect it to afford farmers to what type of milk they'd want and how the packaging and labelling should look. It was a truly collaborative venture that reimagined and redrew the dots between the milk on the shop shelf and the farmers, fields, cows and technology that produced it. It also helped expose the unsustainable consequences of conventional milk production and challenged the power of the supermarket to set prices. Now CQLP has applied the same approach to more than 30 other products, such as steak, sardines and chocolate. For each one, the cooperative's 7,500 members and the public voted on every aspect so that consumers' values and preferences are matched as closely as possible with the sustainably made products, encouraging more responsible production and consumption overall.

In such mission-driven companies, where profits are considered secondary to their overriding social goal, the distinction between the roles of business, consumer, staff and volunteer blurs and the hierarchy of decision-making collapses. It's a similar case at many social enterprises, which are often led by the needs of their local community and more dependent on collaborative working arrangements with stakeholders and volunteers. The aforementioned Giki is a social enterprise, and its founders remarked that their business model means they treat their customers, employees, volunteers and partners as one and the same. 'We're all part of the same sustainability mission', says co-founder James Hand, who gladly admits to prioritizing social and environmental impacts above profits.

Conventional businesses can also connect social value to profits, although perhaps not to the same extent, given most still feel they need to keep owners and investors incentivized first. But there is much they could learn from social enterprises about how to harness the creativity and insight of their consumers in their drive for sustainability. At its most basic, how often do most businesses consult consumers about what they really want as opposed to just focus grouping an existing product? Many scoffed at the UK bakery chain Greggs – famed for its meat-filled pastries – for daring to produce a vegan sausage roll. But the company struck on a huge unmet demand for vegan fast food, with the product becoming a bestseller and helping increase overall sales by 13.5%.[65] Now many other companies are rushing to meet that demand too, but what other ethical gaps in the market are businesses missing out on?

Likewise with a company's sustainability strategy, could a greater role be given to consumers in determining and delivering it? Even if transforming a firm's business model and product line to be more sustainable might prove too difficult in the short term, there are many straightforward ways their customers can be enabled to mitigate any negative impacts in the meantime. There could be the opportunity to offset the carbon footprint of every purchase, for example. It's become the norm to do so when buying a plane ticket, so why not at the petrol station, supermarket till or any other customer transaction too? Moving beyond the 'bag for life', are there more ways for customers to use their own packaging and refill on products to help companies reduce their waste and potentially save costs too? Advertising and signage could provide space for nudging or educational messages about more sustainable choices.

Some PR-wary businesses might feel such consumer-centric initiatives leave them open to accusations of 'woke-washing' business-as-usual activities and shifting the burden onto their customers. But so long as they're viewed as interim measures while the company becomes more sustainable in the long term, they're far better and more excusable than doing nothing at all. At the very least, they engage consumers with the issue of sustainability and empower them to take action, which helps to inform and reinforce consumers' own sustainable values.

However open to consumer participation responsible businesses are, what's important is that they overtly share the same desire for social change with their consumers and provide ways for them to actively support them in this shared goal. As charities have long understood, it's that activism and continual taking part that reaffirms supporters' sense of belonging and identity with a cause – and it is essential for responsible businesses that need to more deeply engage their customers in their social purpose beyond simply sales.

THE INDIVIDUALISM DILEMMA: IS THE WHOLE PREMISE OF PRODUCTION AND CONSUMPTION FLAWED?

This chapter takes aim at the idea of 'consumer sovereignty' and the overemphasis on individualism that underpins much of our understanding of responsible consumption. But does the very premise of production and consumption need rethinking too? It's clear that the paradigm as it currently stands is destroying the planet, being based on an extractive and transactional relationship with the planet and people. Some researchers suggest solutions focused on green innovation and ethical purchasing are just reforming the problem of capitalist consumerism when it should be rejected altogether in favour of a more revolutionary paradigm of frugality, sufficiency, sharing and localism.[66]

Similarly radical is the proposal by the late American anthropologist, David Graeber, to reimagine the idea of production and consumption as caring and freedom instead. Most work is not about producing anything, Graeber argues, but rather 'preserving, maintaining and sustaining things'.[67] Or, in other words, caring. Even building a bridge or a car is less about making a product as caring about people getting across a river or being able to journey around. This urge to care for someone, he suggests, is a potent human driver that goes beyond just catering for basic needs, otherwise a prison would be considered a care-giving institution. 'Caring work is aimed at maintaining or augmenting another person's freedom', says Graeber, and the ultimate expression of freedom is 'self-directed activity', or play.[68]

While undoubtedly idealistic, such a reframing has the benefit of nudging our understanding of work and business towards more holistic social values beyond just the financial. It also recognizes the huge swathes of people engaged in important, unwaged care work, and makes the whole purpose of making, earning and consuming more meaningful and human-focused. But most significantly for Graeber, unlike production and consumption, 'care and freedom ... are things you can increase as much as you like without damaging *anything*'.[69]

Graeber's understanding of people and their motivations fundamentally rejects the selfish individualism that underlies consumerism, which suggests obtaining more material possessions improves a person's wellbeing and happiness.[70] His more generous depiction of people driven by caring and sustaining society is closer to how ethical consumers would describe themselves. If responsible businesses want to appeal to them, they need to demonstrate they understand that powerful sense of interdependency, which is the antithesis of individualism and makes the Global Goals of equal importance to everyone.

As the philosopher Judith Butler explains: 'It makes a difference to understand ourselves as living in a world in which we are fundamentally dependent on others, on institutions, on the Earth, and to see that this life depends on a sustaining organization for various forms of life. If no one escapes that interdependency, then we are equal in a different sense. We are equally dependent, that is, equally social and ecological, and that means we cease to understand ourselves only as demarcated individuals.'[71]

Supporter-owned football clubs, the GAME system and the dangers of woke capitalism

If you were looking for a business exposed to enormous heuristic bias and clashes of human values, where money, social practice and passionate customers combine in occasionally volatile ways, then professional football would fit the bill perfectly. For a seemingly simple game involving 22 players and one ball, it's remarkable how entangled football has become with politics and culture around the world and the array of positive and negative social impacts it can cause.

At any football club, there's often a stark contrast between the teamwork, dedication, balance and structure shown on the pitch and the chaos, violence, racism, sexism, criminality and corruption that can occur off it. But most supporters, staff and players care deeply about their club. While many players are vilified for being playboy millionaires, others are powerful role models and – like Marcus Rashford – even social activists. Of course, outside the top divisions, most footballers are part-timers and don't earn massive wages, while their clubs struggle to get by on no TV money, limited sponsorship and the cash collected at the turnstiles.

Yet football clubs exhibit remarkable resilience and adaptability, outliving most companies. Despite living a precarious financial existence, very few clubs actually die. In an overtly competitive industry, only a tiny minority ever win anything. Most lose very publicly, getting relegated, sold, displaced or forced to sell their best players. But they keep on going, demonstrating a triumph of hope over conflict. So what is it about their extraordinary ability to survive that other businesses can learn from? Well, the most resilient football clubs understand the importance of balancing supporters' interests and the owners' commercial interests with the long-term welfare of the club.

Such was the case at Scottish Premier League club Hearts of Midlothian FC,[72] where a vicious circle of 'new owner–new hope–increased debt–supporter disillusionment' began in 1981 and finally ended with it going into administration in 2014. The last owner, Vladimir Romanov, had initially promised the club would win the European Cup within five years,[73] but he effectively treated Hearts as the UK arm of his Lithuanian bank, and took out crippling loans on the stadium and for player purchases in his pursuit of on-field success. Romanov's increasingly bizarre behaviour, including insisting he was selected for the team in a cup final and impetuous sackings of players and managers, led to a breakdown of relationships with almost all of the club's stakeholders. Any semblance of corporate governance or meaningful stakeholder engagement evaporated completely over his nine-year tenure, and trust with supporters hit an all-time low when he proposed selling the stadium to finance unpaid bills and players' wages before finally putting the club up for sale.[74]

Luckily for Hearts, a group of supporters had set up the Foundation of Hearts in 2010 – a supporter-owned not-for-profit – with the purpose of raising finance to buy the club on behalf of the supporters. They created a unique pledge structure, where fans made small, regular contributions towards a war chest that would cover the costs of initial purchase and the subsequent running of the club.[75] The Foundation also worked incredibly hard to rebuild the network of stakeholders essential for the club's survival that Romanov had alienated and neglected. Unfortunately, at the time of administration the Foundation was not considered sufficiently credible by the Scottish and Lithuanian courts to rescue the club, so local businesswoman Ann Budge led a partnership with them to set up a corporation in 2014 that paid off the club's debts and promised to transfer ownership to the Foundation within five years.

Despite downplaying supporters' expectations of success on the field (there were no grand plans to become champions of Europe), Budge and the Foundation emphasized becoming a responsible and resilient business that recognizes its responsibility and accountability to its communities, which are just as important as winning matches. There would be no return to the past's failed model of concentrated ownership, false dreams and overspending. Instead, the club would work collaboratively across all its stakeholders and invite supporters' scrutiny through the involvement of the Foundation in its governance.

For such an approach to work, Budge said that the club's executives needed to 'think like a supporter' and be transparent in their decision-making. 'I had to engage, from day one, with the supporters in a very positive way', she says. 'And the way to do that was tell them the truth, say it as it is and if we need your help, we'll tell you we need your help.'

In practice, that meant supporters receiving regular explanations for managerial decisions as well as regular opportunities for discussion and democratic input. They also invested money in the club through the Foundation with no expectation of financial return. Six years later, Hearts still hadn't won any trophies but was now debt-free, with a new stand and increased matchday attendances, and had become the UK's largest supporter-owned club after Budge transferred her shares to the Foundation in August 2021.[76] The club had rejected bids from individual investors, preferring to take its chances with a mutually owned, democratic future. While things are never peaceful in the world of football, these arrangements have remained robust despite relegation due to a controversial COVID-19-curtailed season in 2020.

What's remarkable is that although the primary focus of the project was the long-term welfare of the club, its social impact snowballed far beyond it. For instance, the decision to terminate early their shirt sponsorship deal with controversial payday lender Wonga led to the club becoming the first UK football team to have a charity on their shirt for free – Save the Children. Anonymous supporters were so impressed that they made donations to cover the losses. That same concern for the community and maintaining a reputation for responsibility also informed their decision to become the first UK football club to be accredited as a Living Wage employer.

Like the Global Goals, addressing one aspect of responsibility in the business led inexorably to addressing others because they are all interconnected, having a gradual but transformational effect on the whole club. And by acknowledging that interconnection and dependency on the wider network of supporters and community stakeholders in its supporter-owned model, Hearts is much more resilient and successful than it was under the centralized, governance-avoiding regime of Romanov. That's because the Foundation realized that a successful club was dependent on many different resources provided by different stakeholders with a shared interest in the success of the club, including businesses around the stadium, local authorities, the local community and supporters.

They also realized that while footballing success was important, it was a combination of other, more intrinsic values that enabled this stakeholder collaboration to work. Whereas Romanov had played up the individualistic and extrinsic values of hedonism, power and achievement, gambling on results on the field to win over others, the stakeholder network was grounded in more collective and intrinsic values of tradition, benevolence and security. It was these collective values that created systemic resilience for the club through collaboration, rewriting the club's social contract and re-establishing a sense of stewardship in its directors.

Researchers studying Hearts' new, collaborative way of working came up with what they called the 'GAME system' model to show the many complex and dynamic stakeholder relationships around the club's governance, accountability, management and engagement, which make the club so adaptable and resilient.

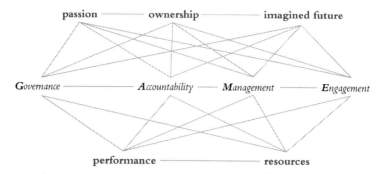

As well as outlining the delicate balance between the operational independence of the club and its oversight by the Foundation, the GAME system incorporated all those other intangibles of a football club: the passion of the fans, the unpredictable performance of the team on the pitch, and that shared, imagined future of the club as a community institution that lives on for generations.

It's these emotional connections that make a football club much more than just a business. What other companies can plead with their customers to pay hundreds of pounds in cash rather than on credit card and get an overwhelming response like this? As Budge recalls:

> I remember looking at season ticket sales and saying right, OK, so we're going to get that amount of money in, and being told no. Because the credit card companies release it on a game-by-game basis. But we needed that money now in order to survive! So the only thing I could do is explain it to the supporters and say please, please – unless you absolutely have to – please pay cash. And a number of the cash machines around here ran out of money. The supporters were incredible.[77]

But all companies are more than just a business – whether they knowingly operate as such or not. They're not only interconnected with the local community and its consumers but also *interdependent* on them, sharing a responsibility for each other's welfare and needs. And while not all ethical consumers may identify with the businesses they transact with as strongly as a football fan does with their club, they still need to trust companies' social values and have that shared imagined future of a more sustainable world. With such personal beliefs and emotions informing their transactions, it's inevitable that a supporter mentality often develops between responsible consumers and producers. But building up the loyalty and expectations of supporters can expose a business to additional risks as well as opportunities.

The Swedish vegan milk brand Oatly built up a hugely loyal following since it started in 1994, which initially consisted of ethical and health-conscious consumers drawn to it as a dairy-free and more eco-friendly alternative to cow's milk. The company's vocal commitment to minimal environmental impact and sustainable, responsible business practices is a central part of the product's appeal,[78] but its popularity really exploded when it recruited independent coffee shops to offer a specially formulated version to their customers, making their baristas enthusiastic supporters of the brand. (Oatly even has an Instagram channel dedicated to baristas.)[79]

However, in 2020, Oatly faced a huge backlash from its consumer supporters after selling a £150 million stake to private equity firm Blackstone, which had ties to Donald Trump and alleged links to the deforestation of the Amazon. Such an occurrence in other businesses would most likely be ignored by consumers, but in the eyes of many of Oatly's customers, while the product may not have fundamentally changed, the company's values had been compromised, and they were now calling for people to boycott it.[80] This vividly demonstrates how values and trust in their veracity are as important as the product itself to ethical consumers, and any sense that there's a misalignment – between them and those of a new investor or owner, for instance – immediately calls them into question as being inauthentic.

Because trust is so integral to the implicit social contract between a responsible business and its stakeholders, inauthenticity can be hugely damaging to a brand.[81] Unfortunately for business, trust can only be granted by others and is based on public perception and terms that are constantly changing. But regardless of these risks, more and more consumers not only welcome brands that actively engage in social issues; they now expect it. This is why it's so important that any such 'brand activism' is an authentic expression of the company's genuinely held social values, which are shared by their consumers. The best way to avoid a clanging misstep (like Pepsi's astonishingly crass advert with Kendall Jenner in 2017 that was accused of trivializing Black Lives Matter and got pulled within 24 hours[82]) is to recognize that those social values are externally and collectively arrived at, and so a business's activism should be too.

Many businesses may not want or be able to instigate the more collaborative and democratic models of ownership that Hearts FC and CQLP have, which make aligning themselves with their communities and consumers a central and obligatory part of how they're governed. But could responsible businesses adopt parts of the GAME system that provide greater input and oversight from their consumer supporters, making them and their values more interconnected and resilient to the risk of inauthenticity?

There are powerful benefits for all involved if businesses get this right, as internationally renowned expert in responsible consumption and marketing Dr Caroline Moraes says: 'When there is congruency among a brand's core activist messaging, its values and corporate practices, brands are seen to engage in authentic brand activism, [which] presents the best potential in terms of both positive consumer responses to the brand and positive societal outcomes.'[83]

Although brand activism has now become a mainstream idea in business – partly because of its proven commercial potential[84] – it's being increasingly cynically employed. While many well-intentioned companies use their profile to amplify good causes, there's been a trend of corporates in particular adopting 'safe' social causes that already have strong public and political support, primarily to boost their consumer appeal rather than benefit society. For instance, how many that publicly supported #BlackLivesMatter are still refusing to publish and address their ethnic pay gap? This exploitative approach to social values by business is reminiscent of old-school CSR and is so common that it's been coined 'woke-washing'.

Professor Carl Rhodes, in his book *Woke Capitalism*, writes particularly damningly about the dangers of woke-washing, seeing it as big companies capitalizing on public morality and capturing it as a corporate resource, which twists that moral outrage into corporate ethics that privilege their interests instead. Its cumulative effect is a 'surreptitious extension of capitalism's reach by backing safe-bet political causes',[85] that ultimately constitutes a threat to democracy by replacing civic debate and democratic dissent with 'the self-congratulatory slickness of marketing and public relations campaigning'.[86]

Rather than counterbalancing a lack of government leadership on social issues and amplifying public demands for change, Professor Rhodes argues that woke-washing brand activism is yet another example of corporates trying to encroach on and take over the public sphere, manipulating social movements to their own ends. 'No longer content to just influence our spending habits and lifestyles, with woke capitalism big businesses enrol the very heart of our moral beliefs into their commercial strategies', he warns.[87]

In an era dominated by social media – in which users and their emotions, loyalty and values are the product – consumers' relationship with business is perhaps uniquely vulnerable to exploitation. Users 'follow' businesses, freely hand over their private data and open themselves up to thousands of behaviour-influencing messages and nudges each day. The fine line between businesses engaging positively in this deeper eliding of private and public to benefit everyone in society rather than abusing it to commercially benefit just themselves is very difficult to tread.

Yet in order for business to play its part in the Global Goals, it will have to engage somewhat in public morality and politics – any social purpose that didn't would be failing by definition. Even if that may make many businesses feel uncomfortable, a company would still make an excellent contribution to responsible consumption and wider society if it aimed to at least be neutral in its operations, minimizing its social and environmental harm and leaving no footprints.

So many businesses feel overwhelmed when first looking to work with the Global Goals and uncertain where to start. Out of all of them, 'responsible production and consumption' (Global Goal 12) is the obvious entry point that falls most directly within their purview and control. After all, production and consumption are what business does! Perhaps those companies ignoring it in favour of addressing more peripheral Global Goals are simply avoiding the necessary changes that will affect them most. But in the end, consumers are becoming wise to companies that fail to acknowledge or use their agency and pass their responsibility for sustainable consumption on to others. However wide the gap between ethical consumers' intentions and behaviours, the expectations of all consumers that business should behave more sustainably is only likely to increase.

Summary: The science of responsible business

Observations to note
Responsible businesses ...

... use easy-to-understand sustainability labelling without being too scientific.

... are honest and transparent in their information.

... use trusted third party certification schemes, backed by governments or NGOs.

... offer carbon offsetting for every purchase.

... don't use being ethical as an excuse to price-gouge.

... accept responsibility for how their products are consumed.

... use social media and personal data sparingly and responsibly.

... understand the limitations of consumer-led transformation.

... have a clear understanding of the behavioural change they're trying to make.

... avoid using magicians' techniques to exploit human biases for their own benefit.

... are aware of the diversity of sometimes conflicting human values and how they relate to emotions in their marketing and communications.

... involve consumers and community stakeholders in their governance, management, accountability and engagement.

... support social and political causes authentically and collaboratively.

Theories to test
Enabling consumers' values
Responsible consumers need clear and trusted information to make good choices.

- How trusted are the organizations you work with to certify the sustainability of your products? (Global Goals 12, 16 and 17)
- Do you measure the carbon footprint of your products and offer consumers the chance to offset? (Global Goals 12, 13 and 15)
- Would your business see a sustainable product-ranking app, like Giki, as a threat or opportunity? (Global Goals 4, 9 and 17)
- Is your pricing a barrier or incentive to responsible consumption? (Global Goals 1, 10 and 12)
- How are you helping your consumers in their desire to pursue the Goodlife Goals? (Global Goals 3, 10 and 14)

Consumers as supporters

Responsible businesses value the trust and support of the people they depend on.

- Have you mapped your dependencies on different stakeholders, including consumers? (Global Goals 9, 12 and 17)
- How well aligned are your values with your consumers'? (Global Goals 5, 13 and 15)
- What facts about your operations and value chain if uncovered could adversely affect your business? (Global Goals 1, 4, 5, 8, 10 and 16)
- How transparent, vocal and engaging are you about your social purpose with consumers? (Global Goals 3, 4 and 5)

Business citizenship

Responsible businesses use their privilege to enhance society and nature.

- Are you paying your staff and your taxes sufficiently to maintain the welfare and infrastructure of society? (Global Goals 1, 2, 6 and 11)
- Do you help support social justice campaigns for changes to the law or government policy? (Global Goals 5, 10 and 16)
- Does your business use its 'purchase power' to buycott and support suppliers with strong environmental standards? (Global Goals 12, 14 and 15)
- Have you audited the alignment of your business values with the Global Goals and your key business activities? (All Global Goals)

First steps to responsible consumption ...

Simple and trusted labelling	Circularity	Consumer activism	Socio-political influence
Use sustainability traffic lights and third party verification	Make it easy for customers to repair, recycle and reuse products	Engage customers in delivering social value	Use your platform and buying power to benefit society

Irresponsible Decisions Are Made by Irresponsible Leaders

The amplifying effect of power, initial framing and solution aversion

'Power tends to corrupt', starts Lord Acton's famous quote about absolute power corrupting absolutely. From lying US presidents to adulterous corporate executives, given the roll call of disreputable politicians and CEOs who have made the headlines in recent years, you'd be forgiven for thinking there was something inherently irresponsible about people in a position of power.[1] And you'd be right. Partly, anyway.

In a series of experimental games by psychologists in 2010, they found powerful people cheated almost a fifth more than powerless people, and were more strict about condemning others' cheating behaviour than their own. As well as this increase in immoral and hypocritical behaviour, the researchers found that by priming their participants with empowering thoughts and emotions, they also became more willing to commit infidelity, break the speed limit, falsify their taxes, keep stolen goods and overclaim on their travel expenses.[2] Other studies have demonstrated how power eliminates people's inhibition and reduces fear and self-reflection, while also increasing their impulsivity, self-interest and sense of invulnerability, control and distance from others.[3]

But it isn't just a simple case of power being bad. Social psychologists have also conducted research demonstrating that the way people *construe* their power affects how they use it.[4] So if leaders see their position as being responsible for others rather than for their own personal attainment, power can have the effect of increasing inclusivity, reducing corruption and discrimination and promoting equality and human rights.[5] So power in the right hands can also be good.

It's been left to more recent behavioural science to explain this seemingly contradictory response to power, which suggests it is neither intrinsically good nor bad but acts as an amplifier for an individual's pre-existing attitudes. A growing body of research around this 'self-validation' theory has shown it's the effect power has on increasing people's confidence that leads them to being more certain about their immediate thoughts and feelings and then acting on them.[6] So power can turn someone into more of a hero or more of a villain depending on their values and emotions – but it definitely can't turn a villain into a hero!

All of which makes it baffling that even long-serving, committed managers within such purpose-driven organizations like Oxfam and Amnesty International have fallen foul of some appalling scandals in recent years.[7] What chance does the average business leader have of making socially responsible decisions if even mission-oriented charity leaders fail? The obvious answer is that nobody's perfect, and power in certain circumstances can unbalance the complex configuration of values all individuals have. Add to the mix stress, urgency for action, scarce resources, competing demands and heuristic biases, then it's no wonder heroes can sometimes act like villains. But it's important to understand why this switch can happen because it's possible that conventional business processes are unintentionally exacerbating the problem.

Obviously, human thoughts and emotions are inconsistent and can change over time or in particular circumstances, but what psychologists call a person's 'moral foundations' – the stable, gut-level concerns about fairness, care, loyalty, authority and moral purity that influence a person's worldview – are far less capricious.[8] So beyond the odd bona fide sociopath, the issue for most well-meaning business leaders is understanding how their responsible worldview, when mediated through business processes and the way our brain works, can still lead to errors of judgement and flawed decision-making.

Drawing on the work of American psychologist Gary Klein, who pioneered the understanding of human decision-making in the workplace, modern management theorists suggest that the brain makes decisions through a process of pattern recognition and emotional tagging – much of it subconscious and therefore difficult to pick up or avoid. Faced with a new situation, the brain makes instant assumptions based on prior experiences and judgements in much the same way an experienced chess player assesses a board and determines their best move. But this cognitive shortcut means that pattern recognition can mislead us in seemingly familiar situations, making us leap to conclusions before we fully understand what's going on. Emotional tagging, on the other hand, are the feelings we attach to past thoughts and experiences that inform our responses to similar situations in the present and determine whether we ignore or pay attention to them.[9]

This instant response of patterns and emotions is analogous to the intuitive System 1 thinking popularized by behavioural economists we looked at in the previous chapter. And together, they mean we're vulnerable to framing a situation in a misleading and distorted way that makes it very difficult for us to revisit and reassess a decision after we've made it – even when applying more analytical System 2 thinking. Hence this 'initial frame', as Klein calls it, can be notoriously difficult to challenge in the workplace.[10] These frames can lurk, unseen and unsaid, in an organization's subconscious, reinforced by a leader's actions or through incentives and sanctions to become powerful myths – even when they're clearly misaligned with the business's purpose. Many will have witnessed the magical thinking of a manager pursuing a pet project long after mounting evidence of its failure. But things can change dramatically when the spell is broken and the myth busted.

Think of how perceptions around plastic changed so quickly. Not long ago, plastic's disposability was considered desirable, even progressive, thanks to it being cheap, single use and hygienic. Now it's become a pariah product, businesses are struggling to replace it and their throwaway mindset fast enough. Similarly, with the explosion in online retail, the environmental and social consequences of fast fashion and same-day delivery goods – from excess packaging to low-paid, insecure work – are challenging the presumption that instant, cheap and global are necessarily desirable. In fact, much of the language used to frame what's good in business needs to be reset and perhaps replaced with words like slow, local and long-lasting instead. This linguistic reframing is a key part of how the slow food movement has successfully challenged public attitudes to factory-farmed and fast food since the 1980s.[11]

There are other important types of frame to note, too. Political, religious and cultural frames all limit our perceptions and rational System 2 thinking when it comes to social justice and environmental issues, like the Global Goals. A recent US study found that – contrary to what you might expect – the most educated Americans with the most scientific literacy were more likely to be stubborn deniers of climate change. The researchers deduced that it was because they drew their conclusions along religious and political lines, not scientific ones.[12] Just as all of us have shifting configurations of personal values, we also have many different, competing frames we use to make decisions. The frame that wins exerts a powerful influence on the outcome.

'What you believe about climate change is more an indicator of whose side you're on', explained Yale Professor of Psychology Dan Kahan, in response to the study. 'It's not a measure of what they know, it's a measure of who they are.'[13] Kahan's own research in this area also found that the more information we have when it comes to these more politicized issues, the more we seem to bend it to serve our own political views. So unfortunately, it's evidently not the case that if business leaders had perfect information, they'd reach the right decisions, while group decision-making will inevitably be fraught with some kind of 'framing contest', as staff approach the same problem with different frames.

This 'sideism' is important for business leaders to recognize because it leads to what academics have labelled 'solution aversion'. It's not necessarily the facts about climate change that many are afraid of or avoid; it's where those facts lead – which is undoubtedly towards more regulation, government intervention and free market reorientation.[14] Many business leaders have a neoliberal antipathy to the state by default, which frames their outlook. Hence, they've already picked their side when it comes to how they evaluate the scientific evidence for climate change and the desirability of its political implications. Their frame only allows them to see part of the problem and excludes many alternative solutions. And this factional bias gives rise to motivated reasoning and active ignorance, instinctively (through pattern and emotion) backing those ideas that support their side and dismissing those that threaten or are uncomfortable for it.

It's clear that as humans in pressurized situations, with shifting configurations of values subject to the amplifying effect of power and initial framing that makes them prone to errors of judgement, business leaders are particularly vulnerable to making irresponsible decisions no matter how good their intentions towards the Global Goals. That's why it's so important leaders are self-aware and alert to these human biases. And why more work needs to be done to promote, educate and embed the Global Goals frame in businesses. For many business leaders, this frame isn't even in their mental toolbox, which means it can't even enter any framing contest, let alone win. Then, beyond that, there's the challenge of making the Global Goals the default frame, when most business leaders will have been socialized into using very different frames for decades.

This socialization and the model and culture of leadership within a particular business are just as influential as any individual who finds themselves in the executive leather chair. They all limit how free a chief executive or senior manager is to choose and construct the way a company and its operations are framed. Moreover, after decades of stereotypes and essentialist theories about what personal traits an ideal leader should have, a new, more participative notion of leadership is becoming more mainstream. This less hierarchical model may not only help to improve business decision-making and forecasting, but is also more compatible with addressing the complex and multidimensional issues behind the Global Goals.

Why we lead, the poison of external motives and the new distributive models of leadership

While any leadership role affords its holder executive powers, there are many different ways that power is constituted, assumed or used by an individual. Power can be taken, seized, granted by a higher authority, appointed by a select group of peers or delegated by the masses. A leader can then choose to use that power either for their own self-advancement and to impose their views, or to further the interests of the people they represent and channel the voices of others.

For the majority of senior business leaders, who are appointed by an owner, company board or executive team, there is usually something of a balancing act performed between these two roles of imposing and representing. But the overall aim is generally always the same: to benefit the company collectively, not the individual in power. It's why humans evolved to create and follow leaders in the first place, because it helped the group perform more effectively when undertaking certain tasks, like hunting, foraging and protecting the vulnerable.[15] That same fundamental aspiration prevails in business today, where leaders are supposed to help the company perform better. It's just what that better performance looks like and how it's framed that has changed.

No longer can a company's performance solely be measured by its financials, such as sales, profit margin and share price. Now, there is an increasing emphasis on 'responsible leadership' in business that aims to make a company more socially and environmentally sustainable in order to be profitable in the long term, with a purview that extends well beyond the welfare of just the leader's 'group' or chosen side. As Boston College's Center for Corporate Citizenship puts it: 'The responsible firm, whether under the label of citizenship, social responsibility or sustainability, aims to minimize harms and maximize benefits in its relationships with stakeholders.'[16]

This far wider scope of performance for a responsible business, which stems from its social purpose and values that are rooted in the Global Goals, demands a different kind of leadership from the simple 'leader–follower' model of bygone times. With such a diversity of stakeholder obligations to manage and include beyond the firm – from working with communities affected by supply chains to collaborating with scientists on environmental protection – the dynamics are far more complex and nuanced. But in truth, most company leaders have always been about more than just the immediate needs of their business. They're often charity partners, community sponsors, sports club board members, political activists, lobbyists and donors too. That's because they're not just concerned with pursuing their company's financial self-interest; they're also bolstering and protecting the systems that support their wider interests. And apart from a minority of ultra-rational, profit-maximizing sociopaths, the vast majority of business leaders are interested in improving society.

Fortunately, research shows that it's these more altruistic leaders, rather than those chasing external incentives and rewards, who actually perform better anyway. Tom Kolditz, director of the Leadership Development Program at the Yale School of Management, led one such study of 10,000 US Army leaders from their initial training at West Point to several years into their careers.[17] He found that those motivated by more intrinsic and collective values (like the obligation to serve) performed better than those driven by extrinsic and individualistic goals (like pay or career progression). He concluded that the results proved how important it was not to let external motives become the primary incentive for leaders, which he called 'leadership poison'. 'If those we seek to develop as leaders adopt external justifications for leading well – such as an increase in shareholder value, better pay or perquisites, or increased profits – they are likely to be less successful as leaders in comparison to those who seek to lead for more internal, intrinsic reasons alone', he said.[18]

This same, intrinsically driven mindset was also found to be true of the most successful responsible business leaders, according to a 2020 study by the UN Global Compact of 55 CEOs and board members with the best track records of pioneering sustainability. It found that all of them were motivated by passionate and personal 'core values and beliefs' about business's interconnectivity with society and the environment and its responsibility to help tackle the issues they face. The study suggests this 'sustainable mindset' or framing is essential to the leaders' success in driving forward transformational changes by simply trying to align all aspects of how their companies are run with these core values.[19]

As we've explored earlier, we know that valuing society and nature is central to any responsible business model committed to the Global Goals. But we have to acknowledge the extensive legacy of values and frames embedded in business that are dominated instead by financial accounting logic. That's why it's so important business leaders truly believe in social purpose, feel a visceral obligation to their wider stakeholders and internalize the Global Goals frame, so they can be more resilient to these ingrained biases and system traps. Otherwise, they'll be far less likely to succeed in implementing a sustainable business model throughout their entire value chain, or make strategic decisions that go beyond short-termism and the profit imperative.

For example, contrast the values and leaders of two very different clothing companies, Trigema and the Boohoo Group. The German firm Trigema has been wholly owned by its CEO, Wolfgang Grupp, for more than 50 years. While its conversion to organic, circular production methods that are 'Cradle to Cradle Certified'[20] is a more recent development, the firm's strong sense of responsibility stems from Grupp's long-term commitment to manufacturing textiles entirely in Germany – and more specifically, in Burladingen, Swabia, where its factory is based. Unlike the vast majority of other textile firms, Trigema doesn't outsource any of its production and only imports cotton. Everything else is made on site so it can maintain control over every aspect of the process.

'Our actions must not be solely guided by goals such as increased power and greater market share, but by solidarity, respect for all members of our community, justice and sustainability', says Grupp about the philosophy of Trigema, stating his number one priority is to look after his workers and protect their jobs.[21] It's clear that Grupp sees his business as part of a bigger system: the community within which it operates. And if the overall system is in trouble, so is the company. As a result, Trigema's social purpose is ultimately focused on supporting that system through fair wages, apprenticeships and the development of its employees. Moreover, Grupp has deliberately chosen not to grow the company and increase profits if it means sacrificing his primary responsibility to these local stakeholders.

The UK-based online retailer, Boohoo Group, on the other hand, is one of the biggest proponents of the 'fast fashion' clothing model, mass-producing cheap clothes in response to the latest trends. It was embroiled in a high-profile scandal in 2020 when there was a COVID-19 outbreak during lockdown in one of its many outsourced factories in Leicester. Journalists uncovered modern slavery conditions of illegal low pay (as little as £3.50/hour), forced attendance and flagrant health and safety violations.[22] Such irresponsible exploitation of its supply chain for short-term profit ended up perpetuating a health crisis and other social miseries for the local community, while ultimately damaging Boohoo's reputation in the long term.

'Our philosophy's pretty simple', say Boohoo on their website, 'we don't take life, or fashion, too seriously.'[23] That certainly seemed the case when it came to the company's attitude to the poor sustainability of its supply chains, which an independent inquiry revealed had been known to the company long before the 2020 scandal broke and blamed on 'weak corporate governance'.[24] Boohoo's CEO John Lyttle has since responded with a raft of initiatives to improve things: from measures to increase compliance to the building of a 'model' factory in Leicester.[25] But while the company's sustainability strategy contained in its annual report is ambitious in intent, there are legitimate questions as to how aggressive plans to expand through acquisitions in Europe and the US fit within that Global Goals frame, and whether they're really more motivated by 'leadership poison'.[26]

And that's a real problem with the current zeitgeist for responsible leadership: many business leaders are simply paying lip-service to sustainability because it's what is expected. All of today's most high-profile business leaders are eager to talk about sustainability and promote their environmental credentials, but how many are just playing to the gallery while continuing to act on problematic myths and doing business as usual? Certainly, the UN Global Compact points out a glaring gap between companies' rhetoric and the reality, with 92% of CEOs proclaiming the importance of sustainability to the future success of their business in 2019 – yet only 48% admitted to doing anything operationally about it, and just 21% said they were making any great strides towards the Global Goals.[27]

In study after study, researchers keep finding evidence that responsibility is ultimately framed as irrational in the world of business. While many leaders talk a good game on sustainability, it can be a hollow misdirection that's as much about reputation building, deception and self-enrichment as actually changing business practice. That lack of substance is evident in companies' recruitment too, which is perpetuating the problem. The UN Global Compact analysed almost 4,000 executive and non-executive role specifications from across different industries around the world in 2019, and found only 15% made reference to sustainability, while just 4% made sustainability experience a requirement. It concluded that: 'businesses are doing a great job embedding talk of sustainability into descriptions about their company, but are falling short in driving decisions about which leaders to hire based on it'.[28]

But performativity will always be an inescapable part of being a leader, since leadership roles tend to be a projection of other people's contemporary values and preconceptions. Right now, the most popular caricature of a 'responsible business leader' seems to be someone who is open, selfless and inspirational, with strong, solid values – a cross between a visionary entrepreneur and social activist (or 'actipreneur', as we'll explore later). Whether or not any individual can hope to live up to such high expectations, they are required to perform this role if they want to take the helm. But however more enlightened that type of leader might seem compared to the slick-suited, commandeering archetypes of bygone-era business leaders, they are all still variations of outdated autocratic and essentialist models of leadership.

What the latest theories of leadership propose, however, is that power doesn't lie within a single, heroic leader. Instead, it is situational and inter-relational, and therefore distributed throughout the workplace wherever decisions are being made. In this model, the leaders with the most appropriate traits emerge as and when the situation arises, and the job of appointed leaders is to facilitate that fluidity by unlocking their employees' potential to innovate and lead. In practice, that could mean investing more time and resources in HR development, encouraging and rewarding staff for their new ideas by allowing room for them to fail, or building peer-to-peer mentoring networks.[29]

But what makes this disruption and democratization of traditional leadership structures in the workplace so potentially transformative is that they unleash the extraordinary collective power of teams and crowds, which are proven to make better decisions, provide greater perspectives and forecast more accurately than any leader or cabal of managers can hope to do on their own.

THE CONSULTATION DILEMMA: DOES INCLUSIVE DECISION-MAKING MAKE A BUSINESS LESS AGILE?

The popular way for businesses to be run now is as 'agile' organizations. Rejecting the top-down hierarchical management approach, the agile operating model sees the workplace as a network of self-managing teams that are empowered and shown direction by the executive – behaving more like a living organism than a rigid machine. Central to its functioning are individual teams going through rapid cycles of decision-making as they learn and respond to what works and what doesn't.[30] But can this process inhibit wider stakeholder consultation and a more responsible, holistic mindset?

For all the slow-going of traditional Japanese business practice, based on the *kaizan* philosophy of continuous improvement involving all employees, the extra time spent meticulously planning and securing the buy-in of all staff and suppliers famously makes delivery that much faster.[31] A recent report into UK employee-owned firms also found a similar trade-off with their necessarily more consultative style of management, acknowledging that 'there were times when things might seem to move a bit more slowly on account of that consultation. But there were also a lot of times when things moved faster, because of a shared understanding of what was needed and a shared commitment to carry it out.'[32] This consensus-based approach is also what drives support for cooperatives and mutual companies, which are owned by their members or customers and are required to have regular democratic votes on key decisions.

Yet none of these different business models preclude the use of agile working practices at some level. In fact, they can enhance a responsible business's effectiveness as long as they're oriented towards delivering on the company's social values and purpose. Besides, being agile and adaptable is essential for the kind of complex and emerging problems associated with the Global Goals. And there is also considerable potential for adapting agile working methods to engage more effectively with stakeholders.

Process-driven decision-making and the power of teams

As individuals, humans are not great decision-makers. We've already seen how power and flawed psychology can easily bias and distort the thinking of leaders. Yet when so many decisions in business – particularly around sustainability – are often novel, complex and uncertain, we ultimately still need someone to have the casting vote and commit the company to a course of action.

Unfortunately, those most certain of themselves can often be the ones who know least. And because self-confidence is normally a prerequisite of leadership, those exhibiting the most certainty tend to scale the management hierarchy and get their voices heard most. Known famously as the 'Dunning–Kruger effect',[33] this cognitive bias of 'the less you know the more certain you are right' is common to many leaders and stems from a fundamental lack of self-awareness and insight about their own incompetence. They overestimate their knowledge and abilities, continuing to think they are doing well while making error after error, as those uncritically following or enabling them confuse confidence with competence. This behaviour gets worse if they're surrounded by sycophants, whose feedback reinforces their lack of knowledge rather than helps to educate them.

But it's important to clarify that this isn't just a shortcoming of the most inept leaders. Even those most skilled and conscientious will have blindspots, ironically because their expertise sometimes also makes them overconfident and more likely to take risks, which can lead to poor decisions – particularly when taken under stressful conditions. And that's where process-driven decision-making can play such a vital role. Whether it's a simple checklist, a series of set questions or a more elaborate role-playing exercise, researchers have found that people improve their ability to achieve their goals by creating a set of conditional rules to follow.

One of the clearest illustrations of how valuable well-designed decision architecture can be was the introduction of the World Health Organization's pre-surgery checklist for operating theatres that staff go through, step by step, before each procedure.[34] The impact was dramatic, with one study showing a 36% drop in major complications and 47% fewer deaths.[35] By following such a process, it activates more purposeful and deliberative System 2 thinking and helps to mitigate against System 1-type biases and presumptions that can lead to mistakes, especially for the overworked surgeon in charge. It also provides an opportunity to introduce counter-arguments and perspectives that can challenge any initial frame.

The Global Goals enable a similar, process-driven way of making decisions about sustainability. Simply working your way, one by one, through all 17 Goals provides a methodical roadmap for examining all aspects of a business's sustainable impacts, exposing blindspots and testing any presumptions. As explored earlier, this process is essential for determining a business's overall social purpose and providing the framework for any sustainability strategy. By aligning purpose with the Global Goals, business leaders can customize how they navigate and prioritize them, clustering together those identified as being core dependencies, important risks or most desirable to influence. These can then be used as a checklist to assess the sustainability of a specific scenario or a sequence of decisions, by applying a process of 'if–then' or algorithmic thinking to each of them. This can be used to triage risks and shape decision-making across the whole business, and is particularly useful when tackling multiple but connected issues, such as adopting a more circular supply chain in the example opposite.

By breaking it down into individual problems in a sequence of proposals, decision-makers will feel less overwhelmed and can strip away unnecessary detail to uncover the critical information required. So for every 'if' the scenario proposes, the 'then' consequences are considered for each of the Global Goals using a traffic light system. The idea is to keep pondering each 'if' until alternative proposals are arrived at that ideally turn the whole matrix green, or at least those areas considered priorities for the business.

It's important to stress that knowing the true impacts for a particular Global Goal is often difficult to predict with precision and certainty (remember the 'unknown unknowns' and unpredictable thresholds discussed earlier). However, just being cognisant of the positive or negative direction and approximate magnitude of the impact will often be enough. For instance, if you know that airfreighting goods emits between 12.5 and 50 times more GHGs than sea transport, the consequences are clear regardless of the exact number.[36] There's a growing body of research that can help provide this sort of general indication of impact. It shows that any toxic substances emitted into watercourses will pollute and harm life, plastic waste pollution usually impacts poorer communities, and products prone to forced or child labour strongly correlate with negative impacts across almost all the Global Goals. Knowing precisely which species or community will be damaged is immaterial: we don't need 100% scientific certainty to know that something is harmful.

Besides, just asking the questions about potential impact on poverty or marine life in this process-driven way prompts awareness of these sustainability issues and highlights what business leaders are ignoring or have no information about and are simply guessing. Then, by acknowledging these blindspots and inviting evidence, business leaders are helping themselves to make better decisions. Moreover, if these Global Goals-based algorithms are co-created and co-administered with businesses and relevant experts – such as the various collaborative initiatives offered by the UN Global Compact, World Benchmarking Alliance, SDG2000, Natural Capital Coalition,

CORE   IMPORTANT   INFLUENTIAL

Circularising supply chain
If we ... then ...

- Design products for easy repair
- Design for recycling of components
- Design for economic reuse

- Purchase based on price ignoring modes of delivery
- Insist on low carbon delivery
- Require reusable components
- Do not check for negative impact of suppliers
- Pay prices that allow for living wage
- Insist on suppliers reducing gender pay gap
- Pay fair taxes in all countries
- Insist on no slavery, forced labour or child labour

- Rely on existing waste and recycling facilities
- Collaborate and invest in recycling/reuse facilities
- Reduce impact on natural systems in our procurement
- Invest in ensuring resilient ecosystems
- Share our sustainable designs with others
- Monitor carbon life cycle consequences of value chain
- If we ...

135

Business in the Community and many local green business clubs – then the benefits to sustainable decision-making will be even greater.

Another example of process-driven decision-making useful for business leaders is the 'six thinking hats' technique, created by psychologist Edward de Bono.[37] Each different-coloured hat forces the metaphorical wearer to adopt a specific way of thinking, encouraging them to be more flexible, reflective and original in their reasoning, to reach a final decision that's been evaluated through a minimum of six different frames.

- *The white hat* is objective and neutral, looking for concrete facts and rejecting interpretations or opinions.
- *The black hat* is negative but logical, searching for complexity and dead-ends that encourages a sense of realism and avoidance of past mistakes.
- *The green hat* is creative and provocative, demanding the wearer be more ambitious and less conservative (thinking 'could' rather than 'should') in looking for alternatives and possibilities.
- *The red hat* is passionate and emotional, freeing the wearer to express their subjective, System 1 intuition about the information they have.
- *The yellow hat* is positive but logical, focusing on a constructive and optimistic assessment of the options while still being rational and factual.
- *The blue hat* is calm and balanced, controlling the whole process. It's worn once at the start to determine the order of the hats and then at the end to make a decision.

What this kind of role-playing does so well is to harness our cognitive limitations and use them to our advantage, channelling the bias of each mode of thought to explore the limits of where they lead and then offset them against each other to reach a more rounded conclusion. Like algorithmic thinking, these methodical decision-making techniques make a virtue of our psychological weaknesses, anticipating and adopting them as part of the process so they can be fully utilized and corrected for. From a behavioural economist's point of view, they can even be viewed as a form of 'choice architecture', altering a leader's environment through external props or checklists to increase the chances of them making the best decision, rather than necessarily trying to change how their brains are wired.

Of course, both these techniques – algorithmic thinking and the six hats – would be quicker and more effective if they involved a team of leaders rather than just an individual. And most companies have an executive team headed up by a CEO to help with strategic decision-making, as well as a board. This senior leadership team needs to fully 'own' the issue of sustainability if they're going to integrate the Global Goals into the firm's business strategy and operations and drive the kind of transformation needed. In addition to the techniques above, it may be useful to assign advocates for particular Global Goals that are a business priority, either permanently or on a rotational basis. Going beyond just six hats, businesses could experiment with introducing hats for nature, diversity or youth, too, since any decision that passes the test of many hats is likely to be more robust and resilient. Or perhaps individuals can be made the lead responsible for championing particular long-term projects, such as net zero carbon, circularity or gender equality.

However the leadership on sustainability is divided among business managers, this individual advocacy approach can be an effective way of harnessing that cognitive propensity for taking sides, and ensuring these competing but interconnected priorities are properly considered in all managerial team decisions. As well as guarding against potential groupthink and the dreaded Dunning–Kruger effect, it also allows for more joint evaluation (rather than separate), which research has shown is better at avoiding unconscious biases and making better decisions when it comes to comparing and choosing new products, alternative investments and changes in strategic direction.[38]

But perhaps the most compelling reason for individual advocacy on sustainability is that it increases accountability on the issue and makes it more likely they will produce results. This has been particularly evident in past efforts to promote diversity in company management. A 2006 study of 708 private sector companies showed that diversity training and evaluations for managers were the least effective at bringing through more women and minority ethnic candidates into managerial roles. The best method was creating dedicated staff roles or committees that were held responsible for hitting diversity targets, which were also found to improve the efficacy of diversity training, evaluation, networking and mentoring schemes too.[39] In the UK, Business in the Community's 'Race at Work Charter' provides a good template for such an approach, as well as resources for creating diversity targets that are both SMART and SIMPLE and so more likely to be effective.[40]

So enabling more collective forms of management is an essential strategy for any CEO or senior leader wanting to make responsible decisions on sustainability. As such, the leader's role is much like that of the blue hat, calmly moderating and orchestrating the process of their executive team's decision-making, but willing to use their casting vote to decide what action to take that best serves the business's purpose. The decisive power and authority, therefore, starts and finishes with an individual, but is substantiated and mediated through the team. As Francesco Starace, CEO of Italian energy firm Enel and one of the pioneering leaders quoted in the UN Global Compact's aforementioned study, describes it: 'At the beginning of the [sustainability] journey, if the CEO is not the engine of this, it cannot work. The CEO must be the ultimate force behind this. But then as time goes on and the topic is established, the group that is involved and supporting it is just as important as the CEO.'[41]

Businesses, then, should break away from the idea of a leader being some kind of maverick figurehead and appoint managers who are skilled in building teams and designing good choice architecture instead. The added cognitive capacity, diversity and experience a team brings is impossible for any one individual to rival, particularly when channelled effectively towards a shared purpose or challenge. Which then begs the question: how big should that leadership team be? Should it include all staff, the whole company, investors, suppliers or even wider stakeholders, such as customers and the local community? Surely the bigger the team is, the greater the benefits? While the logistics of such an all-inclusive approach might make it impossible for day-to-day decision-making, many businesses – including cooperatives, mutual organizations and some crowdfunded companies that are owned by their members, customers, employees or investors – are structured in a way that obliges their leadership team to be democratically elected and consult widely on major decisions.

Whatever the type of business, the principle of involving and responding to as wide a range of stakeholders as possible is fundamental to tackling the complexity and scale of the Global Goals. As the UN Global Compact puts it: 'By bringing in the perspective of diverse stakeholders who have different vantage points and experiences, leaders can substantially improve their coverage of the problem or opportunity space. This reduces risk and opens new opportunities for large-scale impact.'[42] In other words, business leaders need to work with all their stakeholders if they're to have any chance of fully understanding and acting effectively on the Global Goals.

The ways of doing this are manifold and far from unusual: from stakeholder steering groups and staff taskforces to more open investor AGMs and community partnerships. But in essence, all of them are a variation of management by team. The aim is just to encourage a greater proliferation and diversity of teams throughout the company. Ultimately, this all leads to a more widely distributed approach to decision-making and leadership, with those teams best suited to lead and advise on an issue delegated the power and status to do so. This inclusive style of leadership has enormous benefits when it comes to embedding sustainability in a business's everyday operations, primarily because it seeks to release the full potential of one of the firm's most powerful resources: its workforce.

THE CONSISTENCY DILEMMA: DOES YOUR BUSINESS LEAD BY EXAMPLE?

One thing laid bare during the COVID-19 pandemic was the number of businesses that were only too willing to help support external charities to help the hardest hit while failing to look after their own employees. In the UK, one retailer threatened to fire any worker who self-isolated with the disease at the same time as volunteering to help deliver supplies and equipment for the NHS. And a pub chain that had won awards for working with charities to tackle hunger refused to pay its largely low-paid staff for weeks until it had received government furlough payments.[43]

This hypocritical (or at least inconsistent) approach to responsibility is symptomatic of a business that still sees it as a form of external CSR rather than an ethos that informs the whole business – including its internal culture and relationship with staff. But even the most conscientious employers with the best personnel practices may focus all their sustainability efforts on their products and operations while overlooking less output-related elements of the business.

For instance, how many companies bank with an ethical bank, invest their employee pensions sustainably, have insurance policies with a responsible underwriter or make sure their on-site food and drinks are responsibly sourced? All these secondary investments a business makes as a consumer can have a positive impact far beyond the direct scope of the company, as well as enable their employees to make sustainable choices by default.

While they might not offer the same PR opportunity as charitable work, these things do demonstrate a company's integrity to its staff and the wider business ecosystem. Besides, the risk of a company not living its values being communicated externally by staff – who are becoming increasingly engaged with activism – will do far more damage to trust than any philanthropy can repair.[44] Ultimately, business leaders need to ask themselves: why is it okay to do some things responsibly and not others?

Actipreneurialism, workplace culture and the value of diversity and inclusion

One of the most prominent leadership trends in business over the last decade has been the rise of the activist CEO. According to the global 'Trust Barometer' survey by the US PR firm Edelman in 2020, business significantly eclipses national governments as the most trusted institution for governing the world, and three-quarters of the public want CEOs to take the lead on dealing with social issues. But the results for employees are even more decisive, with 92% saying their CEOs should speak out on issues of the day and 73% wanting more opportunities to help change society for the better.[45]

This apparent thirst for more meaningful employment should be a gift for responsible businesses trying to enthuse their workforce with their Global Goals-based social purpose. Staff are increasingly looking for an emotional investment in their work, rather than just robotically pursuing sales and efficiencies, and company leaders need to harness that desire to improve the world. One way of looking at it is like engendering a spirit of actipreneurialism, where employees behave more like dedicated activists for a cause rather than self-interest, bringing the creativity and coordinating skills of an entrepreneur to the task, too. In such a model, the CEO is also an inspiring actipreneur, passionately appealing to the values of staff and their shared purpose rather than looking to command and control.

Research has shown that such a shared values approach is much more effective at rallying the loyalty and support of similarly motivated people and encouraging greater cooperation within teams.[46] And both are essential for mobilizing the kind of mass response needed to tackle the complex social dimensions of sustainability – within and beyond the company. As world-making institutions, businesses already have a powerful role in shaping society. Their actions change the systems they are embedded in, impacting on all who inhabit them, no matter how neutral or unintentional they claim them to be. So responsible business leaders should acknowledge this role and come clean about how they want the world to be and what they are proactively doing to achieve it.

But if a CEO does choose to become a more publicly outspoken activist voice – as many who enjoy a big personal following on social media have done – it's critical they do it with integrity and sincerity. As Professor Carl Rhodes argues in his book *Woke Capitalism*, numerous business leaders seem less interested in agitating for real change and more concerned with aligning their brands with 'safe' causes that will boost their corporate image and increase their commercial appeal. In this way, CEOs aren't so much activists as simply hoary, old-fashioned corporate ambassadors, using the most popular 'woke' causes to create positive brand associations.[47]

Besides, the idea of an activist CEO – whether sincerely done or not – is still very much rooted in outdated notions of the heroic leader. The more radical and progressive outcome of increasing actipreneurialism is the growth in activist employees. Rather than expressions of the personal values of CEOs, employees are taking the moral lead and demanding more strident changes to the way their businesses are run. From mass walkouts at Google over pay awards for executives accused of sexual misconduct[48] to anonymous newspaper adverts from staff at the Big Four accounting firms in support of the Hong Kong protests,[49] employees are using traditional tools of protest with the transparency and instant audience of social media to force companies to stay true to their stated values and purpose. Alison Taylor of New York University's Stern School of Business calls employee activism the antithesis of CEO activism. 'Instead, it constitutes an effort to turn companies into functioning democracies that can operate in the public interest', she says, adding in parentheses: 'That this vision has arisen in the corporate world while becoming much more elusive in the political realm is surely no coincidence.'[50]

Leaders of a responsible business committed to the Global Goals shouldn't be afraid of this employee activism or their demands for greater democracy, since it's entirely in keeping with the kind of management by team and shared values approach to leadership that works so effectively for responsible decision-making and should be embraced within the culture of the workplace. But with respect to the latter, the leadership still has a powerful role in setting the tone of an organization's culture and leading by example. And seeing as one of the Global Goals is providing 'decent work', if a business can't succeed in this most immediate and attainable area of sustainability for its own staff, it's doubtful any commitment to more external and less controllable goals will pass much muster.

One of the most important ways of underpinning a responsible working culture is the various business and personnel structures that are used to encourage or reward staff behaviour. For instance, what personality traits does a particular company tend to recruit, promote, train or incentivize? Are they empathy, integrity and emotional intelligence? Or do they get overlooked in favour of an appetite for risk, personal ambition and assertiveness? As we've seen earlier, fundamental to fostering more responsible behaviours are KPIs that measure more than just sales and productivity and are aligned with the Global Goals. What qualitative measures of staff performance does a company have and how are they connected to its Global Goals-based purpose? Are responsible actions rewarded and irresponsibility penalized in fun and imaginative ways (such as the game-like nudges we looked at previously)?

There is lots of compelling research that for complex, cognitive tasks – like tackling sustainability – financial incentives, excessive control and punitive sanctions don't motivate or encourage the kind of collaborative and innovative behaviour needed for a responsible business to succeed in the long term. They are also likely to drive away the most competent and conscientious employees, while being ignored by those who don't care or have no alternative anyway. Much more effective are human-centred rewards that build on people's desire to improve their skills, feel a sense of belonging and be treated with dignity, such as training, peer recognition and greater autonomy. The author Daniel H. Pink, in his book *Drive* (2009), puts these non-financial motivations into three key categories – mastery, autonomy and making a difference – and attributes their power to the overall sense of purpose they give people.[51]

So giving staff a clear sense of the contribution their work makes to the social purpose of the company and the sustainability of the wider world is not only strategically important for business leaders, but also entirely congruent with providing work that most engages people. As well as enriching even the most routine and mundane of jobs, these more intrinsic and purposeful incentives are far more likely to get people to work together and 'go the extra mile' for each other and – as a consequence – the organization.

This is particularly the case for those who have started or are employed by social enterprises, where the opportunity to work directly on social problems and improve society is what drives them, not large profits or salaries.[52] Many of these social enterprises are still highly profitable and competitive in the conventional sense. It's what they do with these profits that makes the difference. What they don't do is siphon off the value created by others to wealthy investors, many of whom haven't contributed any money to the actual business.[53] Similarly, proponents of employee-owned companies argue that they provide the perfect hybrid of intrinsic and collective incentives, creating a strong bond between staff and the shared success of the business. As a recent report by the Employee Ownership Association puts it, staff 'feel a bond that cannot be fabricated on any away-day or off-site event, no matter how thrilling it might be. This cohesion leads to better and more sustainable results.'[54]

Indeed, so much of a company's working culture is about the dignity of these interpersonal relationships evidenced by the value, trust and respect shown towards each other at all levels. And while it relies on individuals to act responsibly, that behaviour can be encouraged and maintained through staff codes of conduct, SIMPLE KPIs, ethical management guidelines and robust grievance and whistleblowing procedures that make clear everyone's rights and responsibilities. But this dynamic of dignified mutuality rather than commercial exploitation also needs to be backed up by genuine transparency and staff empowerment. This means a responsible company should have some recognized form of employee representation – recommended by the Global Goals as both a key principle of responsible business and a human right.[55]

Whether it's a trade union, employee board members, staff committees or through employee ownership, staff need to have a meaningful say on a company's operations and their material pay and conditions if they're to feel truly valued and listened to by management. And as OECD employment data proves, as well as improving workers' health, training and poverty levels, such collective bargaining is also hugely beneficial for the employer too, with companies that embrace it showing stronger productivity gains and better economic resilience.[56]

Ultimately, all these efforts to promote a culture of teamwork and shared purpose will only succeed if management applies them and its values consistently across the business, because it will be glaringly obvious to staff when management fails to walk the talk, losing the trust it's all so dependent on (see the previous dilemma box on p 139). One of the most obvious is the continuing inequality and lack of diversity in the workforce, especially in leadership positions. Astonishingly, in 2018 there were as many men called Dave or David as there were women who were CEOs of FTSE 100 companies – just seven.[57] Black CEOs are even fewer, numbering just 1% of the Fortune 500 companies in 2019 and making up only 3.2% of all their executives and senior managers.[58]

Having a diverse executive team with a greater range of perspectives is not only good for creative and innovative decision-making; it's also been identified as a key attribute of companies that outperform their industry average. In their latest report, consultancy firm McKinsey & Company found gender-diverse leadership teams were 25% more likely to experience above-average profitability, which rose to 36% if their executive team was ethnically diverse.[59] And the more women and people from minority ethnic groups there were, the greater the likelihood of outperformance, with companies in the US earning 0.8% more for every 10% rise in racial and ethnic diversity among their senior management.[60] Yet somehow, the myth of white, male superiority still prevails in business, and seems to be the default frame for most recruitment and promotion decisions.

This importance of diversity needs to go beyond just the legally protected characteristics of race, gender, disability, age and sexual orientation, and cover the whole of a company's workforce as well as its senior management – because it's inclusion, not just diversity, that a responsible business is striving for, whereby every employee feels part of a safe and respectful workplace in which they can openly be themselves. Unfortunately, recent surveys in the UK found a third of LGBTQ+ staff felt they had to hide their identity at work,[61] and more than half of employees covered up their mental health conditions.[62] This less visible diversity – which also includes class, neurodivergence and parenthood – is often ignored, yet the skills, knowledge and experiences of people from a range of backgrounds all add value to a company. In fact, a poll by the professional services firm, Accenture, of 1,700 senior leaders and 30,300 employees found US companies were missing out on a gargantuan US$1.05 trillion in profits through lost productivity and turnover costs due to a lack of inclusive practices, such as staff feeling able to fail and having the flexibility to work from home.[63]

There are two other major operational benefits to having a diverse and inclusive working culture: better forecasting and wider appeal. With a more heterogeneous workforce you get more cognitive and information diversity, which makes for better predictions and protects against groupthink.

Researchers have shown that more gender-balanced and culturally diverse teams have provided more accurate forecasts in the classroom than on the stock-trading floors of Wall Street.[64] They're also better at solving complex problems faster and designing solutions that are closer aligned to the needs of a more diverse customer base. This wider appeal of diversity and inclusion also helps with attracting the best staff, clients and customers, as well as engaging existing staff and stakeholders, who are more likely to feel they're represented and their needs understood by the business.

'Our research at the Enterprise and Diversity Alliance makes it increasingly clear that organizations with diverse workforces perform better because they attract top talent, yield greater employee satisfaction and are better at problem-solving, decision-making and innovation', says Professor Kiran Trehan, a UK expert on diversity and entrepreneurship, who also argues that inclusive leadership must go further than simply representation. 'Responsible and inclusive leadership is not just about diversity quotas or numbers on boards, it's about ensuring staff, regardless of background, are included in decision-making, strategy and operations. There is now an economic and business imperative for greater leadership inclusivity in addition to the frequently cited social imperative for greater equality.'[65]

Only by proactively embedding this inclusivity in the daily operations of a business can the culture of a workplace be truly transformed, since the ingrained and often tacit norms of any organization's culture have a habit of stubbornly reproducing themselves regardless of executive edicts from above. And such a participative strategy will also have the added benefit of making the business more agile and responsive to the ever-changing expectations of wider society that can seriously impact on people's trust in a company. Yet it's around this area of trust – and the scope and scale of responsibility that a business chooses to exercise to maintain it – that the CEO and senior managers still have the most power to determine.

THE AI DILEMMA: IS YOUR BUSINESS USING TECHNOLOGY RESPONSIBLY?

One of the most powerful new technologies in business today is artificial intelligence (AI), which is transforming operations across the board. Sales, marketing, finance and supply chains are all employing machine learning and algorithms to automate human tasks, target customers, protect against fraud and anticipate demand – to name just a few of their many applications. And there are benefits for responsible business, too. According to Professor Al Naqvi of the American Institute of Artificial Intelligence, AI could help remove human bias from sustainability decision-making, identify better ways to measure impacts, draw on global and dynamic data to monitor progress, and help integrate the Global Goals into a company's overall business strategy.[66]

But there are many serious concerns about the consequences and ethics of AI use in business, which range from data misuse and a lack of knowledge or oversight from company leaders, to mass staff redundancies and automating discrimination. Sadly, most of our datasets are outdated, destructive, exploitative and rife with racism, sexism and other unsustainable logics. Setting AI loose on this data will amplify, not mitigate, our destructive capacity. See how the error rates for facial recognition technology are higher for women and people from minority ethnic groups because the algorithms 'learn' from analysing millions of faces scraped from the internet, which are predominantly white and male.[67] Business has evolved to destroy well enough without AI; the question is how to use AI to change things when most of our datasets are so biased. Government policy and the law are struggling to understand and keep up with all the implications of this new technology, too, so responsible businesses must look to thought leaders such as the Future of Life Institute for best practice guidance.

The charity's 'Asilomar principles' cover the research-related, ethical and long-term issues of AI in 23 points – all of them relevant to business. They recommend programmers create 'beneficial intelligence' that complements human agency and decision-making and not 'undirected intelligence' that replaces it. All AI systems and their decisions should therefore be transparent and auditable by a human authority. The guidance also suggests companies that use AI are responsible for ensuring it doesn't infringe on people's human rights, personal liberties and data privacy, and that the technology should aim to benefit and empower as many people as possible.[68] Responsible business leaders need to embed such principles in their own firm's AI practices, regularly reappraising their implementation to make sure they keep ahead of this rapidly evolving technology so it continues to align with their values and purpose.

Much has correctly been made of the dangers of a robot CEO and the dystopian 'self-driving-autonomous' business. But the reality is that business leaders already make extensive use of digital technology in decision-making and ignore the dystopian present we have managed to create without AI. David De Cremer, in his 2020 book *Leadership by Algorithm: Who Leads and Who Follows in the AI Era?*, maps out this conflict and concludes that AI is unlikely to lead businesses, but has far greater potential to administer them while avoiding the System 1 biases of humans if done responsibly. But how it is designed and used by humans is critical to ensure that what AI provides is beneficial intelligence for responsible leaders.

Managing trust, innovating and adopting a sustainable mindset

If you were to ask people which businesses they most trust, many would undoubtedly include the smaller, local or independent shops and services they've been using in their neighbourhoods for years. Indeed, one such survey by the Better Business Bureau in the US found 84% of people were more likely to trust small businesses over larger ones, and numerous others show an overwhelming public desire to support small and medium-sized enterprises (SMEs) – particularly during the COVID-19 pandemic.[69] So what is it about SMEs that make them so much more appealing to customers?

Well, almost by default, many have to operate as responsible businesses in order to survive. They depend on trusted relationships with their customers, suppliers and the local community to generate loyalty and the repeat business that keeps them sustainable in the longer term. SMEs' tighter business model can't accommodate large amounts of waste, and their susceptibility to word of mouth (made so much acuter by online reviews and social media) means they cannot get away with unethical practices or harmful products and services. Also, because there are fewer employees, there can be a personable immediacy to interacting with an SME – often directly with the owner – that provides a greater feeling of authenticity and transparency.

Many of these SME traits are the envy of big business and are keenly emulated in marketing campaigns and customer services protocols that seldom manage to capture the same feel. But what's essential to businesses of all sizes is that sense of trust. Like diversity, companies deemed trustworthy are more profitable, productive and highly valued by investors, according to analysis by the Great Place to Work Institute.[70] And for business leaders, having trust makes decision-making quicker, easier and less expensive, whether dealing with employees, suppliers, customers or any other key stakeholder. Yet Edelman's 'Trust Barometer' shows trust in business has continued to decline over the years.[71]

Given the value of trust to a company, especially responsible businesses that rightly have higher expectations placed on them, it's remarkable how little executive time is spent trying to actively measure or manage it as a business priority. Ideally, firms should undertake regular trust 'audits' to gauge people's perceptions of their performance against the Global Goals. The results from these audits can then form the basis of KPIs that can be integrated into core business reporting. This needs to be done for all stakeholders and is an invaluable way for leaders to understand how they might gain or lose trust, now and in future.

For instance, at the Finnish oil refining firm Neste, thousands of employees are asked to complete a 'Way Forward' survey every quarter with a series of 10 questions about various aspects of the operating culture, including whether the company is spending enough time focused on its purpose. This information is then used by the CEO and their leadership team to help prioritize decisions that will best help the company achieve a rapid transformation towards renewables.[72]

There are other steps businesses can take to help build trust with stakeholders, which were identified in a recent study into the issue by consultancy firm Grant Thornton. Treating suppliers more like strategic partners than costs to be squeezed was seen as a better way of delivering efficiencies and innovation. By building a long-term relationship that involves suppliers more deeply with the responsible purpose of a company, all kinds of extra value in terms of loyalty, expertise and contribution to the Global Goals could be realized. To improve transparency and trust among the local community, companies could regularly open up their sites for educational visits and public events. And linking executive pay to Global Goals performance would certainly address one of the leading bugbears of responsible investors exasperated by excessive remuneration for failing CEOs.[73]

Not breaking the law would seem to be another obvious way a business can safeguard public trust, but mere compliance won't be enough. Business regulations and governance tend to lag behind science and public opinion. Any changes are often political and fall into the 'shutting the stable door after the horse has bolted' category since they're normally in response to a catastrophe rather than in anticipation of avoiding it. Their aim is to prevent the same thing happening again, not to make the system more resilient. Simply obeying retrospective and inadequate laws or avoiding getting caught won't therefore guarantee trust, which is tried and tested in the public domain and not the courtroom anyway.

So a responsible leader can better protect against a loss of trust when it comes to issues of sustainability by always seeking to make choices that are forward-looking and informed by the latest research and possibilities, rather than waiting for a change in the law to act. In every area of the business, striving to be as fully accountable as possible for the firm's operations will not only safeguard against future regulatory changes and shifting public opinion, but also provide greater transparency, trust and opportunities for improvements – including knowing where there are knowledge gaps and any positive as well as negative impacts to learn and act on. Ancient mapmakers used to leave big sections deliberately blank and add in notations like 'here are lions' or 'Terra Incognita' to denote unknown risks.[74] How many business leaders will have the same courage and curiosity to acknowledge their zones of ignorance and work with others to co-create maps of what they need to know, rather than what they assume they do?

For instance, in the diagram overleaf, you can see the current standard for carbon reporting covers just a small part of the spectrum of carbon

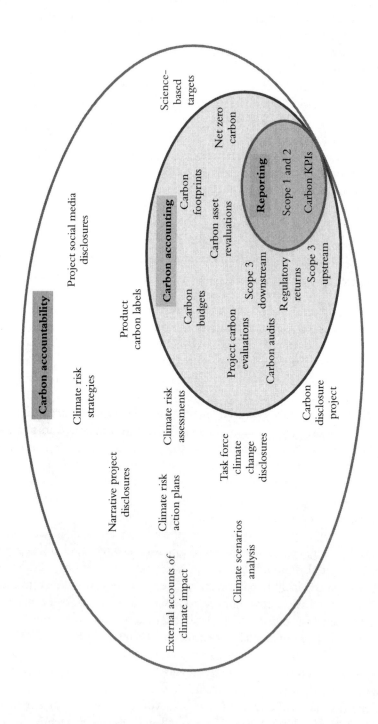

accounting, missing carbon emissions downstream and upstream (the carbon scoping we discuss in detail in Appendix 4). But in addition to missing out on the potentially positive as well as negative impacts of the business beyond its core operations, there's a whole wider area of associated climate risk that leaders could engage with, from climate risk action plans to the latest science-based targets and thresholds. Some of these measures might be beyond the resources of smaller companies, but for multinational corporates like Toyota, there's a real imperative to get on top of climate-related extreme weather that threatens their Just-In-Time manufacturing process, with typhoons and widespread flooding having already halted production at their Thailand factories in 2011.[75]

It's this constant curiosity for greater awareness that's necessary for truly responsible leadership, which then demands ambitious choices be made to properly meet with the full scale of the sustainability issues uncovered. One decisive area is being bold with innovation. The rapid progress needed to meet the 2030 deadline for the Global Goals requires big investment in scientific knowledge, new technologies and disruptive ways of working to accelerate the pace of change from incremental to transformational. This could mean partnering with universities on research, harnessing the power of AI to improve data modelling and decision-making, or transitioning to an employee-owned business model.

Another ambitious choice is to set audacious, long-term sustainability goals as a business priority and persevere with them through any short-term adversity. Of course, the Global Goals themselves are exactly that. But why not go beyond the next 10 years to a 50-year governance plan, or even look a century ahead? Such 100-year strategies are actually commonplace among the big corporations of China and Southeast Asia, with Panasonic's Japanese parent company once even having a 700-year plan for the business.[76] And research shows that directors who focus primarily on the long term are not only better informed about future issues affecting the company but short-term issues too.[77]

Finally, there's being ambitious with knowledge-sharing and collaborative working. A responsible leader should be generous and try to remove barriers to innovation within their business and their wider industry, recognizing that the shared urgency of sustainability and achieving the Global Goals *is* commercial self-interest. How long could the food sector survive without soil, the drinks industry without water or the seafood trade without fish? Organizations like Business in the Community in the UK, or B Corps and the League of Intrapreneurs internationally, provide open forums for companies and their leaders to share best practice and offer peer support. And companies that become sustainable pioneers can foster local business ecosystems that drive up regional and sector sustainability, as we saw earlier in the book with the development of the Kalundborg Eco-Industrial Park in

Denmark and the 'pollinator' programme by carpet manufacturer Interface, involving local businesses around its headquarters in Georgia, USA, and its other factories around the world.

These initiatives required courageous leadership to stand up to the 'winner takes all' myth of conventional business. But it's worth it, because joining together in common cause like this can often create sufficient momentum to overcome barriers that are insurmountable for an individual company. Whether at a global, national or very local level, each responsible action will make something better, not worse. And the cumulative and collective impact of every firm taking small steps towards the Global Goals can become transformative – more so if they encourage changes to the core business model, rather than seeking to offset negative impacts after the fact. By coordinating meaningful and inclusive dialogues, leaders can help build these coalitions for change among their own employees and with other companies, co-creating a more responsible kind of business in a better world.

All of these ways of leading on sustainability – with trust, ambition, long-termism and collaboration – are a natural and logical consequence of what the UN Global Compact calls a 'sustainable mindset', which is essential for responsible leadership.[78] By seeing the fortunes of business as intimately interconnected with the welfare of society and the environment, company leaders are compelled to include wider stakeholders, be more innovative and think about their actions in the long term. The unique scale and shared benefits of sustainability simply demands it.

But perhaps most importantly, it encourages business leaders to think systemically and recognize sustainability as a complex socio-ecological challenge that can only be met by working with other businesses, civic society, academia and governments. Everyone needs to be on board if we're going to be able to live in that systemic 'sweet spot' between the world's social foundation and ecological ceiling, depicted so well in the Doughnut Economics paradigm (see p 72). With a more humble and holistic perspective of business and how it intersects with society and the environment, the idea of trade-offs around the Global Goals disappears. There are no straightforward winners or losers, just intersectional decisions about how a company helps distribute resources and impacts around the socio-ecological system in the most sustainable way.

Thinking systemically like this might sound quite abstract, but Kate Raworth – author of *Doughnut Economics* – suggests several specific ways it fundamentally subverts traditional business thought. Most prominently, it does away with the possibility of endless growth and makes the goal of business about helping wider society and the environment to thrive, whether or not a company grows. It also recognizes consumers and markets aren't rational and self-contained but dynamic and complex, with spiralling feedbacks, emergent trends and surprise tipping points – much like the natural ecosystems in which they're embedded. And it requires businesses to be regenerative and circular, rather than relying on growth to pay for cleaning up its mess.[79]

But perhaps most radically and counterintuitively for responsible business leaders, systems thinking stops the emphasis being on how to make a company completely sustainable (which is impossible anyway) and shifts its focus to how it contributes to the sustainability of the planet. It's a subtle but significant change of perspective that compels a business to always look outward and recognize its relationship with a world in constant flux. It's why being a responsible business is a continuous process rather than an end goal. And it's why – using the Global Goals as their 'senses' – a responsible business leader provides a vital, early feedback loop that helps adjust a company's operations to better align with the wider socio-ecological system. But ultimately, such a holistic perspective also recognizes that the sustainability of the planet is more important than the sustainability of a company. Businesses aren't supposed to be permanent. And if they close because they fail to benefit society and the environment, their resources are released and redistributed elsewhere in the system.

So it's up to business leaders to demonstrate the social value of their firms, both to their workforce and their wider human and non-human stakeholders. While the delivery of a company's purpose and values is a collective effort, leaders have the power to legitimate how every aspect of their work is framed, performance-measured and rewarded. Will you orient your business around the Global Goals with diverse teamworking, rigorous processes and inclusive values? Only such a combination can protect against irresponsible decisions and unleash the full potential of the business to contribute to the sustainability of the planet and thrive with it.

Summary: The science of responsible business

Observations to note
Responsible businesses …

… have self-aware, values-driven leaders who build teams and unlock staff potential.

… make decisions within diverse and inclusive teams in order to co-create rather than command and control.

… use well-designed decision architecture that minimizes the risk of individual bias.

… recognize staff's values and motivate through purpose, not just profits.

… treat suppliers, investors and other stakeholders with dignity as strategic partners.

… make trust a strategic priority with measurable KPIs on all critical relationships.

… use AI, data and emerging digital technology responsibly.

… encourage learning and knowledge-sharing to continually fill zones of ignorance.

… are ambitious about innovation, long-term governance and collaboration.

… prioritize the sustainability of the planet over the business.

Theories to test
Process-driven decision-making
Leaders who use methodical, Global Goals-based processes make more responsible decisions.

- What protocols do you follow to assess the potential impacts of your decision-making on natural systems? (Global Goals 6, 13, 14 and 15)
- Have you discussed with your senior managers what kinds of frame they use when making critical decisions and how they might conflict with the Global Goals? (Global Goals 3, 5, 10, 16 and 17)
- What percentage of your AI, data science or digital technologies have been formally assessed or certified as meeting ethical standards? (Global Goals 5, 9, 10 and 16)
- What 'hat(s)' do you wear when making critical decisions? (Global Goals 5, 10, 16 and 17)

Diverse and inclusive teams
An inclusive working culture that respects the dignity of staff and stakeholders will be more sustainable and appealing.

- Does your business have an inclusion team and/or working group with set targets? (Global Goals 3, 5, 10 and 11)

- Do you have staff representation at executive and board level? (Global Goals 1 and 8)
- What measures are in place to accommodate neurodivergence and mental health conditions among your staff? (Global Goal 3)
- How effectively do you consult with your key stakeholders on major business decisions? (Global Goals 11, 12, 14, 15, 16 and 17)
- Do your staff incentives reward irresponsible behaviour and create a hostile workplace culture? (Global Goals 3, 8, 12, 16 and 17)

Intersectional leadership

Leaders who take a systemic approach are better able to anticipate, innovate and collaborate on issues of sustainability.

- How extensively are you sharing your knowledge of sustainable working with others to help drive up performance across industry and wider society? (Global Goals 8, 9, 10, 11, 12, 13, 14, 15, 16 and 17)
- What beneficial impacts do you want your business to provide for others in 20, 50, 100 or 200 years' time? (All Global Goals)
- What measures do you take to gauge trust in your business? (Global Goals 3, 8, 9, 11, 12, 16 and 17)
- Which other businesses and organizations do you work with to keep up to date with the latest scientific knowledge and joint initiatives on sustainability? (Global Goals 4, 9, 11, 16 and 17)

First steps to responsible leadership ...

Team leadership	Inclusive decision-making	Trust monitoring	Systemic thinking
Build diverse teams that lead on key sustainability issues	Treat stakeholders as strategic partners	Measure trust as a core KPI for the business	Always be aware of how the firm contributes to the planet's sustainability

Do Something

Creating your own business roadmap to responsibility

It may come as a disappointment to some readers (although hardly a surprise, given what you've read so far!), but there is no straightforward answer to how to be a 'responsible business'. Being responsible will mean different things in different places at different times. The priorities for responsible actions in Malawi, with its high levels of poverty and extreme vulnerability to changing weather patterns, will be different from what is responsible in Sweden, which is generally regarded as the most sustainable of countries. That's because responsibility is co-created between a business and the priorities of the various systems in which it is embedded.

Moreover, at different times, different businesses will be responding to different priorities and will be at different points on different paths to responsibility. There are many starting points and pathways to becoming more responsible and sustainable. And even though they take different routes, they should all head towards a shared destination, which, in the medium term, is the Global Goals. Given the unique makeup of each business, it's not practical or useful to prescribe a fixed roadmap to sustainability, so this book offers five suggested pathways for businesses wanting to begin their own journey towards more responsible governance, accountability, production, consumption and leadership.

Stage one is to take stock of where you are on each path, where you want to be at the end of each year up until 2030, which steps you can take relatively easily, and what needs to change to get to the end of each path. Since businesses often don't have a clear understanding of what sustainability is, many find they are further along than they think they are once they start exploring the Global Goals. Many are already addressing historic gender and ethnic discrimination (Global Goals 5 and 10), paying living wages for employees and tier 1 suppliers (Global Goals 1, 2, 3 and 8), and ensuring their product and its packaging can be easily recycled (Global Goals 12, 14 and 15).

In fact, while almost all businesses could be doing more, very few are not, in some way, contributing towards the Global Goals. That's because they

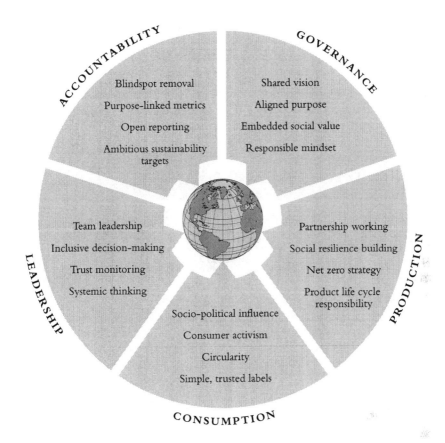

represent human values that we have been striving towards for millennia. Creating and maintaining safe, sustainable communities (Global Goal 11), for example, is a primordial and intrinsic part of being human, not some global conspiracy initiated by the UN in 2015. So there is much value in using the Global Goals to interrogate all that your business does and to own what you are doing, as well as what you still need to do.

Stage two is to draw up a list of milestones, obstacles and critical activities, identifying fellow travellers who will help you along the way. If you customize your targets based on the Global Goals that are core to your purpose, that you are dependent on, that you negatively impact and that you benefit (see p 25), your milestones will also function as signposts for your business, showing you where to go next. Taken together, all these different elements should allow you to construct a sustainability roadmap customized for your business that will see you through to 2030. Given how dynamic the future always is, it's important to revisit and readjust this map on a regular basis, building in agility and adaptability.

Finally, stage three is to create a strong visualization of your sustainability journey for the business and to update your progress regularly. This should be an inclusive and democratic process that's done as a highly visible event, so that the roadmap is both owned by and relevant to all the critical actors in this journey – from staff to suppliers and other key external stakeholders. Any decision to move where you are on the map must also be collaboratively agreed and collectively celebrated when progress is made, particularly if any milestone is reached. Periodically coming together in this way, you can reflect on the profile of your company's progress, work out next steps and even construct new pathways.

The visualization of your roadmap can take any form deemed most appropriate and understandable for those using it, but the rules and criteria for moving forward should be transparent and adaptable to changing circumstances. For example, you could create a simple Global Goals abacus, with the rods representing the pathways towards each Global Goal from left to right, which are stacked in order of importance to the business (see opposite).

But you can be even more creative and get a graphic designer, artist or other visual expert involved to come up with something really engaging. You can even enlist the help of local school children, colleges or community groups to do it with you – the results can be spectacular!

When using your roadmap, make sure you don't just plough through it all or try to perfect a single pathway before starting on another. With the complex, multidimensional problems of sustainability, there are advantages in advancing incrementally on many fronts – because moving forward in one area will unlock possibilities in others, allowing you to raise the floor on many Global Goals at the same time and avoid unnecessary antagonisms. All your positive pathways will invariably intersect at some shared milestones and have this positive multiplier effect. Paying a living wage to your workers will also reduce gender, ethnic and disability-related issues. Similarly, reducing your carbon footprint not only contributes to action on climate change, but benefits life on land and life under water too.

Concentrating on these key intersections will provide much more return on your efforts as single actions will have multiple sustainability payoffs. But the timing, sequencing and coordination of your efforts along your roadmap also matter a lot. For example, to make credible claims about the sustainability of your product, it won't be sufficient for it to have a net zero carbon footprint but still use materials that are toxic in their extraction, production and disposal or place natural ecosystems under extreme stress. However, demonstrating progress on many different responsible pathways and critical milestones will make for far more credible labelling of your product.

Ultimately, whatever progress you make on your roadmap, there is no final point of arrival where you become fully sustainable or responsible; it's a continuous process. This is why being responsible isn't really a goal but

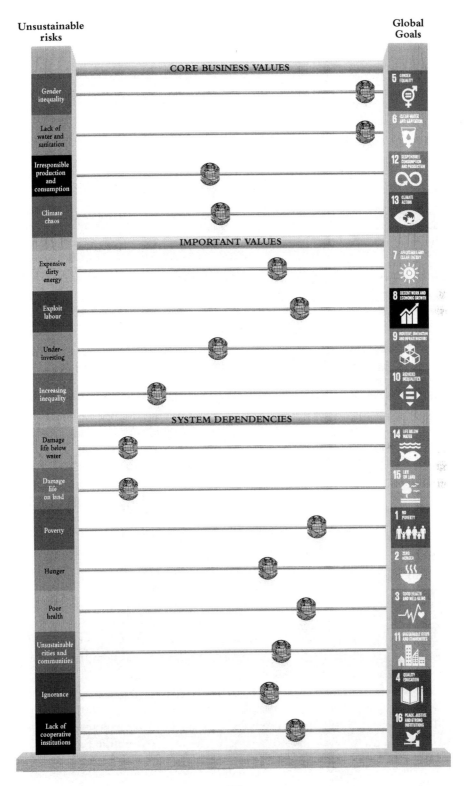

a mindset that frames every decision and business performance measure, constantly triggering questions about where you are already responsible, how you can be more so, and which areas are in most urgent need. Hopefully, having debunked five of the most pervasive business myths that frame conventional business thinking, this book has helped you to foster this more questioning and scientific mindset around responsible business practice based on observations and theories of what currently seems to work best.

But even today's theories and solutions have a sell-by date. History shows us what is acceptable to society and nature now will change – sometimes incredibly quickly. Asbestos was once a lifesaver, and then it became a killer. Fossil fuels freed individuals from manual toil, and now choke our atmosphere and disrupt our climate. Plastics protected us from infection before polluting our land and seas. While there is no magic switch to instantly make a business responsible at any given time, companies can turn on their responsibility radar and peer into the future using the Global Goals to see what they are currently blind to. Complacency is the enemy of responsibility, and any business wanting a successful future will need to search out and be responsive to these new risks as they're exposed, investing in knowledge and innovation to learn and stay ahead of them.

Working collaboratively with others and sharing knowledge will make this learning and problem-solving much quicker. It's also likely to be cheaper and more effective in the long term, given the shared nature of sustainability issues. Standing back or freeloading, on the other hand, could mean any solution found may not deal with your specific circumstances, delaying your response and prolonging your suffering. Besides, the sheer scale and urgency of the Global Goals demands we all work together. Reading one book won't be enough, but it's a start. So continue learning and exploring with the Appendices, Further Reading list and various tools and resources (both in this book and on our website at www.birmingham.ac.uk/urgent-business).

However you choose to act, putting your head in the sand and your fingers in your ears certainly won't save your company. History shows that businesses very seldom win against the combined might of society and nature. Society is becoming ever more sensitive to the damage some businesses have inflicted on them and nature. The tide is turning and surfing is much easier than trying to push back the tide. But you need to find out when and where the tide will take you. This requires intelligence, human and artificial, if needed, to ask the right questions and interpret the answers – especially if they are contradictory.

Be on guard for fake news, as too many have an incentive to spread mistruths and amplify doubt for selfish reasons. This requires understanding the psychological aspects and motivated reasoning that's inherent in our post-truth culture. Always ask who benefits – cui bono – from the provision of alternative facts. Our inherent cognitive biases make us ripe for manipulation and exploitation by those who have an agenda to push. And when we are emotionally invested in a subject, experimental evidence shows that our ability to reason well will be negatively affected.

So it's worth investing in a few safeguards to distinguish between useful knowledge and fake news, adopting the same scepticism you might use to interpret customer reviews on Amazon or Tripadvisor. First, investigate the author. What can you find out about them? What else have they written? What's their day job and what sources do they quote to support their opinion? Check out their webpages, who funds them and what else they have said. Are there patterns in their opinions?

Second, look for corroboration from other sources and how other people have interpreted the same facts. Look for helpful pointers such as a named author, author affiliation and publication date. It's relatively easy to sound authoritative to non-experts on a study completed in the 1950s and ignore any developments or studies since then. No author, no date, no sources, no corroboration equals no usable facts. Just as you should never rely solely on the evidence provided by a salesperson, you should always confirm things from more independent sources. This advice applies just as much to journalism, policy statements and academic papers as it does to tweets. We are all human.

Remember also that while we can't know anything about the future with 100% certainty, that doesn't mean we don't know anything about the future. All decisions and outcomes involve elements of doubt as well as predictions and plausible scenarios. It's hypocritical of businesses to demand total certainty before acting on climate change, while happily investing in new products with only a 50% chance of making money. Dealing with living systems means making do with the best available evidence and plausible future scenarios – however imperfect – in the hope that our actions prevent them from happening. We will never know for sure what would have happened if we hadn't acted, but that shouldn't undermine the enormity of their preventive impact.

Every one of our decisions makes our future world. And we need vision and aspirations to act as our guide to those decisions. We may not necessarily be able to predict with absolute certainty what future global and local crises will come after COVID-19 or identify the next niche sustainability strategy that may become mainstream, such as hyper-recycling or blockchain carbon accounting are becoming now. But right now, the Global Goals are our best bet to help us navigate away from the catastrophes we do currently know about. The 'known knowns' are a certain and big enough threat to us already, and acting on them must be our priority. We have ideas that are good enough to inform meaningful action with a high chance of success now. If we don't hit enough of the Global Goals by 2030, we won't know what future awaits us or the future for business. So do what you can, when you can, but please do something.

THE 'TOO LATE' DILEMMA: WHAT IF THE GLOBAL GOALS WERE OUR LAST CHANCE?

How did we miss our golden ticket for a better future in 2015? Our leaders had been pushed, prodded and cajoled into agreeing something amazing with the Global Goals: a radical vision of a harmonious, equitable and resilient world. They were a rainbow-coloured blueprint of hope, mapping out a better way to be and providing a set of shared values to build back better after COVID-19. Now the only time you hear them mentioned is on satirical panel shows or historical documentaries, poked at as a grim checklist of our collective failure.

Back then, everyone seemed to agree there was a problem to be solved – even the children knew things were wrong and needed fixing. Despite the post-truthers and trolls, the evidence of undeniable harm was mounting and momentum was with those looking to end our slow ecological violence and societal self-harm. The news was full of transformative technologies and ways to make a difference, and businesses were stepping up to pledge their allegiance to a sustainable future. We seemed to have defined the problems, found countless solutions and committed to change – at least in public. Yet in private, government offices, town halls and boardrooms, infectious stupidity prevailed.

Did we really become virtue-fatigued and tired of pursuing purpose rather than profit? When did humanity replace empathy with self-pity? Was it when the last rhino horn was ground into virility powder? Or when dignity in the workplace was abolished and steady employment became as rare as giant pandas? Was it when we stopped counting crimes, coronavirus deaths or food banks? Or when children were obliged to bring their smartphones into school to pay for their education by the hour?

Now we nostalgically rewatch old Attenborough documentaries and dream of fresh fish and chips or salad that doesn't have to be decontaminated before eating. How much of the planet has to become uninhabitable before new restrictions are placed on fossil fuels? How many days of summer without forest fires is acceptable? There was a time when you could be sick or decide to change job without worrying about hunger and homelessness. Not anymore. Did we really do our best when we had the chance in 2015? We followed the leaders and look where we are now. Perhaps there never was such a thing as society.

Beyond 2030 and the Global Goals

While the world almost certainly won't end in 2030 (thankfully), the Global Goals represent our best chance for a sustainable upgrade that can be achieved with the coordinated efforts and goodwill of everyone. But they are a milestone on a much longer journey to ensure harmonious interrelationships among people and between us and non-humans. They build on the Millennium Development Goals (MDGs) and will inevitably be replaced by a new set of goals. As with the unevenly achieved MDGs, it's likely that not all the targets and outcomes of the Global Goals will be fully met, but the very act of striving to achieve them will make a huge difference to billions of our fellow citizens and future generations.

While there is a broad consensus as to the Global Goals' validity, we have to remember that they are political as well as scientific, and informed by pragmatism as well as hope. They're designed to start an evolutionary process, nudging governments, businesses and communities back on to a more sustainable track. But we don't know with certainty that hitting them all will solve all of our problems. Our history is full of examples of where success and progress have uncovered new or hidden problems and inequities that then also need addressing. The internet may have unlocked vast treasures of knowledge and enabled collaborative efforts unimaginable a few decades ago, for instance, but it also created systemic invasion of privacy, horrendous bullying and the promulgation of fake news. Similarly, with the paradox of medical advances, no matter how numerous and successful they are, there will always be another number one killer to fight against.

Set against our human efforts and ingenuity, the non-human world also continues to evolve, triggering more natural feedback mechanisms that may or may not be compatible with people's ways of life – such as the rise in sea levels as a result of the melting polar icecaps. The natural adaptive process of mutation also continues apace, dancing to the rhythms and rationalities of each ecological niche. So, like antibiotic-resistant bacteria, our human solutions to these natural phenomena can become weaknesses and sources of instability in the same way our carefully constructed defences against influenza-like pandemics were insufficient to deal with COVID-19. But because humanity has evolved to evolve quickly, we have collaborated and responded to these health crises, eliminating the worst excesses of many killer diseases like cholera, smallpox, measles, TB, Ebola and eventually HIV. It would seem perfectly possible, then, for us to take similarly successful action against the worst of our sustainability crises too – even without being fully certain yet of how they're caused or best remedied.

Only historians, pathologists and forensic scientists can know anything with any certainty thanks to the hindsight of postmortems. But even then, they often change their judgements with the development of new knowledge and technology. Eventually, we work out why it was past societies were wiped out, species became extinct and fertile land turned into sterile deserts. But too many of us seem happy to wait until death occurs or systems collapse before we accept the truth. After-the-fact knowledge is too late to act on, and too many irresponsible leaders are happy to dismiss risks and evidence of possible harm and suffering, including predictions that, with hindsight, could have prevented catastrophes. No doubt over the next few years we'll discover a host of experts whose suggestions would have prevented the impact of COVID-19-type pandemics who were ridiculed, their reports shelved and proposals rejected. Labelled as doomsayers, Cassandras, out-of-touch academics and interfering bureaucrats, they could well have saved more than a million lives if we had listened properly at the time. We can't let the same thing happen when it comes to business and sustainability.

The crux of this book's argument is that it's time to stop 'business as usual' and embrace fresh thinking infused by the Global Goals. Too many business truisms simply don't stand up to contemporary scrutiny. They may have worked in times of plenty, when it was acceptable for a small elite to take far more than their fair share and invest in themselves rather than a future for all, but in our current precarious state, these myths are impractical fables, as irrelevant and unacceptable as the flat Earth theory or slavery. It's time to move on and develop new concepts that will help us co-create a dynamic and adaptive business ecosystem and avoid a dystopian future. We don't want to motivate through fear, but we do need a healthy dose of realism as to where we could end up. There is sense that we are at a crossroads, and maybe this is our last best chance to manage the transformations urgently needed, rather than leave it to the vagaries of chance.

Like any crossroads there is a need to stop, reflect and think about where you want to go (or where you don't want to go). This requires thinking about the route ahead – the pitfalls and obstacles as well as the opportunities and benefits – and accurately remembering what led you to this point. Do you like where you are or where you came from? Are you escaping danger or looking for something better, or a bit of both? Without a hopeful vision or honest history, choosing the next step will be difficult.

Throughout this book, we've tried to provide ways to help you choose that next step and make responsible choices wherever you have the power to. This book also set out to challenge the fatalism and oppressive nature of business myths and to help you reclaim your agency to make a difference. Assumptions such as continual growth and the need for ever-increasing profits are oppressive and destructive, as well as being far removed from what actually motivates most people. Hopefully we've demonstrated that the values underpinning the Global Goals are far more natural to much more of society than the cartoon version of economics that dominates our thinking. Unfortunately, we've evolved a number of cognitive biases that make some goals more difficult to achieve than others. These are amplified by incomplete and poorly designed performance measures, accountability and reward schemes, which tend to incentivize irresponsibility and unsustainability. It's these inherent biases, together with flawed decision-making processes, regressive social attitudes and practices, misdirected leadership and distorted mental frames, that explain some of the irrational choices made by even well-meaning people in business.

Blaming individuals in this context seems rather pointless, just as blaming consumers for their choices between really unsustainable and slightly less unsustainable products misses the point. What the planet needs is for business to recognize these limitations, understand and accept the consequences of doing nothing and then change. Companies should rewire how they operate so that they represent the dynamics of the world in the 21st century and reflect their dependencies on other systems. Removing businesses' sense of exceptionalism, reconnecting them with society and nature, and taking account of all their critical relationships and impacts is urgently required.

Businesses aren't armies, even though irresponsible business practices have massive destructive powers and have inflicted slow ecological and systemic social violence. And competition is nothing like war, with businesses usually prospering during periods of peace and collaboration. Yet business myths and leadership models draw heavily on military metaphors, hero worship, destructive strategies and command hierarchy. Unsurprisingly, such conflictual thinking reinforces individualism, machismo, aggression and 'them and us' frames unhelpful to sustainability. Instead, responsible businesses need to reimagine leadership as someone who mobilizes resources, enables collaboration and fosters coalitions that will co-create social value and help further the Global Goals-based purpose of their companies.

An important part of this co-creative approach will be harnessing and curating the collective wisdom of the crowd – among staff, stakeholders and the wider public – which has been shown to pay dividends in the long term. Underpinning this wisdom should be reliable evidence, open source data and the beneficial use of digital technologies, such as AI. Through such methods, our capacity to usefully model the complexity of the world in a way that helps predict the consequences of business actions has never been greater. Yet we're dramatically underutilizing this potential and our working knowledge is seriously out of date.

Things considered 'unknown unknowns' or just plain unknowable only a few years ago have been shifted into the 'known knowns' or 'known unknowns' categories. Climate change models have moved from the labs into pragmatic scenarios and roadmaps for use by governments, regulators, businesses and civil society. But we need to pause before we rush into naively trusting these models. The dissemination of untrustworthy data is widespread, and our historic datasets are an archive of irresponsible and unsustainable thinking and past actions. We must not make AI based on dirty data. It needs to be trained on clean, uncorrupted datasets that represent positive pathways to desired outcomes, such as the Global Goals and whatever eventually replaces them after 2030.

So how, in summary, does this book propose a responsible business should look and behave? Well, it isn't just growing and profitable but purposeful; it manages what it can't measure and is fully transparent to its stakeholders; it recognizes the value of connected and circular thinking and respects planetary boundaries; it knows that it's wrong to wait for the consumer to instigate sustainable products and practices and embraces its role as citizen in society; and it recognizes that without appropriate decision architecture and inclusive, collaborative working, its leaders will make irresponsible decisions.

We don't underestimate the challenges in aligning and connecting all these different dots into a coherent whole. Big businesses that pioneered Global Goals-based strategies, such as Danone and Unilever, have already faced high-profile pushbacks from activist investors concerned that sustainability was being used as an excuse for lower earnings and potential mismanagement.[1] Now some business leaders are reportedly reluctant to jump wholeheartedly into purpose-led business models for fear of similar backlashes from stakeholders.[2] But these contradictions and potential conflicts were always an inherent part of being a responsible business that pursues both purpose and profit, while also encouraging stakeholder scrutiny and collaboration. Of course it won't be easy.

Which is why it's so important to hang on to the fundamental principles of responsible business, set out in our 15-point manifesto, to guide you and prevent the damaging myths that still dominate business thinking from creeping back in. Together with the Global Goals, they should help you and your stakeholders reimagine a responsible version of your business and ask the right questions of each other. In the spirit of our arguments, we don't want these points to become dogma or myths in themselves, but rather to help frame any future dialogues between business, society and nature. Please make use of them and all the other tools and ideas in this book to set out and further your journey towards responsibility and sustainability. There really is no business more urgent.

THE RESPONSIBLE BUSINESS MANIFESTO

1. Make profits in pursuit of purpose rather than maximizing profits.
2. Choose whether to grow or not and minimize any damage of expansion.
3. Balance the interests of all stakeholders and ecosystems, not just of the owners.
4. Use performance metrics that accurately measure impact and align with the Global Goals.
5. Be fully transparent by using open-access reporting based on the Global Goals.
6. Use technology, including AI, to help avoid triggering unforeseen tipping points in our ecosystems.
7. Respect planetary boundaries and seek collaborative, circular solutions.
8. Work collectively to build society and nature's resilience and avoid systemic risks.
9. Understand the systemic nature of any problem to find its most effective solution.
10. Give consumers clear and trusted information to enable responsible choices.
11. Value the trust and support of the people you depend on.
12. Use your privilege to enhance society and nature.
13. Don't reward or incentivize irresponsible behaviour.
14. Create an inclusive culture that respects the dignity of staff and stakeholders.
15. Prioritize the sustainability of the planet over your business.

Appendix 1:
Get to Know Your Global Goals

It's worth taking a little time to familiarize yourself with the 17 Global Goals and how they relate to your business mission, purpose, vision, values and strategy. A good way to start this process is to play a Global Goals game such as the one developed by the Institute of Chartered Accountants in England and Wales (ICAEW, see https://gamethegoals.com). Getting to know what they are about helps to domesticate them from the language of international conventions into everyday business activities. The Global Goals can be grouped in many different ways, but it is useful to think of them in three clusters: economic, societal and planetary.

As you read down this list, you will realize what you are already contributing to each goal, and it is likely that many are already part of your business mission, purpose or values. As you read each one, think about your products or services, your supply chain, your sites, your logistics, your activities, your influence and your potential. Initially, some will jump out as directly connected to your business and others will seem harder to connect with what you do. But remember that in the near future, your ability to create value will be determined by your contribution to these goals.

Economic Goals

7. Ensure access to affordable, reliable, sustainable and modern energy for all.
8. Promote sustained, inclusive and sustainable economic growth, full and productive employment and decent work for all.
9. Build resilient infrastructure, promote inclusive and sustainable industrialization and foster innovation.
12. Ensure sustainable consumption and production patterns.

Societal Goals

1. End poverty in all its forms everywhere.
2. End hunger, achieve food security and improved nutrition and promote sustainable agriculture.
3. Ensure healthy lives and promote wellbeing for all at all ages.
4. Ensure inclusive and equitable quality education and promote life-long learning opportunities for all.
5. Achieve gender equality and empower all women and girls.
10. Reduce inequality within and among countries.
11. Make cities and human settlements inclusive, safe, resilient and sustainable.
16. Promote peaceful and inclusive societies for sustainable development, provide access to justice for all and build effective, accountable and inclusive institutions at all levels.
17. Strengthen the means of implementation and revitalize the global partnership for sustainable development.

Planetary Goals

6. Ensure availability and sustainable management of water and sanitation for all.
13. Take urgent action to combat climate change and its impacts.
14. Conserve and sustainably use the oceans, seas and marine resources for sustainable development.
15. Protect, restore and promote sustainable use of terrestrial ecosystems, sustainably manage forests, combat desertification, and halt and reverse land degradation and halt biodiversity loss.

After you have read through this list, take your business mission, purpose, values and strategy documents and read them through, ticking off the connections and looking for gaps and possibilities. Also look for any accreditations, pledges, certification schemes, policies and labels your business has, and begin to join the dots between those and the Global Goals. Don't be disheartened if you don't feel you can solve these grand challenges. Rather, think about what you can do to make a difference, no matter how small.

Appendix 2:
Connecting Purpose with the Global Goals and Systems that Underpin Them

The Global Goals represent an optimal configuration of the different systems that impact all of our lives. Businesses are familiar with these systems as they engage with them on a daily basis. The systems aren't new, it's just the outcomes of these systems that are. So, to achieve the Global Goals, these formal systems and how they operate need to be reformed, which include health systems, education systems, welfare systems, transportation systems, legal systems, taxation systems, international trade systems, market systems, environmental protection systems and so on. They also include more informal systems such as cultural values, customs, habits, religious values, respect for nature, charities and so on.

Businesses need to reflect on how their actions impact on the different Global Goals at this systemic level. For example, a company impacts positively and negatively on levels and distribution of poverty through its remuneration practices, employment practices, procurement practices, pricing policies, training opportunities, taxation, scholarships or corporate philanthropy. Decisions in respect of these practices can also be seen to impact other Global Goals, such as zero hunger (Global Goal 2), gender equality (Global Goal 5) or economic growth and decent work (Global Goal 8), whereas decisions on product design, where to locate operations, logistics and raw material sourcing affect and are affected by the systems underpinning Global Goals such as 11, 12, 13, 14, 15 and 16.

The following is a synthetic purpose statement derived from several leading financial institutions. All of these phrases are drawn from real life and demonstrate how contemporary businesses' purpose connects to the Global Goals.

Purpose statement

We create innovative financial products that make a positive difference to the lives of individual customers, their families and communities, helping to build a global economy that protects human rights, enhances quality of life and has a beneficial rather than a negative impact on the natural environment.

Purpose statement with links to Global Goals

We create innovative financial products (Global Goals 9 and 12) that make a positive difference to the lives of our customers, their families and communities (Global Goals 11, 12, 16 and 17), helping to build a global economy (Global Goals 8 and 9) that protects human rights (Global Goals 3, 4, 5 and 10), enhances quality of life (Global Goals 1, 2 and 8) and has a beneficial rather than a negative impact on the natural environment (Global Goals 6, 7, 13, 14 and 15).

Appendix 3:
The Resilience Assessment
Workbook

Resilience is a phrase whose time seems to have come. However, its ubiquitous use seems to lack a solid definition. It's hard to nail down what others mean by 'resilience' or how it can be usefully put into practice, but resilience is generally understood as the level of disturbance a system can absorb without shifting to a different configuration. It's possible for an institution to appear resilient yet still be morally problematic or socially irresponsible – for example North Korea. This book argues that resilience means that resolving a specific problem should not compromise the resilience and integrity of the system as a whole.

Valuable lessons for businesses can be learned from the governance of natural resource systems that deliver environmental benefits to human wellbeing while maintaining the sustainability of other interconnected systems. And the most effective strategies for building business resilience are those that understand where the vulnerabilities and opportunities for changes in an unsustainable system configuration are, as a precursor to identifying possible points of leverage where they can intervene and have the most transformational impact.

Resilience needs businesses to consider themselves simultaneously dependent on the state of multiple interconnected systems and able to control some of the intersections between these interconnected systems, while also providing benefits to, and negatively impacting on, other systems. At any point in time, each business is managing a unique configuration of dependencies, vulnerabilities, resource deployment, internal impacts and external consequences, and accounting for these relationships to a multitude of different governing institutions, each with a range of intervention powers, rewards and sanctions.

A coalition of world-leading research centres, called the Resilience Alliance, has produced a Resilience Assessment Workbook with a variety of methods informed by innovative approaches to resource management (available at www.resalliance.org/resilience-assessment and summarized below). There is much for business leaders to learn from this workbook, and much that these resilience researchers can also learn from responsible business.

Appendix 4:
Carbon Scoping

One area where systemic thinking is still often surprisingly absent is in carbon emissions. Despite carbon neutrality and going 'net zero' being among the most prominent sustainability targets for many responsible businesses, it's striking how many businesses are unclear about what constitutes greenhouse gases (GHGs), how to properly measure them and what their social impacts are. This lack of carbon literacy can lead to an oversimplistic understanding of the issue and seriously undermine genuine efforts by business to address it.

For instance, carbon emissions aren't just a measure of carbon dioxide (CO_2) but of the whole cocktail of chemicals that make up GHGs, which exacerbate global warming and climate change. Two of them, methane and sulphur hexafluoride, are 25 times and 22,800 times more damaging than CO_2 respectively. So you can see how important it is for business to identify these extreme gases and eliminate them as well as CO_2.

And when it comes to measuring, our research has found widespread unawareness among business leaders of the different ways to account for carbon emissions and how to interpret them. The gold standard is the Greenhouse Gas Protocol methodology, which divides up and reports emissions in four different categories – or 'scopes' – that represent different stages of the entire business value chain.

For most businesses, scope 2 emissions from energy are the most accurately accounted for since they are purchased from a sector that is well established at measuring its carbon footprint, whereas scope 3 downstream emissions, being the most removed from a business's direct control and oversight, are the least accurately measured. But it's this area that will be most important to reduce if a company wants to achieve net zero status. Because, unlike the less stringent, internationally recognized standard of carbon neutrality, PAS 2060, scope 3 emissions are included in net zero measurements and only certified methods of greenhouse gas removal are allowed as offsets.

It's also important businesses understand how different actions will impact on these scopes in both the short and long term – building an on-site wind farm, for example, will initially increase upstream carbon emissions (scope 3 upstream) involved in its manufacture and construction. Over subsequent

Scope	Definition	Examples of reduction activities
1	Direct emissions from the business's sources	Investing in lower carbon assets
2	Emissions from generation of purchased electricity, gas (based on volume purchased)	Reducing energy use, producing own renewable energy, changing to low carbon supplier
3 upstream (pre-sale)	Goods and services from supply chain, capital goods, fuel, transport and distribution, waste from operations, business travel, employee commuting, leased assets	Buying lower carbon alternatives, changing increased public transport, active travel, buying local, water efficiency, video conferences, cutting waste
3 downstream (post-sale)	Transport and distribution, processing sold products, product use, end-of-life treatment, leased assets, franchises, investments	Low carbon distribution, more efficient logistics, design for reuse, reduce electricity consumption, low carbon pension investments

years, purchased energy emissions will decline (scope 2), although direct emissions (scope 1) may increase due to the servicing and maintaining of the wind farm. In this way, responsible businesses should try to avoid making decisions based on one year's total carbon emissions and instead assess the long-term impact of any actions.

Action and overall impact	Total	Short-term scopes				Long-term scopes			
		1	2	3 up	3 down	1	2	3 up	3 down
Build on-site wind farm	↙	↔	↔	↗	↔	↗	↙	↔	↔
Energy efficiency programme	↙	↙	↙	↔	↔	↙	↙	↙	↔
New renewable energy supply	↙	↙	↙	↔	↔	↙	↙	↔	↔
Low carbon product redesign	↙	↔	↙	↙	↙	↔	↙	↙	↙
Buy from local suppliers	↙	↔	↔	↙	↔	↔	↔	↙	↔
Reduce plastic packaging	↙	↔	↔	↙	↙	↔	↔	↙	↙
Buy low emission delivery vans	↙	↔	↔	↗	↙	↔	↔	↔	↙

Breaking down and measuring a business's carbon emissions across its whole value chain like this – from resources, investments and procurement to productivity, logistics and product design and marketing – is a really helpful way of translating the seemingly insurmountable problem of climate change into normal business decision-making. Although getting to net zero is likely to be a long-term journey, every bit of carbon not emitted helps contribute to the Global Goal of climate action and dramatic reductions can be achieved quicker than you might expect.

Further Reading

Below is a selection of key books, research papers and resources – divided by topic – that have inspired the ideas and theories in this book, and helped constitute a science of responsible business.

Responsible business

Aras, G. and Crowther, D. (2009) *The Durable Corporation*, Farnham: Gower Publishing.

Brammer, S.J. and Pavelin, S. (2006) 'Corporate reputation and social performance: The importance of fit', *Journal of Management Studies*, 43(3), 435–55.

Business in the Community (2017) 'The responsible business map', www.bitc.org.uk/what-responsible-business (accessed 25 February 2019).

Carroll, A.B. (1991) 'The pyramid of corporate social responsibility: Toward the moral management of organizational stakeholders', *Business Horizons*, 34(4), 39–48.

Claydon, J. (2011) 'A new direction for CSR: The shortcomings of previous CSR models and the rationale for a new model', *Social Responsibility Journal*, 7(3), 405–20.

Du, S., Bhattacharya, C.B. and Sen, S. (2010) 'Maximizing business returns to corporate social responsibility (CSR): The role of CSR communication', *International Journal of Management Reviews*, 12(1), 8–19.

Elkington, J. (1994) 'Toward the sustainable corporation: Win-win-win business strategies for sustainable development', *California Management Review*, 36, 90–100.

Freeman, R.E. (1984) *Strategic Management: A Stakeholder Approach*, London: Pitman Publishing.

Hill Collins, P. and Bilge, S. (2020) *Intersectionality* (2nd edn), Cambridge: Polity Press.

Lehmann, M., Toh, I., Christensen, P. and Ma, R. (2010) 'Responsible leadership? Development of CSR at Danfoss, Denmark', *Corporate Social Responsibility and Environmental Management*, 17(3), 153–68.

Levitt, T. (2017) *The Company Citizen: Good for Business, Planet, Nation and Community*, London: Routledge.

Oreskes, N. and Conway, E.M. (2010) *Merchants of Doubt: How a Handful of Scientists Obscured the Truth on Issues from Tobacco Smoke to Global Warming*, London: Bloomsbury.

Porter, M.E. and Kramer, M.R. (2011) 'Creating shared value', *Harvard Business Review*, 89(1–2), 62–77.

Sachs, J. (2018) *Unsafe Thinking: How to be Creative and Bold When You Need It*, London: Random House Business.

SRC (Stockholm Resilience Centre) (2016) 'Contributions to Agenda 2030', www.stockholmresilience.org/research/research-news/2017-02-28-contributions-to-agenda-2030.html (accessed 27 February 2019).

Susskind, R. and Susskind, D. (2015) *The Future of the Professions: How Technology Will Transform the Work of Human Experts*, Oxford: Oxford University Press.

Visser, W. (2010) 'CSR 2.0: The Evolution and Revolution of Corporate Social Responsibility', in M. Pohl and N. Tolhurst (eds) *Responsible Business: How to Manage a CSR Strategy Successfully* (pp 311–28), Chichester: Wiley.

Wahba, H. (2008) 'Does the market value corporate environmental responsibility? An empirical examination', *Corporate Social Responsibility and Environmental Management*, 15(1), 89–99.

Welford, R., Chan, C. and Man, M. (2007) 'Priorities of corporate social responsibility: A survey of businesses and their stakeholders', *Corporate Social Responsibility and Environmental Management*, 15(1), 52–62.

Retail and consumerism

Bowd, R., Bowd, L. and Harris, P. (2006) 'Communicating corporate social responsibility: An exploratory case study of a major UK retail centre', *Journal of Public Affairs*, 6, 147–55.

Hultman, J. and Elg, U. (2018) 'Developing CSR in retail–supplier relationships: A stakeholder interaction approach', *The International Review of Retail, Distribution and Consumer Research*, 28(4), 339–59.

Marin, L. and Ruiz, S. (2007) '"I need you too!" Corporate identity attractiveness for consumers and the role of social responsibility', *Journal of Business Ethics*, 71, 245–60.

Morsing, M. and Roepstorff, A. (2015) 'CSR as corporate political activity: Observations on IKEA's CSR identity–image dynamics', *Journal of Business Ethics*, 128, 395–409.

Pomering, A. and Dolnicar, S. (2009) 'Assessing the prerequisite of successful CSR implementation: Are consumers aware of CSR initiatives?', *Journal of Business Ethics*, 85, 285–301.

Sarvaiya, H., Eweje, G. and Arrowsmith, J. (2018) 'The roles of HRM in CSR: Strategic partnership or operational support?', *Journal of Business Ethics*, 153, 825–37.

Utgård, J. (2018) 'Retail chains' corporate social responsibility communication', *Journal of Business Ethics*, 147, 385–400.

Ecology and sustainability

Castree, N. (2013) *Making Sense of Nature*, London: Routledge.

Cronon, W. (1992) *Nature's Metropolis*, New York: W.W. Norton.

Kohn, E. (2013) *How Forests Think*, Berkeley, CA: University of California Press.

Resilience Alliance (no date) *Resilience Assessment Workbook*, www.resalliance. org/resilience-assessment (accessed 9 April 2021).

Tsing, A. (2015) *The Mushroom at the End of the World*, Princeton, NJ: Princeton University Press.

Walker, B., Salt, D. and Reid, W. (2006) *Resilience Thinking: Sustaining Ecosystems and People in a Changing World*, Washington, DC: Island Press.

Wohlleben, P. (2015) *The Hidden Life of Trees*, London: William Collins.

Society and psychology

Akala (2018) *Natives*, London: Two Roads.

Burnett, D. (2017) *The Idiot Brain: A Neuroscientist Explains What Your Head Is Really Up To*, London: Guardian Faber Publishing.

Joy, M. (2019) *Powerarchy*, San Francisco, CA: Berrett-Koehler Publishers.

King, M.P. (2020) *The Fix*, New York: Simon & Schuster.

McGarvey, D. (2017) *Poverty Safari*, London: Pan Macmillan.

Pink, D. (2009) *Drive: The Surprising Truth About What Motivates Us*, New York: Riverhead Books.

Storr, W. (2019) *The Science of Storytelling*, London: William Collins.

Politics and economics

Karpik, L. (2010) *Valuing the Unique: The Economics of Singularities*, Princeton, NJ: Princeton University Press.

Raworth, K. (2017) *Doughnut Economics: Seven Ways to Think Like a 21st-Century Economist*, White River Junction, VT: Chelsea Green Publishing.

Stiglitz. J. (2019) *People, Power and Profits*, London: Penguin.

Future studies

De Cremer, D. (2020) *Leadership by Algorithm: Who Leads and Who Follows in the AI Era?*, Petersfield: Harriman House.

Harari, Y.N. (2016) *Homo Deus: A Brief History of Tomorrow*, New York: HarperCollins.

Kelly, K. (2016) *The Inevitable: Understanding the 12 Technological Forces that Will Shape Our Future*, New York: Viking Press.

Lovelock, J. (2019) *Novacene: The Coming Age of Hyperintelligence*, London: Penguin.

Tetlock, P. and Gardner, D. (2015) *Superforecasting: The Art and Science of Prediction*, New York: Crown Publishers.

Science and knowledge

Beck, U. (1998) *World at Risk*, Hoboken, NJ: Wiley.

Fuller, S. (2018) *Post Truth: Knowledge as a Power Game*, London: Anthem Press.

Rosling, H. (2018) *Factfulness: Ten Reasons We're Wrong About The World – And Why Things Are Better Than You Think*, London: Sceptre.

Glossary

AI (artificial intelligence)   Uses algorithmic programming, modelling and machine learning to automate human tasks, such as visual perception, speech recognition and decision-making.

Behavioural economics   The study of the effects of psychology on decisions by consumers and businesses, and how they contradict traditional economic thinking around consumer sovereignty and the profit motive.

Buycotts   Deliberately shopping at ethical companies to support responsible business practices; often done in conjunction with a consumer boycott of unethical firms.

Carbon footprint   The amount of carbon dioxide released into the atmosphere as a result of a business's activities. Can include other greenhouse gas emissions and extend across supply chains and secondary operations.

CAS (complex adaptive system) theory   Sees the world as a series of systems with a large number of components or agents that interact and adapt or learn from each other, such as climate change and natural ecosystems.

Circular economy   Or circularity, a model of production and consumption that aims to eliminate waste and pollution by regenerating and reusing as many materials as possible, rejecting the business practices of 'make-take-waste' and end-of-life for products, and instead working with natural ecosystems to minimize impact and aid their restoration.

Citizen scientist   Any member of the general public who helps collect and analyse data as part of a collaborative project with professional scientists.

Closed-loop solution   Any strategy that addresses or takes ownership of the full circularity of a company's products and operations, from extraction of raw materials to the disposal, recycling and reuse of unwanted products.

Community ownership   A business owned or run by a community, often as a legally designated 'community asset' in the UK.

Consumer sovereignty   An economic concept that sees the consumer as an entirely rational and self-interested operator, who is the best judge of their own welfare and is the controlling power of what goods and services are produced.

CSR (corporate social responsibility)   Also known as 'corporate citizenship', CSR is the idea that companies should be accountable to their stakeholders and wider society for the impacts of their operations. It's generally considered to be an outdated model that offsets irresponsible activities through philanthropic projects, rather than incorporating responsibility into everyday strategy and operations, such as the responsible business model.

ESG (environmental, social and governance)   Factors that are used to measure the sustainability and social impact of a company or investment.

Externalities   A cost or benefit caused by a business that isn't financially accounted for, which are usually social or environmental impacts.

Financialization   The increasing dominance of the financial sector in Western economies since the 1980s, and the resulting marketization of every aspect of society and the environment for profit.

Global Goals   The United Nation's 17 Sustainable Development Goals.

Greenwashing   The superficial promotion of green values by a company without any substantive changes to their 'business-as-usual' activities, in order to boost their commercial appeal and appear more environmental or ethical to their customers and stakeholders. Purpose-washing and woke-washing have similar meanings.

Intersectionality   The interconnected nature of business, society and the environment, which means any issue has multiple dimensions that intersect. Traditionally, intersectionality was used to describe the overlapping social categories of race, class, sexuality and gender, but it is expanded in this book to include how the 17 Global Goals and socio-ecological systems intersect too.

Net zero   Or carbon neutrality, is the idea that a business offsets or sequesters as much carbon dioxide as it produces in emissions from its operations. How those total emissions are measured is still a source of debate.

Purpose   Or social purpose, is the reason a business exists and adds value to society beyond just making money and gives meaning to its activities, employees and stakeholders.

Resilience   The level of disturbance a system can absorb without shifting to a different, often hostile or undesirable, configuration. A responsible business should try to avoid compromising the resilience and integrity of the planet's many life support systems as a whole.

Responsible business   A company that judges its purpose and practices against all of the Global Goals, embedding them in its business strategy and operations. Sustainability is just one vital part of being a responsible business.

Social contract   In business, this is the convention that companies operate with the consent of society according to obligations and rules that benefit everyone. The contract can be formally written and agreed as part of a company's charter, but is usually informal and subject to changing public opinion.

Social value   The benefits to the wellbeing of society and the environment from a company's activities beyond just its financial value.

Socio–ecological system   A concept that refutes any delineation between society and nature, seeing the world as an interaction between humans and the natural world. Any human activity, such as business, is done within this overarching complex and adaptive system (CAS).

SRI (socially responsible investing)   Being ethically conscious about the social impacts of a company's activities. This usually means eschewing investments in firms involved in alcohol, tobacco, pornography, arms and animal testing as standard, but can also involve investors working with firms to improve their behaviour and social or environmental impacts.

Stakeholder   Anyone (person, animal or entity, such as government) that has an interest in a company or is affected by its activities, including staff, suppliers, investors, customers and their wider communities and ecosystems.

Sustainability   Meeting the needs of society without compromising the planet's ability to replenish itself or function properly. More specifically in business, the concept of balancing people, planet and profit in a way that benefits all three.

System 1 and System 2 thinking   Conceived by psychologist Daniel Kahneman to describe the emotional and rational ways the mind processes information. System 1 thinking is fast, automatic and intuitive; System 2 is slower and more analytical.

Value chain   A business model that describes the full range of activities needed to create a product or service, including all stakeholders and the full life cycle of a product or process.

Endnotes

Joining the Dots

1. See www.un.org/sustainabledevelopment
2. Wildhearts (2020).
3. Interface (2019).
4. 'The 5 Whys' model has proved remarkably powerful across history and in organizations as varied as the UK National Health Service (NHS), Toyota and many universities, where its use in seminars yields impressive results after the third 'why?'
5. This involved releasing young Atlantic salmon into the sea, but using a mixture of static lights, bubbles and robot 'salmon-dogs' to keep track of them and herd them back when needed. This would replace offshore salmon cages, and avoid any artificial feeding or the need for medical treatment.
6. From Chapter 8 of the novel.
7. Deane (2020).
8. Taylor (2021).

Myth 1: A Successful Business Is a Growing and Profitable One

1. Apple history derived from Flannelly (2014); Wall Street Survivor (2014); Lee (2015).
2. Apple values quoted from Dormehl (2020).
3. Frasers Group and Wetherspoons, from *Management Today* (2020).
4. See www.euractiv.com/section/aviation/news/coronavirus-redraws-battle-lines-on-airline-emissions
5. The idea of social values being complex, fluid and dynamic, unlike social impacts, is explored in Potter (2012).
6. Bhattacharjee and Dana (2017).
7. Makower (2016).
8. Interface (2019).
9. Quoted in Dean (2007).
10. Makower (2016).
11. Gies (2011).
12. Anderson (2005).
13. See NPR (2019).
14. Sources for the brief history of CSR and corporations that follows include https://accp.org/resources/csr-resources/accp-insights-blog/corporate-social-responsibility-brief-history; Asbury and Ball (2016: Chapter 2); Zhang et al (2017: Chapter 2); and *New Internationalist* (2002).
15. See www.history.co.uk/history-of-death/trends-in-death
16. Rao (1973).

[17] These are the Rochdale Principles of cooperatives in the UK, which survive in the current International Co-operative Alliance principles: www.ica.coop/en/cooperatives/cooperative-identity

[18] The idea of a social contract extends right back to the days of Plato and the realization that justice doesn't occur naturally or through divine intervention but by mutual agreement of laws between people. The idea was popularized during the 17th and 18th centuries by Enlightenment philosophers such as Hobbes and Rousseau, who argued that individuals should surrender some of their freedoms to state authority in exchange for the protection of their remaining rights.

[19] Ormiston (2013).

[20] Cofino (2013).

[21] Cofino (2012).

[22] Marchal (2008).

[23] Atkins (2020).

[24] Friedman (2002: 133).

[25] Schwab (2019).

[26] Domini (2020).

[27] See the definition of 'social enterprises' at www.socialenterprise.org.uk/what-is-it-all-about

[28] See www.swissinfo.ch/eng/corporate-offenders-in-the-dock/5663826

[29] Taylor and Watts (2019).

[30] Behar (2020).

[31] Anderson (2005).

[32] Co-operatives UK (2015: 8).

[33] Jones (2019).

[34] See www.anglianwater.co.uk/about-us/our-purpose

[35] Anglian Water (2019: 50).

[36] See www.anglianwater.co.uk/news/anglian-water-honoured-with-queens-award-for-enterprise-sustainable-development

[37] https://businessinsider.mx/apple-knew-a-supplier-was-using-child-labor-but-took-3-years-to-fully-cut-ties-despite-the-companys-promises-to-hold-itself-to-the-highest-standards-report-says; see also Bergen (2021).

[38] Morrison (2017).

[39] UNGSII (2019).

[40] Oxfam (2017: 23).

[41] Nieuwenkamp (2016).

[42] See www.wildlifetrusts.org/citizen-science

[43] Ki-moon (2015).

Myth 2: Only Manage What You Can Measure

[1] See Francis (2020).

[2] See www.respect.international/products-of-slavery-map

[3] See www.sedex.com

[4] Nieuwenkamp (2016).

[5] See www.ethicalbiotrade.org/leadingvoices/leontino-balbo

[6] See www.bipiz.org/en/csr-best-practices/natives-success-story-15-000-ha-of-sugar-cane-30-more-profitable-thanks-to-organic-culture.html

[7] See www.coop.co.uk/communities?_ga=2.114288911.966838409.1601983905-1109501611.1601983905

[8] See https://communitywellbeing.coop.co.uk

[9] Frandsen (2009).

10 Sullivan (2019).

11 This paradox of needing financial values for political and commercial decision-making processes, yet recognizing the impossibility of a perfect single measure of nature, is central to *The Dasgupta Review* into the economics of biodiversity, published in February 2021 (HM Treasury, 2021).

12 HM Government (2019: 15).

13 Business in the Community (2020a).

14 See www.pwc.com/gx/en/services/sustainability/sustainable-development-goals/sdg-challenge-2019.html

15 Russell and Thomson (2009).

16 See https://nationalperformance.gov.scot

17 Bates (2015b).

18 See www.ungsii.org/research

19 Govindarajan et al (2018).

20 Atkins (2020).

21 Biehl et al (2020).

22 See www.worldwidegeneration.co/g17eco

23 Betley (2019).

24 Yankelovich (1972).

25 Yankelovich (1972: 286).

26 Andriani (2020).

27 Wildhearts (2020).

28 See www.msci.com/index-carbon-footprint-metrics

29 Brander (2017).

30 Koshy (2018).

31 Thomson and Cooper (2018).

32 Denedo et al (2018).

33 Buller (2020).

34 Chami et al (2019).

35 Chenet et al (2020).

36 Chenet et al (2020).

37 See https://applyingresilience.org/en/principle-3

38 Rosling (2018)

39 Titley (2017).

40 Buis (2019).

41 Haines-Young et al (2006).

42 Carpenter et al (2005).

43 See www.reutersevents.com/supplychain/technology/estee-lauder-uses-blockchain-boost-supply-chain-traceability

44 Bebbington et al (2020).

45 George (2020).

46 Mace (2020).

47 See https://tcocertified.com/pressrelease/tco-certified-generation-8-now-open-for-application

48 See www.wbcsd.org/Overview/News-Insights/General/News/Can-sustainable-business-really-save-the-world

Myth 3: Laser-Like Focus Gets Results

1 See www.bbc.co.uk/mediacentre/latestnews/2018/plastics-watch

2 Aldous (2018).

3   See https://plasticoceans.org/the-facts

4   See https://plasticoceans.org/the-facts

5   ITV News (2018).

6   See www.greenpeace.org.uk/news/supermarket-plastic-rises-above-900000-tonnes-per-year-despite-plastic-reduction-pledges

7   Stanislaus (2018). Organic cotton still has the same large water footprint as non-organic cotton, however.

8   Allen (2018).

9   BioMed Central (2015).

10 Rosling (2018: 186).

11 Lautenbach et al (2012).

12 Hallmann et al (2017).

13 Genersch (2010).

14 Schroeder (2011).

15 Biehl and Macpherson (2016)

16 Correlation is a measurable pattern between different sets of observations, whereas causation is when one event can be shown to be the direct consequence of another. Causation cannot be determined statistically but needs some form of experimentation. In German villages of old, the number of babies born in a year statistically correlated with the number of storks in that village. The more storks, the more babies. Of course, the number of storks was related to the number of nesting sites on chimneys. More houses = more chimneys, storks, people and babies. The storks didn't directly *cause* babies.

17 See www.buzzaboutbees.net/German-Bee-Monitoring-Project.html

18 Bates (2015c).

19 Oreskes and Conway (2010).

20 See www.overshootday.org/newsroom/country-overshoot-days

21 Business in the Community (2020b: 10).

22 Developed by Kate Raworth in the Oxfam paper *A Safe and Just Space for Humanity* and elaborated on in her 2017 book *Doughnut Economics: Seven Ways to Think Like a 21st-Century Economist.*

23 Williams et al (2019).

24 See John Evelyn's *Fumifugium or, The inconveniencie of the aer and smoak of London* (1661), considered the seminal modern text on environmental pollution.

25 de los Reyes and Scholz (2019).

26 See www.seabos.org

27 The idea of keystone actors was developed by the Stockholm Resilience Centre and refers to a human or non-human element of a system that has a disproportionate influence on the structure and functioning of the systems in which they operate. The COVID-19 virus is an example of a contemporary non-human keystone actor. The World Benchmarking Alliance has developed five principles for identifying keystone businesses that have the power to trigger seven critical transformations. See World Benchmarking Alliance (2019).

28 Thamotheram and Biehl (2018).

29 See www.benjerry.com/about-us/media-center/dismantle-white-supremacy

30 See www.ceres.org/about-us

31 See www.refugeecouncil.org.uk/get-involved/support-us-through-your-company/employment-partnerships

32 Willard (2019).

33 Business in the Community (2019: 28).

34 See www.interface.com/APAC/en-AU/about/press-room/Carbon-Storing-Tile-Release-en_AU

35 Beuret (2019).

36   See www.foeeurope.org/time-stop-dumping-plastic-waste-global-south-290419
37   Gibbens (2019).
38   Penny (2020).
39   Business in the Community (2019: 27).
40   Business in the Community (2020a: 24).
41   See www.nationalgrid.com/uk/electricity-transmission/Keeping-36-million-electric-vehicles-on-the-mov
42   Bonsu (2020).
43   See www.ukbic.co.uk
44   Domenech and Davies (2011).
45   Sakr et al (2011).
46   See WHO (2006).
47   BBC News (2019).
48   Griffiths (2019).
49   See https://wwf.panda.org/our_ambition/wwf_together_possible/managing_the_forest_factory
50   Business in the Community (2020a: 26).
51   See www.toyotauk.com/environment/biodiversity.html
52   See https://biomimicry.net/what-we-do/speakers-bureau
53   King (2015); Mathew (2018).
54   Mori et al (2012).

Myth 4: The Consumer Is Always Right

1   Devinney (2011). Interestingly, Marylyn Carrigan revisited the topic in 2017 for the *Journal of Consumer Ethics*, and concluded that 'the ethical consumer in 2017 appears as mythical as ever'.
2   Townsend (2018).
3   The Goodlife Goals were shaped through a multi-stakeholder collaboration between Futerra and the 10YFP (10 Year Framework of Programmes) on Sustainable Lifestyles and Education Programme, co-led by the governments of Sweden and Japan, represented by the Stockholm Environment Institute (SEI) and the Institute for Global Environmental Strategies (IGES), with UN Environment, UNESCO and WBCSD. See https://sdghub.com/goodlifegoals
4   Pailhès et al (2020).
5   This can be contrasted with the Dunning–Kruger effect, whereby the less you know about a topic, the more certain you are that you're right. Fortunately, the vast majority of people exist somewhere in the middle of these two polar opposites.
6   See https://impact.ref.ac.uk/casestudies/CaseStudy.aspx?Id=21769
7   Emrich et al (2017).
8   Muller et al (2019).
9   Vlaeminck et al (2014).
10   Liu et al (2015).
11   Cho (2014).
12   Dekhili (2014).
13   Darnall et al (2018).
14   Georgakopoulos and Thomson (2005).
15   Hainmueller et al (2015).
16   See Bauer et al (2013); Husted et al (2014).
17   Coburn (2019).
18   Bates (2015a).

19 See https://about.iceland.co.uk/environment

20 FSC-Watch (2020).

21 See www.ikea.com/gb/en/this-is-ikea/about-us/wood-a-material-with-many-qualities-pubd4deffde

22 Grunert et al (2014).

23 Hilger (2019).

24 Frank and Brock (2018).

25 See https://giki.earth

26 Peachey (2019).

27 See www.findgreen.co

28 See www.overshootday.org/newsroom/country-overshoot-days

29 Carrington (2020).

30 See https://eatforum.org/eat-lancet-commission

31 Longo et al (2017).

32 Hollingworth and Barker (2019).

33 This table contains a range of heuristics but there are many more detailed in informative and entertaining books, such as Dan Pink's *Drive*, Dean Burnett's *The Idiot Brain*, Will Storr's *The Science of Storytelling*, Hans Rosling's *Factfulness* and Jonah Sachs' *Unsafe Thinking*.

34 DeMarree et al (2014).

35 Petty et al (2002).

36 Briñol et al (2018).

37 Goenka and van Osselaer (2019).

38 Haidt (2003); Horberg et al (2011).

39 Schwartz (1994).

40 These observations and the adapted basic human values chart are taken from the excellent and insightful *The Common Cause Handbook* (Holmes et al, 2011).

41 Warde (2017: 195).

42 Wrap (2020).

43 Warde (2017: 194).

44 This is the division of social norms that psychologist Robert Cialdini and his associates make between 'descriptive norms' based on individual situational behaviour and 'injunctive norms' based on moral or social approval. See Nicholson (2019).

45 Warde (2017: 197–8).

46 Kroese et al (2015).

47 The Behavioural Insights Team (2015).

48 See www.youtube.com/watch?v=zSiHjMU-MUo

49 See www.youtube.com/watch?v=iynzHWwJXaA

50 See www.activistbrands.com/what-is-brand-activism

51 Dolšak and Prakash (2017); Endres and Panagopoulos (2017).

52 Warde (2017: 203).

53 Singer (2019).

54 Check out the documentary at www.whokilledtheelectriccar.com for how an EV lost the battle to the fossil fuel industry in the 1990s.

55 Knobloch et al (2020).

56 Sovacool et al (2020).

57 European Court of Auditors (2020).

58 Townsend (2018).

59 See www.marketingsociety.com/the-library/2010-ariel-marketing-sustainable-consumption-case-study

60 See www.colgate.com/en-us/everydropcounts

61 Warde (2017: 192).

62 See www.skyoceanrescue.com

63 See www.theunileverfoundry.com

64 Henley (2019).

65 Ro (2020).

66 Carrigan (2017: 14).

67 Graeber (2011).

68 Moreau (2019).

69 Graeber (2019).

70 Hayes (2021).

71 Quoted in Ferber (2020).

72 We believe that Hearts is the only top-flight football club to be named after a novel, *The Heart of Midlothian*, by Walter Scott. Rather aptly, it's a rip-roaring epic involving riots, murder, court cases and political intrigue! Hearts was founded in 1874 and plays its home games in Edinburgh.

73 See www.scotsman.com/news/high-and-lows-vladimir-romanovs-time-hearts-1696357

74 Afterwards, Romanov returned to Lithuania to win the country's equivalent of *Strictly Come Dancing* and subsequently had a failed bite at becoming president. He is currently on the run somewhere in Russia, with an international warrant out for his arrest.

75 At the time of writing, the pledgers have contributed over £11 million to the club.

76 See: www.skysports.com/football/news/11790/12395375/hearts-become-largest-fan-owned-club-in-the-uk-as-ann-budge-transfers-shares-to-foundation-of-hearts

77 Quoted in Thomson et al (2021: forthcoming).

78 See www.oatly.com/int/the-oatly-way

79 Gutierrez (2020).

80 Whitbread (2020).

81 Mukherjee and Althuizen (2020).

82 Victor (2017).

83 Moraes (2020).

84 Vrendenburg (2020).

85 Rhodes (2021: 15).

86 Rhodes (2021: 11).

87 Rhodes (2021: 15).

Myth 5: Irresponsible Decisions Are Made by Irresponsible Leaders

1   Namely Donald Trump and Harry Stonecipher, CEO of Boeing.

2   Lammers et al (2010).

3   Power eliminates inhibition and increases impulsivity: Hirsh et al (2011); reduces fear and increases action: Keltner et al (2003); increases accessibility of your own goals: Guinote (2017); reduces processing: Weick and Guinote (2008); increases distance: Magee and Smith (2013); increases perceived invulnerability: Lammers et al (2011); and increases control: Galinsky et al (2003).

4   Scholl et al (2015).

5   Power increases inclusivity: Chen et al (2004); promotes equality and human rights: Gruenfeld et al (2008); reduces corruption: Overbeck and Park (2001); reduces discrimination: Overbeck and Park (2006); and promotes gender equality: Vescio et al (2003).

6   Briñol et al (2017).

7   Dolšak and Prakash (2020).

8   Haidt and Joseph (2004).

9   Campbell et al (2009).

10 Quoted in Sieck et al (2007).

11 See www.slowfood.org.uk
12 Drummond and Fischhoff (2017).
13 Quoted in Irfan (2017).
14 Hockley (2018).
15 van Vugt and Ronay (2013).
16 Quoted in Morgan et al (2009).
17 Wrzesniewski et al (2014).
18 Kolditz (2014).
19 UN Global Compact (2020: 12).
20 See www.c2ccertified.org/get-certified/product-certification
21 See www.trigema.de/en/company/philosophy
22 Kenway (2020).
23 See www.boohoo.com/page/about-us.html
24 Clark (2020).
25 Whelan (2020).
26 See www.boohooplc.com/sites/boohoo-corp/files/all-documents/result-centre/2020/boohoo-com-plc-annual-report-2020-hyperlink.pdf
27 UN Global Compact (2020: 7).
28 UN Global Compact (2020: 8).
29 Trehan (2018).
30 Aghina et al (2018).
31 Carreira et al (2020).
32 Stern (2020).
33 See https://en.wikipedia.org/wiki/Dunning–Kruger_effect
34 See www.who.int/teams/integrated-health-services/patient-safety/research/safe-surgery/tool-and-resources
35 Beshears and Gino (2015).
36 See https://timeforchange.org/co2-emissions-for-shipping-of-goods
37 See https://exploringyourmind.com/edward-de-bono-six-thinking-hats
38 Beshears and Gino (2015).
39 Kalev et al (2006).
40 See www.bitc.org.uk/race
41 UN Global Compact (2020: 7).
42 UN Global Compact (2020: 13).
43 FareShare (2018); Partridge (2020).
44 Powell-Smith (2020).
45 See www.edelman.com/news-awards/2020-edelman-trust-barometer
46 Tyler (2002).
47 Rhodes (2021: 98–110).
48 Lee (2018).
49 See https://gogetfunding.com/blog-single-update/?blogpre=6243314&single=40332
50 Taylor (2019).
51 See www.youtube.com/watch?v=u6XAPnuFjJc
52 Ghalwash et al (2017).
53 Unless the investors purchased shares in the initial public offering, the company doesn't receive the proceeds of the vast majority of transactions on equity markets. Most of these are trades in second-hand shares and bonds with the money going to the existing owner of the shares. It's very much like the second-hand car market – the car company only gets the money from the first sale and nothing of any future trades.
54 Stern (2020: 15).
55 See www.unglobalcompact.org/what-is-gc/mission/principles

[56] Alpman et al (2020).

[57] Thomson (2018).

[58] Connley (2019).

[59] See www.mckinsey.com/featured-insights/diversity-and-inclusion/diversity-wins-how-inclusion-matters

[60] See www.mckinsey.com/business-functions/organization/our-insights/why-diversity-matters

[61] McCulloch (2018).

[62] Churchill (2019).

[63] Sweet and Shook (2020).

[64] Wilck and Lynch (2018); Merkley et al (2020).

[65] Trehan (2019).

[66] Naqvi (2018).

[67] Malito (2018).

[68] See https://futureoflife.org/ai-principles

[69] See www.bbb.org/globalassets/local-bbbs/council-113/media/smallbusiness/shop-small-biz-infographic.pdf

[70] Grant Thornton (2017: 8).

[71] See www.edelman.com/news-awards/2020-edelman-trust-barometer

[72] UN Global Compact (2020: 17).

[73] Grant Thornton (2017: 14–15).

[74] Dempsey (2012).

[75] Associated Press (2011).

[76] McGrath (2013).

[77] Cooper et al (2020).

[78] UN Global Compact (2020: 12).

[79] See www.kateraworth.com/animations

Do Something

[1] See www.ft.com/content/668d9544-28db-4ad7-9870-1f6671623ac5

[2] Henderson (2020: 123).

References

Aghina, W., Ahlback, K., De Smet, A., Lackey, G., Lurie, M., Muraka, M. and Handscomb, C. (2018) 'The five trademarks of agile organizations', McKinsey & Company, 22 January, www.mckinsey.com/business-functions/organization/our-insights/the-five-trademarks-of-agile-organizations (accessed 20 January 2021).

Aldous, P. (2018) 'Plastic pollution – What was the tipping point?', *Water & Wastewater Treatment*, 20 June, https://wwtonline.co.uk/Blog/plastic-pollution---what-was-the-tipping-point (accessed 19 January 2021).

Allen, T. (2018) 'Food prices must drop in Africa: How can this be achieved?', *OECD Development Matters*, 9 February, https://oecd-development-matters.org/2018/02/09/food-prices-must-drop-in-africa-how-can-this-be-achieved (accessed 19 January 2021).

Alpman, A., Cohen, G. and Murtin, F. (2020) *Social Dialogue in the 2030 Agenda*, www.theglobaldeal.com/news/newsrelease/Social-Dialogue-2030-Agenda-Global-Deal-Thematic-Brief-June-2020.pdf (accessed 20 January 2021).

Anderson, R. (2005) 'On Responsibility in the Private Sector', Keynote speech to Second International Conference on Gross Happiness, www.gpiatlantic.org/conference/proceedings/anderson.htm (accessed 20 January 2021).

Andriani (2020) *Sustainable Development Report 2019*, www.andrianispa.com/en/sustainable-development-report-2019 (accessed 19 January 2021).

Anglian Water (2019) *Annual Integrated Report 2019*, www.anglianwater.co.uk/siteassets/household/about-us/aws-air2019.pdf (accessed 19 January 2021).

Asbury, S. and Ball, R. (2016) *The Practical Guide to Corporate Social Responsibility: Do the Right Thing*, London: Routledge.

Associated Press (2011) 'Toyota extends suspension of Thai auto production', *The San Diego Union-Tribune*, 21 October, www.sandiegouniontribune.com/sdut-toyota-extends-suspension-of-thai-auto-production-2011oct21-story.html (accessed 20 January 2021).

Atkins, B. (2020) 'Demystifying ESG: Its history and current status', *Forbes*, 8 June, www.forbes.com/sites/betsyatkins/2020/06/08/demystifying-esgits-history--current-status/#35fe10dc2cdd (accessed 19 January 2021).

Bates, D. (2015a) 'The chocolate companies on the hunt for a sustainable Easter egg', *The Guardian*, 27 March, www.theguardian.com/sustainable-business/2015/mar/27/chocolate-palm-oil-easter-egg-nestle-mars-lindt-cadbury-ferrero (accessed 19 January 2021).

Bates, D. (2015b) 'The military spy turned sustainability warrior – drones have come of age', *The Guardian*, 20 May, www.theguardian.com/sustainable-business/2015/may/20/drone-technology-military-spy-turned-sustainability-warrior (accessed 19 January 2021).

Bates, D. (2015c) 'Who is winning the PR battle over neonicotinoids?', *The Guardian*, 19 March, www.theguardian.com/sustainable-business/2015/mar/19/pr-battle-neonicotinoids-decling-bee-colonies-food-security (accessed 19 January 2021).

Bauer, H.H., Heinrich, D. and Schäfer, D.B. (2013) 'The effects of organic labels on global, local, and private brands: More hype than substance?', *Journal of Business Research*, 66(8), 1035–43.

BBC News (2019) 'McDonald's paper straws cannot be recycled', 5 August, www.bbc.co.uk/news/business-49234054 (accessed 19 January 2021).

Bebbington, J., Schneider, T., Stevenson, L. and Fox, A. (2020) 'Fossil fuel reserves and resources reporting and unburnable carbon: Investigating conflicting accounts', *Critical Perspectives on Accounting*, 66.

Behar, A. (2020) 'What does "business with purpose" actually mean?', *Eco-Business*, 29 January, www.eco-business.com/opinion/what-does-business-with-purpose-actually-mean (accessed 19 January 2021).

Behavioural Insights Team, The (2015) *EAST: Four Simple Ways to Apply Behavioural Insights*, www.behaviouralinsights.co.uk/wp-content/uploads/2015/07/BIT-Publication-EAST_FA_WEB.pdf (accessed 19 January 2021).

Bergen, M. (2021) 'Microsoft and Apple wage war on gadget right to repair laws', Bloomberg News, 20 May, www.bnnbloomberg.ca/microsoft-and-apple-wage-war-on-gadget-right-to-repair-laws-1.1606259 (accessed 7 September 2021).

Beshears, J. and Gino, F. (2015) 'Leaders as decision architects', *Harvard Business Review*, May, https://hbr.org/2015/05/leaders-as-decision-architects (accessed 20 January 2021).

Betley, C. (2019) 'Tobacco companies pay billions to compensate for smoking-related illness. Is it enough?', *PBS*, 16 April, www.pbs.org/newshour/health/tobacco-companies-pay-billions-to-compensate-for-smoking-related-illness-is-it-enough (accessed 19 January 2021).

Beuret, N. (2019) 'Emissions inequality – A gulf between global rich and poor', *Social Europe*, 10 April, www.socialeurope.eu/emissions-inequality (accessed 19 January 2021).

Bhattacharjee, A. and Dana, J. (2017) 'People think companies can't do good and make money. Can companies prove them wrong?', *Harvard Business Review*, 28 November, https://hbr.org/2017/11/people-think-companies-cant-do-good-and-make-money-can-companies-prove-them-wrong (accessed 20 January 2021).

Biehl, C.F. and Macpherson, M.N. (2016) 'Bees and Accountability in Germany', in J.F. Atkins and B. Atkins (eds) *The Business of Bees* (pp 277–330), Sheffield: Greenleaf.

Biehl, C.F., Thomson, I. and Travers, M. (2020) 'Leading viewpoint: Rethinking materiality: the missing link', *IPE*, November, www.ipe.com/reports/leading-viewpoint-rethinking-materiality-the-missing-link/10048668.article (accessed 9 March 2021).

BioMed Central (2015) 'Two degree Celsius climate change target "utterly inadequate", expert argues', *ScienceDaily*, 27 March, www.sciencedaily.com/releases/2015/03/150327091016.htm (accessed 19 January 2021).

Bonsu, N.O. (2020) 'Towards a circular and low-carbon economy: Insights from the transitioning to electric vehicles and net zero economy', *Journal of Cleaner Production*, 256.

Brander, M. (2017) 'Comparative analysis of attributional corporate greenhouse gas accounting, consequential life cycle assessment, and project/policy level accounting: A bioenergy case study', *Journal of Cleaner Production*, 167, 1401–14.

Briñol, P., Petty, R.E., Durso, G.R.O. and Rucker, D.D. (2017) 'Power and persuasion: Processes by which perceived power can influence evaluative judgments', *Review of General Psychology*, 21(3), 223–41.

Briñol, P., Petty, R., Stavraki, M., Lamprinakos, G., Wagner, B. and Diaz, D. (2018) 'Affective and cognitive validation of thoughts: An appraisal perspective on anger, disgust, surprise, and awe', *Journal of Personality and Social Psychology*, 114(5), 693–718.

Buis, A. (2019) 'A degree of concern: Why global temperatures matter', *Nasa*, 19 June, https://climate.nasa.gov/news/2865/a-degree-of-concern-why-global-temperatures-matter (accessed 19 January 2021).

Buller, A. (2020) 'What's the value of a whale?', *Novara Media*, 16 October, https://novaramedia.com/2020/10/16/whats-the-value-of-a-whale (accessed 19 January 2021).

Business in the Community (2019) *Raising the Bar*, www.bitc.org.uk/report/responsible-business-tracker-insights-raising-the-bar (accessed 17 March 2021).

Business in the Community (2020a) *An Opportunity to Build Back Better*, www.bitc.org.uk/wp-content/uploads/2020/05/BITC-Report-RBTrackerreport2019-2020-webready-May2020.pdf (accessed 20 January 2021).

Business in the Community (2020b) *Lifting the Lid on Waste*, www.bitc. org.uk/wp-content/uploads/2020/03/BITC-Report-Environment-LiftingtheLidonWasteGuideV4-March2020.pdf (accessed 17 March 2021).

Campbell, A., Whitehead, J. and Finkelstein, S. (2009) 'Why good leaders make bad decisions', *Harvard Business Review*, February, https://hbr. org/2009/02/why-good-leaders-make-bad-decisions (accessed 20 January 2021).

Carpenter, S.R., Turner, M.G. and Westley, F. (2005) 'Surrogates for resilience of socio-ecological systems', *Ecosystems*, 8, 941–4.

Carreira, D., Horii, M., Kim, M. and Rocha, A. (2020) 'Organizing for speed: Agile as a means to transformation in Japan', McKinsey & Company, 20 November, www.mckinsey.com/business-functions/organization/our-insights/organizing-for-speed-agile-as-a-means-to-transformation-in-japan (accessed 20 January 2021).

Carrigan, M. (2017) 'Revisiting "The myth of the ethical consumer": Why are we still not ethical shoppers?', *Journal of Consumer Ethics*, 1(1), 11–21.

Carrigan, M. and Attalla, A. (2001) 'The myth of the ethical consumer – Do ethics matter in purchase behaviour?', *Journal of Consumer Marketing*, 18(7), 560–77.

Carrington, D. (2020) 'World's consumption of materials hits record 100bn tonnes a year', *The Guardian*, 22 January, www.theguardian.com/environment/2020/jan/22/worlds-consumption-of-materials-hits-record-100bn-tonnes-a-year (accessed 20 January 2021).

Chami, R., Cosimano, T., Fullenkamp, C. and Oztosun, S. (2019) 'Nature's solution to climate change: A strategy to protect whales can limit greenhouse gases and global warming', *Finance & Development*, 56(4), www. imf.org/external/pubs/ft/fandd/2019/12/natures-solution-to-climate-change-chami.htm#author (accessed 19 January 2021).

Chen, S., Ybarra, O. and Kiefer, A.K. (2004) 'Power and impression formation: The effects of power on the desire for morality and competence information', *Social Cognition*, 22(4), 391–421.

Chenet, H., Ryan-Collins, J. and van Lerven, F. (2020) 'Dealing with the "unknown unknowns": A precautionary approach to financial regulation in the face of climate change', *UCL Institute for Innovation and Public Purpose*, 13 January, https://medium.com/iipp-blog/dealing-with-the-unknown-unknowns-a-precautionary-approach-to-financial-regulation-in-the-face-33e6eedd84ec (accessed 19 January 2021).

Cho, Y. (2014) 'Different shades of green consciousness: The interplay of sustainability labeling and environmental impact on product evaluations', *Journal of Business Ethics*, 128, 73–82.

Churchill, F. (2019) 'Workers call in physically sick to hide mental ill-health, poll reveals', *People Management*, 29 August, www.peoplemanagement.co.uk/news/articles/workers-call-in-physically-sick-hide-mental-ill-health (accessed 20 January 2021).

Clark, J. (2020) 'Major Boohoo shareholders fail to denounce CEO over Leicester factory conditions', *City AM*, 5 October, www.cityam.com/major-boohoo-shareholders-fail-to-denounce-ceo-over-leicester-factory-conditions (accessed 20 January 2021).

Coburn, C. (2019) 'Why industry is going green on the quiet', *The Guardian*, 8 September, www.theguardian.com/science/2019/sep/08/producers-keep-sustainable-practices-secret (accessed 19 January 2021).

Cofino, J. (2012) 'Unilever's Paul Polman: Challenging the corporate status quo', *The Guardian*, 24 April, www.theguardian.com/sustainable-business/paul-polman-unilever-sustainable-living-plan (accessed 20 January 2021).

Cofino, J. (2013) 'Interview: Unilever's Paul Polman on diversity, purpose and profits', *The Guardian*, 2 October, hwww.theguardian.com/sustainable-business/unilver-ceo-paul-polman-purpose-profits (accessed 20 January 2021).

Connley, C. (2019) 'Corporate America's diversity and inclusion efforts are still failing black employees, new report says', *CNBC*, 13 December, www.cnbc.com/2019/12/13/report-corporate-americas-diversity-efforts-fail-black-employees.html (accessed 20 January 2021).

Cooper, S., Babcock, A.F., Loat, A., Neal, P.J., Safferstone, T. and Williamson, S.K. (2020) 'Tone at the top: The board's impact on long-term value', Russell Reynolds Associates, 22 April, www.russellreynolds.com/insights/thought-leadership/tone-at-the-top-the-boards-impact-on-long-term-value (accessed 20 January 2021).

Co-operatives UK (2015) *The co-operative economy 2015*, www.yumpu.com/en/document/read/39880623/co-op-economy-2015 (accessed 19 January 2021).

Darnall, N., Ji, H. and Vázquez-Brust, D.A. (2018) 'Third-party certification, sponsorship, and consumers' ecolabel use', *Journal of Business Ethics*, 150, 953–69.

Dean, C. (2007) 'Executive on a mission: Saving the planet', *The New York Times*, 22 May, www.nytimes.com/2007/05/22/science/earth/22ander.html (accessed 19 January 2021).

Deane, M.T. (2020) 'Top 6 reasons new businesses fail', *Investopedia*, 28 February, www.investopedia.com/financial-edge/1010/top-6-reasons-new-businesses-fail.aspx#:~:text=According%20to%20the%20U.S.%20Bureau,to%2015%20years%20or%20more (accessed 10 August 2021).

De Cremer, D. (2020) *Leadership by Algorithm: Who Leads and Who Follows in the AI Era?*, Petersfield: Harriman House.

Dekhili, S. (2014) 'The influence of the country-of-origin ecological image on ecolabelled product evaluation: An experimental approach to the case of the European eolabel', *Journal of Business Ethics*, 131, 89–106.

de los Reyes, G. and Scholz, M. (2019) 'The limits of the business case for sustainability: Don't count on "Creating Shared Value" to extinguish corporate destruction', *Journal of Cleaner Production*, 221, 785–94.

DeMarree, K.G., Briñol, P. and Petty, R.E. (2014) 'The effects of power on prosocial outcomes: A self-validation analysis', *Journal of Economic Psychology*, 41, 20–30.

Dempsey, C. (2012) 'The map myth of here be dragons', *GIS Lounge*, 21 October, www.gislounge.com/here-be-dragons (accessed 29 March 2021).

Denedo, M., Thomson, I. and Yonekura, A. (2018) 'Accountability, maps and inter-generational equity: Evaluating the Nigerian Oil Spill Monitor', *Public Money and Management*, 38(5), 355–64.

Devinney, T. (2011) 'The myth of the ethical consumer', *The Conversation*, 11 April, https://theconversation.com/the-myth-of-the-ethical-consumer-204 (accessed 19 January 2021).

Dolšak, N. and Prakash, A. (2017) 'Yes, consumers can change public policies – sometimes. Here are the challenges', *The Washington Post*, 27 February, www.washingtonpost.com/news/monkey-cage/wp/2017/02/27/yes-consumers-can-change-public-policies-sometimes-here-are-the-challenges (accessed 19 January 2021).

Dolšak, N. and Prakash, A. (2020) 'Restoring the reputations of charities after scandals', *The Conversation*, 13 February, https://theconversation.com/restoring-the-reputations-of-charities-after-scandals-130639 (accessed 20 January 2021).

Domenech, T. and Davies, M. (2011) 'Structure and morphology of industrial symbiosis networks: The case of Kalundborg', *Procedia – Social and Behavioral Sciences*, 10, 79–89.

Domini, A. (2020) 'Thoughts on meaning and mission: ESG, CSR and SRI', *GreenMoney*, https://greenmoney.com/thoughts-on-meaning-and-mission-esg-csr-and-sri (accessed 19 January 2021).

Dormehl, L. (2020) 'Today in Apple history: Apple lays out its core company values', *Cult of Mac*, 23 September, www.cultofmac.com/446380/today-apple-history-apple-lays-core-company-values (accessed 19 January 2021).

Drucker, P. ([1954] 2007) *The Practice of Management*, London: Routledge.

Drummond, C. and Fischhoff, B. (2017) 'Individuals with greater science literacy and education have more polarized beliefs on controversial science topics', *PNAS*, 114(36), 9587–92.

Emrich, T.E., Qi, Y., Lou, W.Y. and l'Abbe, M.R. (2017) 'Traffic-light labels could reduce population intakes of calories, total fat, saturated fat, and sodium', *PLOS ONE*, 12(2), e0171188.

Endres, K. and Panagopoulos, C. (2017) 'Boycotts, buycotts, and political consumerism in America', *Research & Politics*, 4(4).

European Court of Auditors (2020) *Sustainable Urban Mobility in the EU: No Substantial Improvement Is Possible without Member States' Commitment*, www.eca.europa.eu/Lists/ECADocuments/SR20_06/SR_Sustainable_Urban_Mobility_EN.pdf (accessed 19 January 2021).

FareShare (2018) 'JD Wetherspoon scoops Waste No Food prize for work with FareShare', 4 October, https://fareshare.org.uk/news-media/press-releases/jd-wetherspoon-scoops-waste-no-food-prize-for-work-with-fareshare (accessed 20 January 2021).

Ferber, A. (2020) 'Judith Butler on the culture wars, J.K. Rowling and living in "anti-intellectual times"', *New Statesman*, 22 September, www.newstatesman.com/international/2020/09/judith-butler-culture-wars-jk-rowling-and-living-anti-intellectual-times (accessed 20 January 2021).

Flannelly, M. (2014) 'The complete history of Apple stock', *Dividend.com*, 29 December, www.dividend.com/dividend-education/the-complete-history-of-apple-aapl (accessed 20 January 2021).

Francis, C. (2020) 'How many senses do we have?', Sensory Trust, 15 October, www.sensorytrust.org.uk/blog/how-many-senses-do-we-have (accessed 17 August 2021).

Frank, P. and Brock, C. (2018) 'Bridging the intention–behavior gap among organic grocery customers: The crucial role of point-of-sale information', *Psychology & Marketing*, 35(8), 586–602.

Frandsen, A.-C. (2009) 'Psoriasis to a number and back', *Information and Organization,* 19, 103–28.

Friedman, M. (2002) *Capitalism and Freedom*, Chicago, IL: University of Chicago Press.

FSC-Watch (2020) 'IKEA's Ukrainian illegal timber problem. That FSC didn't notice...', 2 August, https://fsc-watch.com/2020/07/02/ikeas-ukrainian-illegal-timber-problem-that-fsc-didnt-notice (accessed 20 January 2021).

Galinsky, A.D., Gruenfeld D.H. and Magee, J.C. (2003) 'From power to action', *Journal of Personality and Social Psychology*, 85(3), 453–66.

Genersch, E. (2010) 'The German bee monitoring project: A long term study to understand periodically high winter losses of honey bee colonies', *Apidologie*, 41(3), 332–52.

Georgakopoulos, G. and Thomson, I. (2005) 'Organic salmon farming: Risk perceptions, decision heuristics and the absence of environmental accounting', *Accounting Forum*, 29(1), 49–75.

George, S. (2020) 'Investors ask most-emitting companies to prove their climate lobbying is Paris-Agreement-aligned', *edie*, 27 October, www.edie.net/news/9/Investors-ask-most-emitting-companies-to-prove-their-climate-lobbying-is-Paris-Agreement-aligned (accessed 19 January 2021).

Ghalwash, S., Tolba, A. and Ismail, A. (2017) 'What motivates social entrepreneurs to start social ventures?', *Social Enterprise Journal*, 13(3), 268–98.

Gibbens, S. (2019) 'You eat thousands of bits of plastic every year', *National Geographic*, 5 June, www.nationalgeographic.com/environment/2019/06/you-eat-thousands-of-bits-of-plastic-every-year (accessed 19 January 2021).

Gies, E. (2011) 'Interface founder Ray Anderson leaves legacy of sustainability success', *Forbes*, 10 August, www.forbes.com/sites/ericagies/2011/08/10/interface-founder-ray-anderson-leaves-legacy-of-sustainability-success/?sh=5d527874174a (accessed 10 August 2021).

Goenka, S. and van Osselaer, S.M.J. (2019) 'Charities can increase the effectiveness of donation appeals by using a morally congruent positive emotion', *Journal of Consumer Research*, 46(4), 774–90.

Govindarajan, V., Rajgopal, S. and Srivastava, A. (2018) 'A blueprint for digital companies' financial reporting', *Harvard Business Review*, 3 August, https://hbr.org/2018/08/a-blueprint-for-digital-companies-financial-reporting (accessed 9 March 2021).

Graeber, D. (2011) 'Consumption', *Current Anthropology*, 52(4), 489–511.

Graeber, D. (2019) 'From managerial feudalism to the revolt of the caring classes', *Open Transcripts*, 27 December, http://opentranscripts.org/transcript/managerial-feudalism-revolt-caring-classes (accessed 19 January 2021).

Grant Thornton (2017) *The Business Case for Trust*, www.grantthornton.co.uk/globalassets/1.-member-firms/united-kingdom/pdf/publication/the-business-case-for-trust.pdf (accessed 20 January 2021).

Griffiths, G. (2019) 'Blog: What is the Global Living Wage Initiative?', *Living Wage Foundation*, 12 November, www.livingwage.org.uk/news/blog-what-global-living-wage-initiative%3F#:~:text=The%20principles%20of%20a%20Global,to%20participate%20fully%20in%20society (accessed 19 January 2021).

Gruenfeld, D.H., Inesi, M.E., Magee, J.C. and Galinsky, A.D. (2008) 'Power and the objectification of social targets', *Journal of Personality and Social Psychology*, 95(1), 111–27.

Grunert, K.G., Hieke, S. and Wills, J. (2014) 'Sustainability labels on food products: Consumer motivation, understanding and use', *Food Policy*, 44, 177–89.

Guinote, A. (2017) 'How power affects people: Activating, wanting, and goal seeking', *Annual Review of Psychology*, 68, 353–81.

Gutierrez, E. (2020) 'A traditional marketing success story: How Oatly dominated plant milks without using social media', *Digital Marketer*, 17 August, www.digitalmarketer.com/blog/oatly-marketing-success-story (accessed 19 January 2021).

Haidt, J. (2003) 'The Moral Emotions', in R.J. Davidson, K.R. Scherer and H.H. Goldsmith (eds) *Handbook of Affective Sciences* (pp 852–70), Oxford: Oxford University Press.

Haidt, J. and Joseph, C. (2004) 'Intuitive ethics: How innately prepared intuitions generate culturally variable virtues', *Daedalus*, 133(4), 55–66.

Haines-Young, R., Potschin, M. and Cheshire, D. (2006) *Defining and Identifying Environmental Limits for Sustainable Development*, Final Overview Report to Defra, http://randd.defra.gov.uk/Default.aspx?Menu=Menu& Module=More&Location=None&ProjectID=13901 (accessed 19 January 2021).

Hainmueller, J., Sequeira, S. and Hiscox, M.J. (2015) 'Consumer demand for fair trade: Evidence from a multistore field experiment', *Review of Economics and Statistics*, 97(2), 242–56.

Hallmann, C.A., Sorg, M., Jongejans, E., Siepel, H., Hofland, N., Schwan, H., ... de Kroon, H. (2017) 'More than 75 percent decline over 27 years in total flying insect biomass in protected areas', *PLOS ONE*, 12(10), e0185809.

Hayes, A. (2021) 'What is consumerism?', *Investopedia*, 18 March, www. investopedia.com/terms/c/consumerism.asp (accessed 7 September 2021).

Henderson, R. (2020) *Reimagining Capitalism: How Business can Save the World*, London: Random House.

Henley, J. (2019) 'How millions of French shoppers are rejecting cut-price capitalism', *The Guardian*, 4 December, www.theguardian.com/ world/2019/dec/04/french-shoppers-rejecting-cut-price-capitalism-nicolas-chabanne (accessed 19 January 2021).

Hilger, J. (2019) 'Measuring willingness to pay for environmental attributes in seafood', *Environmental and Resource Economics*, 73, 307–32.

Hirsh, J.B., Galinsky, A.D. and Zhong, C.-B. (2011) 'Drunk, powerful, and in the dark: How general processes of disinhibition produce both prosocial and antisocial behavior', *Perspectives on Psychological Science*, 6(5), 415–27.

HM Government (2019) *Voluntary National Review of Progress towards the Sustainable Development Goals*, https://assets.publishing.service.gov.uk/ government/uploads/system/uploads/attachment_data/file/818212/ UKVNR-web-accessible1.pdf (accessed 20 January 2021).

HM Treasury (2021) *The Economics of Biodiversity: The Dasgupta Review – Full Report*, London: TSO, www.gov.uk/government/publications/ final-report-the-economics-of-biodiversity-the-dasgupta-review (accessed 17 August 2021).

Hockley, T. (2018) 'Solution aversion', *Behavioural Public Policy Blog*, 27 March, https://bppblog.com/2018/03/27/solution-aversion (accessed 20 January 2021).

Hollingworth, C. and Barker, L. (2019) 'New frontiers: Re-establishing System1/System 2 truths', *Research Live*, 7 August, www.research-live.com/article/opinion/new-frontiers-reestablishing-system1system-2-truths/id/5057422 (accessed 20 January 2021).

Holmes, T., Blackmore, E., Hawkins, R. and Wakeford, T. (2011) *The Common Cause Handbook*, Machynlleth: Public Interest Research Centre, www.commoncause.com.au/uploads/1/2/9/4/12943361/common_cause_handbook.pdf (accessed 19 August 2021).

Horberg, E.J., Oveis, C. and Keltner, D. (2011) 'Emotions as moral amplifiers: An appraisal tendency approach to the influences of distinct emotions upon moral judgment', *Emotion Review*, 3(3), 237–44.

Husted, B.W., Russo, M.V., Basurto Meza, C.E. and Tilleman, S.G. (2014) 'An exploratory study of environmental attitudes and the willingness to pay for environmental certification in Mexico', *Journal of Business Research*, 67(5), 891–9.

Interface (2019) *Lessons for the Future*, http://interfaceinc.scene7.com/is/content/InterfaceInc/Interface/EMEA/WebsiteContentAssets/Documents/25th%20anniversary%20report/English/wc_eu-lessonsforthefuture-en.pdf (accessed 19 January 2021).

Irfan, U. (2017) 'People furthest apart on climate views are often the most educated', *Scientific American*, 22 August, www.scientificamerican.com/article/people-furthest-apart-on-climate-views-are-often-the-most-educated (accessed 20 January 2021).

ITV News (2018) 'Plastic bag charge: Why was it introduced and what impact has it had?', 25 August, www.itv.com/news/2018-08-25/plastic-bag-charge-why-was-it-introduced-and-what-impact-has-it-had (accessed 20 January 2021).

Jones, H. (2019) 'UK banks sign up to UN-backed responsible banking code', *Reuters*, 18 September, https://uk.reuters.com/article/uk-britain-banks/uk-banks-sign-up-to-u-n-backed-responsible-banking-code-idUKKBN1W32QE (accessed 19 January 2021).

Kalev, A., Dobbin, F. and Kelly, E. (2006) 'Best practices or best guesses? Assessing the efficacy of corporate affirmative action and diversity policies', *American Sociological Review*, 71(4), 589–617.

Keltner, D., Gruenfeld, D.H. and Anderson, C. (2003) 'Power, approach, and inhibition', *Psychological Review*, 110(2), 265–84.

Kenway, E. (2020) 'Priti Patel is wrong, modern slavery in Leicester is built on her government's failures', *The Guardian*, 14 July, www.theguardian.com/commentisfree/2020/jul/14/priti-patel-modern-slavery-leicester-cultural-sensitivities (accessed 20 January 2021).

Ki-moon, B. (2015) 'Secretary-General's remarks at the United Nations Private Sector Forum [as prepared for delivery]', *UN.org*, 26 September, www.un.org/sg/en/content/sg/statement/2015-09-26/secretary-generals-remarks-united-nations-private-sector-forum (accessed 19 January 2021).

King, B. (2015) 'Can a carpet factory run like a forest?', *GreenBiz*, 12 June, www.greenbiz.com/article/can-carpet-factory-run-forest (accessed 19 January 2021).

Knobloch, F., Hanssen, S.V., Lam, A., Pollitt, H., Salas, P., Chewpreecha, U. ... Mercure, J.-F. (2020) 'Net emission reductions from electric cars and heat pumps in 59 world regions over time', *Nature Sustainability*, 3, 437–47.

Kolditz, T. (2014) 'Why you lead determines how well you lead', *Harvard Business Review*, 22 July, https://hbr.org/2014/07/why-you-lead-determines-how-well-you-lead (accessed 20 January 2021).

Koshy, V. (2018) 'What are vanity metrics and how to avoid them', *Hubstaff*, 10 July, https://blog.hubstaff.com/vanity-metrics (accessed 19 January 2021).

Kroese, F.M., Marchiori, D.R. and de Ridder, D.T.D. (2015) 'Nudging healthy food choices: A field experiment at the train station', *Journal of Public Health*, 38(2), e133–e137.

Lammers, J., Stapel, D.A. and Galinsky, A.D. (2010) 'Power increases hypocrisy: Moralizing in reasoning, immorality in behavior', *Psychological Science*, 21(5), 737–44.

Lammers, J., Stoker, J.I., Jordan, J., Pollmann, M.M.H. and Stapel, D.A. (2011) 'Power increases infidelity among men and women', *Psychological Science*, 22(9), 1191–7.

Lautenbach, S., Seppelt, R., Liebscher, J. and Dormann, C.F. (2012) 'Spatial and temporal trends of global pollination benefit', *PLOS ONE*, 7(4), e35954.

Lee, D. (2018) 'Google staff walk out over women's treatment', BBC News, 1 November, www.bbc.co.uk/news/technology-46054202 (accessed 20 January 2021).

Lee, T.B. (2015) 'How Apple became the world's most valuable company', *Vox*, 9 September, www.vox.com/2014/11/17/18076360/apple (accessed 20 January 2021).

Liu, L., Chen, R. and He, F. (2015) 'How to promote purchase of carbon offset products: Labeling vs calculation?', *Journal of Business Research*, 68(5), 942–8.

Longo, C., Shankar, A. and Nuttall, P. (2017) '"It's not easy living a sustainable lifestyle": How greater knowledge leads to dilemmas, tensions and paralysis', *Journal of Business Ethics*, 154, 759–79.

Mace, M. (2020) 'WBCSD launches net-zero criteria for new and existing business members', *edie*, 27 October, www.edie.net/news/7/WBCSD-launches-net-zero-criteria-for-new-and-existing-business-members (accessed 19 January 2021).

Magee, J.C. and Smith, P.K. (2013) 'The social distance theory of power', *Personality and Social Psychology Review*, 17(2), 158–86.

Makower, J. (2016) 'Inside Interface's bold new mission to achieve "Climate Take Back"', *GreenBiz*, 6 June, www.greenbiz.com/article/inside-interfaces-bold-new-mission-achieve-climate-take-back (accessed 20 January 2021).

Malito, A. (2018) 'Your facial recognition software may be racist and sexist', *MarketWatch*, 13 February, www.marketwatch.com/story/your-facial-recognition-software-may-be-racist-and-sexist-2018-02-13 (accessed 29 March 2021).

Management Today (2020) 'COVID-19 key developments: Furlough scheme cut-off to be announced, the UK's fiscal shackles', 20 May, www.managementtoday.co.uk/coronavirus-live-blog-furlough-scheme-extended-rent-change-covid-secure-guidelines-issued/coronavirus/article/1677347 (accessed 20 January 2021).

Marchal, J. (2008) *Lord Leverhulme's Ghosts: Colonial Exploitation in the Congo*, London: Verso.

Mathew, M. (2018) 'Factory as a forest: Reimagining facilities as ecosystems', *Interface*, 24 August, https://blog.interface.com/factory-forest-reimagining-facilities-ecosystems (accessed 19 January 2021).

McCulloch, A. (2018) 'Third of LGBT employees hide their sexual orientation at work', *Personnel Today*, 30 April, www.personneltoday.com/hr/third-of-lgbt-employees-conceal-their-sexual-orientation-at-work (accessed 20 January 2021).

McGrath, R.G. (2013) 'CEOs no longer have the luxury to focus on the next 100 years', *Quartz*, 25 July, https://qz.com/107479/ceos-no-longer-have-the-luxury-to-focus-on-the-next-100-years (accessed 20 January 2021).

Merkley, K., Michaely, R. and Pacelli, J. (2020) 'Cultural diversity on Wall Street: Evidence from consensus earnings forecasts', *Journal of Accounting and Economics*, 70(1), 101330.

Moraes, C. (2020) 'The Oatly–Blackstone deal: How will consumers respond?', Birmingham Business School Blog, 10 September, https://blog.bham.ac.uk/business-school/2020/09/10/the-oatly-blackstone-deal-how-will-consumers-respond (accessed 20 January 2021).

Moreau, A. (2019) 'David Graeber on capitalism's best kept secret', *Philonomist*, 8 February, https://medium.com/philonomist/david-graeber-on-capitalisms-best-kept-secret-704f13914a88 (accessed 20 January 2021).

Morgan, G., Ryu, K. and Mirvis, P.H. (2009) 'Leading corporate citizenship: Governance, structure, systems', *Corporate Governance*, 9(1), 39–49.

Mori, A.S., Furukawa, T. and Sasaki, T. (2012) 'Response diversity determines the resilience of ecosystems to environmental change', *Biological Reviews of the Cambridge Philosophical Society*, 88(2), 349–64.

Morrison, D. (2017) 'US companies rank miserably low on the UN's new corporate responsibility rankings', *Quartz*, 19 April, https://qz.com/963033/us-companies-rank-miserably-low-on-the-uns-new-corporate-responsibility-rankings (accessed 19 January 2021).

Mukherjee, S. and Althuizen, N. (2020) 'Brand activism: Does courting controversy help or hurt a brand?', *International Journal of Research in Marketing*, 37(4), 772–88.

Muller, L., Lacroix, A. and Ruffieux, B. (2019) 'Environmental labelling and consumption changes: A food choice experiment', *Environmental and Resource Economics*, 73(2).

Naqvi, A. (2018) 'How AI and robotics can transform CSR', *Reuters Events*, 18 January, www.reutersevents.com/sustainability/how-ai-and-robotics-can-transform-csr (accessed 20 January 2021).

New Internationalist (2002) 'A short history of corporations', 5 July, https://newint.org/features/2002/07/05/history (accessed 20 January 2021).

Nicholson, J. (2019) '4 steps for using social norms to persuade and influence', *Psychology Today*, 29 June, www.psychologytoday.com/gb/blog/persuasion-bias-and-choice/201906/4-steps-using-social-norms-persuade-and-influence (accessed 20 January 2021).

Nieuwenkamp, R. (2016) '2016: CSR is dead! What's next?', *OECD Insights*, 22 January, http://oecdinsights.org/2016/01/22/2016-csr-is-dead-whats-next (accessed 19 January 2021).

NPR (2019) 'Transcript: Greta Thunberg's speech at the UN Climate Action Summit', 23 September, www.npr.org/2019/09/23/763452863/transcript-greta-thunbergs-speech-at-the-u-n-climate-action-summit?t=1614863664739&t=1628600372593 (accessed 10 August 2021).

Oreskes, N. and Conway, E.M. (2010) *Merchants of Doubt: How a Handful of Scientists Obscured the Truth on Issues from Tobacco Smoke to Global Warming*, London: Bloomsbury.

Ormiston, M. (2013) 'Companies' CSR policies may be leading to corporate irresponsibility', *The Guardian*, 10 December, www.theguardian.com/sustainable-business/comapanies-csr-policies-corporate-irresponsibility-new-study (accessed 20 January 2021).

Overbeck, J.R. and Park, B. (2001) 'When power does not corrupt: Superior individuation processes among powerful perceivers', *Journal of Personality and Social Psychology*, 81(4), 549–65.

Overbeck, J.R. and Park, B. (2006) 'Powerful perceivers, powerless objects: Flexibility of powerholders' social attention', *Organizational Behavior and Human Decision Processes*, 99(2), 227–43.

Oxfam (2017) *Raising the bar: Rethinking the role of business in the Sustainable Development Goals*, www-cdn.oxfam.org/s3fs-public/dp-raising-the-bar-business-sdgs-130217-en_0.pdf (accessed 19 January 2021).

Pailhès, A., Kuhn, G. and Kumari, S. (2020) 'The magician's choice: Providing illusory choice and sense of agency with the Equivoque forcing technique', *Journal of Experimental Psychology: General*, 30 November, 1–15.

Partridge, J. (2020) 'Which companies are coming through during the coronavirus crisis?', *The Guardian*, 29 March, www.theguardian.com/business/2020/mar/29/which-companies-are-coming-through-during-the-coronavirus-crisis (accessed 20 January 2021).

Peachey, J. (2019) 'My startup: Giki app', *Prolific London*, 17 September, www.prolificlondon.co.uk/features/2019/09/my-startup-giki-app (accessed 19 January 2021).

Penny, E. (2020) 'Filth: Space junk is always somebody else's problem – But eventually someone is going to have to clean it up', *Novara Media*, 8 May, https://novaramedia.com/2020/05/08/filth-space-junk-is-becoming-a-problem-we-cant-ignore-but-whose-job-is-it-to-clean-it-up (accessed 19 January 2021).

Petty, R.E., Briñol, P. and Tormala, Z.L. (2002) 'Thought confidence as a determinant of persuasion: The self-validation hypothesis', *Journal of Personality and Social Psychology*, 82(5), 722–41.

Pink, D. (2009) *Drive: The Surprising Truth About What Motivates Us*, New York: Riverhead Books.

Potter, D. (2012) 'Beyond social impact to social value', *The Guardian*, 2 May, www.theguardian.com/social-enterprise-network/2012/may/02/beyond-social-impact-social-value (accessed 20 January 2021).

Powell-Smith, A. (2020) 'Ten sustainability signals for the new normal', *Forster Communications*, 20 May, www.forster.co.uk/insight/ten-sustainability-signals-for-the-new-normal (accessed 20 January 2021).

Rao, S.L.N. (1973) 'On long-term mortality trends in the United States, 1850–1968', *Demography*, 10(3), 405–19.

Raworth, K. (2017) *Doughnut Economics: Seven Ways to Think Like a 21st-Century Economist*, White River Junction, VT: Chelsea Green Publishing.

Rhodes, C. (2021) *Woke Capitalism: How Corporate Morality Is Sabotaging Democracy*, Bristol: Bristol University Press.

Ro, C. (2020) 'How did the vegan sausage roll get so popular?', BBC News, 3 February, www.bbc.com/worklife/article/20200202-how-did-the-vegan-sausage-roll-get-so-popular (accessed 19 January 2021).

Rosling, H. (2018) *Factfulness*, London: Sceptre.

Russell, S.L. and Thomson, I. (2009) 'Analysing the role of sustainable development indicators in accounting for and constructing a *Sustainable Scotland*', *Accounting Forum*, 33(3), 225–44.

Sakr, D.A., El-Haggar, S., Bass, L. and Huisingh, D. (2011) 'Critical success and limiting factors for eco-industrial parks: Global trends and Egyptian context', *Journal of Cleaner Production*, 19, 1158–69.

Scholl, A., Ellemers, N., Sassenberg, K. and Scheepers, D. (2015) 'Understanding Power in Social Context: How Power Relates to Language and Communication in Line with Responsibilities or Opportunities', in R. Schulze and H. Pishwa (eds) *The Exercise of Power in Communication* (pp 312–34), London: Palgrave Macmillan.

Schroeder, A. (2011) 'Struktur und Ergebnisse des DeBiMo', *ADIZ*, 9, 8–9.

Schwab, K. (2019) 'Davos Manifesto 2020: The universal purpose of a company in the Fourth Industrial Revolution', *World Economic Forum*, 2 December, www.weforum.org/agenda/2019/12/davos-manifesto-2020-the-universal-purpose-of-a-company-in-the-fourth-industrial-revolution (accessed 19 January 2021).

Schwartz, S.H. (1994) 'Are there universal aspects in the structure and contents of human values?', *Journal of Social Issues*, 50(4), 19–45.

Sieck, W.R., Klein, G., Peluso, D.A., Smith, J.L. and Harris-Thompson, D. (2007) 'A Model of Sensemaking', www.researchgate.net/publication/266217173_A_Model_of_Sensemaking (accessed 20 January 2021).

Singer, M. (2019) 'Is there really such a thing as "ethical consumerism"?', *Vogue*, 4 February, www.vogue.com/article/ethical-consumer-rentrayage-batsheva-lidia-may (accessed 20 January 2021).

Sovacool, B.K., Ali, S., Bazilian, M., Radley, B., Nemery, B., Okatz, J. and Mulvaney, D. (2020) 'Sustainable minerals and metals for a low-carbon future', *Science*, 367(6473), 30–3.

Stanislaus, M. (2018) 'Banning straws and bags won't solve our plastic problem', World Resources Institute, 16 August, www.wri.org/blog/2018/08/banning-straws-and-bags-wont-solve-our-plastic-problem (accessed 19 January 2021).

Stern, S. (2020) *Redesigning Work: Employee Owners Speak*, Ownership at Work, https://employeeownership.co.uk/wp-content/uploads/REDESIGNING-WORK-PDF-0720.pdf (accessed 20 January 2021).

Sullivan, S. (2019) 'The balance sheet of nature? On making monetary value of UK "natural capital"', 12 December, https://the-natural-capital-myth.net/2019/12/12/the-balance-sheet-of-nature (accessed 20 January 2021).

Sweet, J. and Shook, E. (2020) *Getting to Equal 2020*, Accenture, www.accenture.com/_acnmedia/Thought-Leadership-Assets/PDF-2/Accenture-Getting-To-Equal-2020-Research-Report.pdf (accessed 20 January 2021).

Taylor, A. (2019) 'Employees have given rise to something far more powerful than "CEO activism"', *Quartz*, 6 September, https://qz.com/work/1703005/ceo-activism-has-given-way-to-employee-activism (accessed 20 January 2021).

Taylor, M. (2021) 'Climate crisis hits "worst case scenario" levels – Environment Agency head', *The Guardian*, 23 February, www.theguardian.com/environment/2021/feb/23/climate-crisis-hitting-worst-case-scenarios-warns-environment-agency-head (accessed 10 August 2021).

Taylor, M. and Watts, J. (2019) 'Revealed: The 20 firms behind a third of all carbon emissions', *The Guardian*, 9 October, www.theguardian.com/environment/2019/oct/09/revealed-20-firms-third-carbon-emissions (accessed 19 January 2021).

Thamotheram, R. and Biehl, C. (2018) 'Long-term matters: What world are we creating by saving the world?', *IPE*, September, www.ipe.com/long-term-matters-what-world-are-we-creating-by-saving-the-world/10026416.article (accessed 19 January 2021).

Thomson, A. (2018) 'Guys named Dave equal number of women in FTSE 100 CEO roles', *Bloomberg*, 15 August, www.bloomberg.com/news/articles/2018-08-14/guys-named-dave-equal-number-of-women-in-ftse-100-ceo-roles (accessed 20 January 2021).

Thomson, I. and Cooper, S. (2018) 'Privilege, Detachment, Concealment and Omission: Normalisation and GHG Reporting', presented at Interdisciplinary Perspectives on Accounting Conference, Edinburgh, July.

Thomson, I., Morrow, S. and Adams, A. (2021: forthcoming) 'Building a responsible resilient football club: Institutional entrepreneurship, adaptive governance, and accountability'.

Titley, D. (2017) 'Why is climate change's 2 degrees Celsius of warming limit so important?', *The Conversation*, 23 August, https://theconversation.com/why-is-climate-changes-2-degrees-celsius-of-warming-limit-so-important-82058 (accessed 19 January 2021).

Townsend, S. (2018) '88% of consumers want you to help them make a difference', *Forbes*, 21 November, www.forbes.com/sites/solitairetownsend/2018/11/21/consumers-want-you-to-help-them-make-a-difference/#3209cee46954 (accessed 19 January 2021).

Trehan, K. (2018) 'How can leaders unlock human potential?', *Drucker Forum Anniversary Report 2018*, https://issuu.com/revistabibliodiversidad/docs/drucker_digital_version (accessed 20 January 2021).

Trehan, K. (2019) 'Small is sustainable', *Edge*, Autumn, https://issuu.com/revistabibliodiversidad/docs/edge_autumn_2019 (accessed 20 January 2021).

Tyler, T.R. (2002) 'Leadership and cooperation in groups', *American Behavioral Science*, 45(5), 769–82.

UN (United Nations) Global Compact (2019) *The Decade to Deliver: A Call to Business Action*, https://ceowatermandate.org/resources/the-decade-to-deliver-a-call-to-business-action-2019 (accessed 20 January 2021).

UN Global Compact (2020) *Leadership for the Decade of Action*, https://unglobalcompact.org/library/5745

UNGSII (United Nations Global Sustainability Index Institute) (2019) *SDG Commitment Report: Empowering Investors on Both Profit and Impact*, https://docs.wixstatic.com/ugd/d97ebd_cbba48f780c04d9ebf0037029d6c6686.pdf (accessed 19 January 2021).

van Vugt, M. and Ronay, R. (2013) 'The evolutionary psychology of leadership: Theory, review, and roadmap', *Organizational Psychology Review*, 4(1), 74–95.

Vescio, T.K., Snyder, M. and Butz, D. (2003) 'Power in stereotypically masculine domains: A social influence strategy x stereotype match model', *Journal of Personality and Social Psychology*, 85(6), 1062–78.

Victor, D. (2017) 'Pepsi pulls ad accused of trivializing Black Lives Matter', *The New York Times*, 5 April, www.nytimes.com/2017/04/05/business/kendall-jenner-pepsi-ad.html (accessed 20 January 2021).

Vlaeminck, P., Jiang, T. and Vranken, L. (2014) 'Food labeling and eco-friendly consumption: Experimental evidence from a Belgian supermarket', *Ecological Economics*, 108, 180–90.

Vrendenburg, J. (2020) 'Brands taking a stand: Authentic brand activism or woke washing?', *Journal of Public Policy & Marketing*, 39(4), 444–60.

Wall Street Survivor (2014) 'Why did Steve Jobs only make $1 a year? (and what can you learn from it)', *The Motley Fool*, 1 February, www.fool.com/personal-finance/2014/02/01/why-did-steve-jobs-only-make-1-a-year-and-what-you.aspx (accessed 20 January 2021).

Warde, A. (2017) *Consumption: A Sociological Analysis*, London: Palgrave Macmillan.

Weick, M. and Guinote, A. (2008) 'When subjective experiences matter: Power increases reliance on the ease of retrieval', *Journal of Personality and Social Psychology*, 94(6), 956–70.

Whelan, G. (2020) 'Boohoo boss pledges to clean up supply chain', *Drapers*, 30 September, www.drapersonline.com/news/sustainability-a-key-focus-for-boohoo-says-ceo (accessed 20 January 2021).

Whitbread, L. (2020) 'Oatly Blackstone investment: If you need a new milk alternative, try these instead', *Independent*, 3 September, www.independent.co.uk/extras/indybest/food-drink/oatly-oat-milk-blackstone-investment-barista-edition-whole-gluten-dairy-free-vegan-a9701281.html (accessed 19 January 2021).

WHO (World Health Organization) (2006) *WHO Guidelines on Hand Hygiene in Health Care* (Advanced Draft), www.who.int/patientsafety/information_centre/Last_April_versionHH_Guidelines%5B3%5D.pdf (accessed 7 September 2021).

Wilck, J. and Lynch, P.C. (2018) 'Diverse teams build better forecasts', *ASEE Annual Conference and Exposition, Conference Proceedings*, June, https://pennstate.pure.elsevier.com/en/publications/diverse-teams-build-better-forecasts (accessed 20 January 2021).

Wildhearts (2020) *Impact Report 2019*, www.wildheartsgroup.com/wp-content/uploads/2020/08/WildHearts-Impact-Report-2019-compressed-3.pdf (accessed 19 January 2021).

Willard, B. (2019) '7 ways companies can contribute to the SDGs', *Sustainability Advantage*, 30 July, https://sustainabilityadvantage.com/2019/07/30/7-ways-companies-can-contribute-to-the-sdgs (accessed 19 January 2021).

Williams, A., Whiteman, G. and Kennedy, S. (2019) 'Cross-scale systemic resilience: Implications for organization studies', *Business & Society*, 60(1), 95–124.

World Benchmarking Alliance (2019) *Measuring What Matters Most: Seven Systems Transformations for Benchmarking Companies on the SDGs*, July, https://assets.worldbenchmarkingalliance.org/app/uploads/2020/09/WBA-sevensystemstransformations-report.pdf (accessed 7 September 2021).

Wrap (2020) 'Food surplus and waste in the UK – key facts', wrap.org.uk/sites/files/wrap/Food-surplus-and-waste-in-the-UK-key-facts-Jan-2020.pdf (accessed 20 January 2021).

Wrzesniewski, A., Schwartz, B., Cong, X., Kane, M., Omar, A. and Kolditz, T. (2014) 'Multiple types of motives don't multiply the motivation of West Point cadets', *PNAS*, 111(30), 10990–5.

Yankelovich, D. (1972) *Corporate Priorities: A Continuing Study of the New Demands on Business*, Stanford, CA: Yankelovich Inc.

Zhang, D., Morse, D., Kambhampati, U. (2017) *Sustainable Development and Corporate Social Responsibility*, London: Routledge.

Index

A

Accenture 143
accounting 36–65
    alternative accounting 52–3
    ambitious 63
    collecting and sharing data 60–1
    data 44–5
    decarbonization 61–2
    and feedback loops 55–6
    financialization 41–2, 54
    Global Goals-based 41, 46–50, 64–5
    market-led 61–2
    materiality 47
    measures 42–5
    misleading metrics 50–1
    non-financial 37, 40–2
    responsible accounting 55–6, 64–5
    sanctions 53–4
    selective reporting 45–9
    SIMPLE measures 43–4
    SMART measures 36, 42–4
    statistics dilemma 56–7
    and thresholds 57–60
    traditional 53–4
    and uncertainty 54–5, 65
actipreneurialism 140–1
Acton, Lord 124
Adams, Douglas 7
Adidas 32
agile-business practice 132
air pollution 73–4, 83
algae blooms 56
algorithmic thinking 134–6
alternative accounting 52–3
American Institute of Artificial Intelligence
    144–5
Amnesty International 53, 125

Anderson, Ray 16, 17, 29
Andriani 49
Anglian Water 30, 89
animal welfare 66, 98, 99, 112
annual reports 31, 45–9
    open reporting 64–5
anti-profit beliefs 15–18
Anti-Slavery International 38–9
Apple 13–14, 31
Apple Values 14
artificial intelligence (AI) 44–5, 144–5,
    178
Asilomar principles 145
Attalla, Ahmad 93
auditing 33, 39, 146
authenticity 119–20

B

B Corps 23, 149
B Impact Assessment 43
bag for life schemes 7, 67
Bakker, Peter 62–3
Balbo, Leontino Jr 40
Ban Ki-moon 33
Bangladesh 39
banking industry 29
Basic Human Values 104–6
batteries 85–6
Battery Industrialization Centre 86
Bayer AG 69–70
bees 68–71
Behar, Amitabh 28
behavioural economics 126, 136, 178
behavioural science
    and consumers 101–10
    and leadership 124–6

Ben & Jerry's 76
Benyus, Janine 89–90
Better Alignment Project 46
Better Business Bureau 146
biases 102–3, 127, 129, 133, 136, 137, 144, 162–3
Bierce, Ambrose 23
biodiversity 40, 89, 90
biomimicry 89–90
Biomimicry 3.8 90
Black and minority ethnic groups 120, 137, 143, 145
Black Lives Matter 76, 110, 120
black plastic 84
Blackout Tuesday 76
Blackstone 119
blame instinct 57
blindspots 37–8, 133–4
blockchain 61, 99–100
Blue Planet II 66
Boohoo Group 130
Borneo 74–5
Boston College's Center for Corporate Citizenship 128
BP 28, 45
brand activism 108, 119–20
Budge, Ann 116–17, 118
business citizenship 109–10, 123
business ecosystems 88–91
business exceptionalism 71–3
Business in the Community 26, 43, 136, 137, 149
business roadmap 154–9
Butler, Judith 115
buycotts 108, 110, 123, 178

C
Cadbury 19, 20
Capgemini 80
carbon accounting 50–1, 82, 147–9
carbon footprint 16, 28, 68
    and carbon literacy 79–83
    current standards of accountability 147–9
    definition 178
    impact of 6–7
    and markets 61–2
    metrics 50–1

outsourcing emissions 83
    unequal responsibility for 83
    see also net zero carbon
carbon intensity ratio 50–1, 61–2
carbon literacy 79–83
carbon negativity 16, 85
carbon off-setting 28–9, 58, 81, 82, 85, 97, 113
carbon scoping 148, 149, 172–3
Cargill 45
caring and freedom 114–15
Carrigan, Marylyn 93
Ceres Investor Network 62
certification schemes 62, 96–100
C'est qui le patron?! (CQLP) 112–13
Chabanne, Nicolas 112
charities 104
child labour 29, 31, 38–9, 134
choice architecture 136
circular economy/circularity 84–7, 91–2, 129–30, 178
Circular Economy Action Plan (EU) 86
citizen scientists 33, 60, 178
Climate Action 100+ 62
climate change deniers 126–7
Climate Disclosure Standards Board (CDSB) 46
climate collapse 56, 91
closed loop solution 178
closing the loop 84, 91–2, 178
Co-operative Group 41
Colgate 111
collective bargaining 142
collective solutions 111
Committee for Economic Development (US) 20
community ownership model 23, 178
Community Wellbeing Index 41
complex adaptive systems theory (CAS) 73–5, 178
confirmation bias 102
consistency dilemma 139
consumer sovereignty 8, 101–2, 109, 114, 178–9
consumers 8, 93–123
    biases 102–3
    brand activism 108
    business as social movement 111–14
    businesses as 139

consumers (continued)
   digital sources of information 99–100
   and emotions 103–4
   engaging with 112–14, 119–20, 121
   ethical consumer 8, 93–100, 103–4,
     108, 115, 119–21
   exploitation of 121
   football supporters 115–19
   Global Goals (UN) 94–5, 109, 121,
     122–3
   Goodlife Goals 50, 94–5, 185n3
   herd mentality 108
   labelling of products 94, 96–100
   marketing 96
   paralysis 101–2
   self-validation theory 103–4
   social practice 106–8
   sovereignty of 8, 101–2, 109, 114, 178–9
   as supporters 111–14, 123
   sustainable consumption level 100–1
   and trust 97, 99–100, 119
   and values 104–6, 122
   woke-washing 120
consumption
   individualism 114–15
   responsible 123
   sustainable consumption level 100–1
cooperatives 20, 23, 29, 112–13, 132
Corporate Reporting Dialogue 46
corporate social responsibility (CSR)
     19–23, 179
correlation 69, 184n16
coveillance 60–1
COVID-19 58, 60, 139
cross-sector partnerships 75–6, 77
   circular economy 84–6
crowdsourcing 99, 112
culture of the workplace 141–4

D
dairy-free alternatives 119
Dale, Caroline 20
Danone 164
data 44–5
   biased datasets 145, 163–4
   blockchain 61
   collecting and sharing 60–1
   statistics dilemma 56–7

Davos Manifesto 22
de Bono, Edward 136
De Cremer, David 145
DeBiMo 69–70
decarbonization 61–2, 82
decision-making
   artificial intelligence (AI) 144–5
   consumer involvement 112–13
   Global Goals (UN) 133–5
   inclusive 132
   of leaders 125–7, 133–8
   process-driven 133–6, 152
   six thinking hats technique 136
   and team leadership 136–8
degrowth movement 18
Denmark 86–7
Derbyshire Wildlife Trust 89
destiny instinct 57
Dieselgate 29
distributed ledger technologies 47, 61
distributive leadership 131–2
diversity 137, 143–4, 152–3
Divine Chocolate 23
Domini, Amy 22
Doughnut Economics 72–3, 150
Dow Jones Sustainable Indices 46
drone mapping 45
Drucker, Peter 36
due diligence 33
Dunning–Kruger effect 133, 137

E
EAT-Lancet Commission 101
eco-industrial parks 86–7
ecological performance standards 90
ECOMUSA 88–9
economic goals (Global Goals) 166
Edelman 139–40, 146
electric vehicle (EV) industry 85–6,
     110–11
emotional tagging 125–6
employee-owned companies 132, 142
Employee Ownership Association 142
employees
   actipreneurialism 140–1
   diversity and inclusion 143
   Global Goals (UN) 141, 142, 152–3
   human-centred rewards 141–2

as owners 132, 142
performance measuring 141
slavery 11, 20, 23, 38, 38–9, 130
staff representation 142
in supply chains 24, 31, 38–9, 111, 130
and trust 143, 146–7
working culture 141–4
Enel 137–8
Enron 20–1, 54
Enterprise and Diversity Alliance 144
environmental, social and governance (ESG) 21–2, 45–6, 47, 61, 62, 179
equality 32, 104, 108, 144
Esteé Lauder 61
ethical consumer 8, 93–100, 103–4, 108, 115, 119–21
  see also consumers
Ethical Trading Initiative 32
ethnic diversity 137, 143
ethnic pay gap 120
European Professional Beekeeper Association 70
European Union 70
  Circular Economy Action Plan 86
  Non-Financial Reporting Directive 46
exceptionalism 71–3
executive pay 147
external accountability 52
external motives 129–30
externalities 40, 41–2, 54, 179
extrinsic values 105, 106

F

Factfulness (Rosling) 56–7, 68
Fair For You 23
Fair Labor Association 32
Fairtrade 93, 97, 99
fake news 158–9
feedback loops 55–6, 71, 151
Financial Accounting Standards Board (FASB) 46
financial markets 71–2
financialization 41–2, 54, 179
Find Green app 99
fishing industry 75–6
FitBee 70

Floyd, George 76
food waste 107
football clubs 115–19
forced labour 21, 38–9
forest as factory 88–9, 90
Forest Stewardship Council (FSC) 98
forestry 59, 88–9, 90, 97–8
Foundation of Hearts 116–17
framing 126–7
Friedman, Milton 22
Friends Provident 20
full-scope carbon accounting 82
Futerra 94
Future-Fit 26, 43, 94
Future of Life Institute 145

G

G17Eco platform 47, 52
GAME system 118, 120
gamification 108
Gandhi, Mahatma 77
Gap 32
gap instinct 57
gender issues 32, 143–4
Geolytix 41
Germany 68–71
Giki 99, 113
Global Compact 26, 129, 131, 134, 138, 150
global financial crisis (2008) 29, 45–6, 55, 71–2
Global Footprint Network 100
Global Goals (UN) 3–5, 22, 161–4, 166–7
  17-dimensional analysis 38–9
  accounting 41, 43–52, 64–5
  business citizenship 123
  closing the loop 91–2
  and consumers 94–5, 109, 121, 122–3
  diversity and inclusion 152–3
  economic goals 166
  employees 141, 142, 152–3
  governance 35
  growth and profit 34–5
  impact at systemic level 168
  and keystone actors 75
  as last chance 160

Global Goals (continued)
    leadership 127, 129, 131, 133–8, 141,
        147, 149–50, 152–3
    and localism 88
    planetary goals 167
    power of common goals 31–3
    process-driven decision-making 133–5,
        152
    production and consumption 121
    purpose mapping 24–7
    purpose statement 169
    resilience-building 77–8, 92
    risk of ignoring 37–8
    roadmap 154–9
    societal goals 167
    stakeholders 138
    system traps dilemma 78–9
    systemic agency 92
    team leadership 136–8
Global Living Wage Initiative 88
Global Reporting Initiative (GRI) 46, 49
Global Sustainability Index Institute
    (UNGSII) 31, 45–6
global warming 45, 58, 62, 68
Good Business Charter initiative 23
Goodlife Goals 50, 94–5, 185n3
Google 140
governance 22, 35, 147
Graeber, David 114–15
Grant Thornton 147
Great Place to Work Institute 146
Great Smog of London (1952) 73–4
green growth 18
Green New Deal 18
greenhouse gas emissions 16, 45, 62, 63,
    172
Greenhouse Gas Protocol methodology
    172
Greenvest Solutions 44
greenwashing 20, 28, 31, 179
Greggs 113
growth
    anti-profit beliefs 15–17
    degrowth movement 18
    dilemma of 18
    green growth 18
    responsible growth 34
    zero growth 18
Grupp, Wolfgang 129–30

H
Haefeker, Walter 70
Hand, James 113
Harrison, Adam 98
Hearts FC 116–19
herd mentality 87, 102, 108
Hitchhiker's Guide to the Galaxy, The (Adams)
    7
Honda 85
human-centred rewards 141–2

I
Iceland 98
IKEA 23, 98
inclusion 143–4, 152–3
individual advocacy 137
individualism 114–15
industrial revolution 19–20
industrial symbiosis 86–7
information paralysis 101–2
Ingoldisthorpe, Norfolk 89
initial framing 126–7
Institute of Chartered Accountants in
    England and Wales 166
Institutional Investors Group on Climate
    Change 62
intention–behaviour gap 94, 107
interconnectedness 1–2, 40, 67, 68, 73, 83,
    117, 119, 170
interdependency 115, 119
Interface 16–17, 29, 85, 90, 150
Intergovernmental Panel on Climate
    Change (IPCC) 58
International Accounting Standards Board
    (IASB) 46
International Integrated Reporting Council
    (IIRC) 46
International Monetary Fund (IMF) 54
International Organization for
    Standardization (ISO) 46
intersectionality 32, 150, 153, 156, 179
investors 21, 45–6, 61–2, 76, 164, 180

J
Jackson, Tim 18
Jaguar Land Rover 85
Jobs, Steve 13

John Lewis 23
Just-In-Time manufacturing 149

K

Kahan, Dan 126–7
Kahneman, Daniel 101
Kalundborg Eco-Industrial Park, Denmark 86–7, 149
key performance indicators (KPIs) 40, 41, 43, 45, 141, 146
keystone actors 75, 184n27
Keystone Dialogues 75–6
Klein, Gary 125, 126
knowledge-sharing 149–50, 158
Kolditz, Tom 129

L

labelling 94, 96–100
leadership 8–9, 124–53
    actipreneurialism 140–1
    agile-business practice 132
    altruistic 128–9
    artificial intelligence (AI) 144–5
    biases 127, 129, 133
    collaborative working 149–50
    decision-making 125–7, 133–8, 152
    distributive model 131–2
    diversity and inclusion 143–4
    Global Goals (UN) 127, 129, 131, 133–8, 141, 147, 149–50, 152–3
    human-centred rewards 141–2
    innovation 149
    intersectionality 153
    knowledge-sharing 149–50
    long-term goals 149
    moral foundations 125
    motivation 129–30
    participative 127
    performativity 131
    and power 124–5, 128
    process-driven decision-making 133–6, 152
    recruitment 131
    responsible 128–31
    rhetoric vs reality 130–1
    solution aversion 127
    sustainable mindset 150–1
    team leadership 136–8
    and trust 146–7
    values 129–30
Leadership Development Program, Yale School of Management 129
League of Intrapreneurs 149
leasing model 85
Lever Brothers 21
LGBTQ+ staff 108, 143
life cycle of products 38, 61, 80, 82, 84–7, 99–100
    carbon scoping 148, 149, 172–3
lithium-ion batteries (LIBs) 85–6
living wage 88, 117, 156
Lloyds Banking Group Centre for Responsible Business 47
localism 87–8
long-term planning 149
loyalty 119, 146
Lyttle, John 130

M

machine learning (ML) 44, 45, 144–5
management by objectives 36, 63
management by team 136–8
market failure 62
marketing 96, 104
markets, decarbonization 61–2
Marks & Spencer 32
materiality 47
McDonalds's 87
McKinsey & Company 143
McNamara, Robert 48
meat-free alternatives 93, 113
MeToo 110
metrics
    align with Global Goals 45–50
    misleading 50–2
    purpose-led 64
    SIMPLE measures 43, 44
    SMART measures 36, 42–4
    of value 40–1
    vanity metrics 51, 56–7
    see also accounting
Microsoft 13–14
Millennium Development Goals (MDGs) 161
minimum wage 32

modelling 58–60
Mondelez International 98
monocausal narratives 68–71
Moraes, Caroline 120
moral currency 21
moral foundations 125
Myanmar 32

N
Naqvi, Al 144–5
NASA 58
Native 40
natural capital 41–2
nature
    value of 41–2, 54–5
    working with 88–90
nature reserves 89
negativity instinct 57
neonicotinoids 69–70
Neste 146–7
Nestlé 98
net zero carbon 16, 28, 29, 58, 62, 68, 82
    definition 81, 179
New York University's Stern School of
      Business 141
Nieuwenkamp, Roel 33
Nigerian Delta 52–3
Nike 29, 108
Norfolk Rivers Trust 89
nudges 107–8

O
Oatly 119
Ocean Rescue 112
OECD 33
Ofwat 30
Oil Spill Monitor (OSM) 52–3
open reporting 47, 52, 64–5
Operation Pollinator 70
overconsumption 100
Overton window 17
Owen, Robert 20
Oxfam 28, 72, 125

P
palm oil 74–5, 97–8

Panasonic 149
Paris Agreement 62, 81
partnerships 75–6, 77, 86
pattern recognition 125–6
pay, executives 147
peer pressure 108
Pepsi 119–20
Peru 88–9
pesticides 69–70
philanthropy 19–20
Pink, Daniel H. 141–2
planetary goals (UN Global Goals) 167
plastic bags 7, 66–7
plastics 66–7, 83, 84, 87, 112, 126
political consumerism 108
politics 44, 76–7, 126–7
pollinators 69–70, 90, 150
Polman, Paul 21
positive multiplier effect 32–3, 63, 78
post-truth world 63
poverty 24, 67, 168
power 124–5, 128
    see also leadership
precautionary principle 55, 65
price-gouging 99
price points 97
Primark 32
Principles for Responsible Banking 29
Principles for Responsible Investment
    21
process-driven decision-making 133–6,
    152
Proctor & Gamble 111
procurement 50–1, 80
product life cycle analysis 38
profit maximising 6, 13–35
    anti-profit beliefs 15–17
    business as more than 13–15, 17
    business exceptionalism 71–2
    governance 35
    growth dilemma 18
    positive multiplier effect 32–3
    purpose-mapping 24–7
    resilience and public trust 28–30
    responsible business and Global Goals
      34–5
    responsible profit and growth 34
    rise of responsible business 19–23
    trade-off fallacy 17

purpose
    accounting 49–50
    and anti-profit beliefs 15–17, 28
    backlash 164
    connecting with the Global Goals
        168–9
    and consumer support 111–14, 123
    definition 179
    employees 140–2
    mapping and measuring 24–7, 43, 45,
        134
    purpose-led metrics 64
    purpose-washing 28
    re-imagining 3
    statement of 14, 30, 169
purpose mapping 24–7
purpose-washing 28
PwC 43

Q

quantitative fallacy 48

R

Race at Work Charter 137
radical uncertainty 54–5
Rainforest Alliance 98
Rana Plaza, Bangladesh 39
raw materials 61, 80, 81, 85–6, 99–100,
    110
Raworth, Kate 18, 72, 150
recruitment 131
recycling 16, 84–7, 100
Refugee Councils 77
regulation 110–11
repair 31, 84, 85
resilience
    assessing 170–1
    complex adaptive systems theory (CAS)
        74–5
    definition 179
    resilience-building 29, 77–9, 89–90,
        92
    socio-ecological 59, 74–8
    system traps 79
Resilience Alliance 170–1
response diversity 90
Responsibility Reports 31

responsible business
    definition 179
    power of 33
    science of 34–4, 64–5, 91–2, 122–3,
        152–3
responsible business manifesto 9–10
Responsible Business Tracker 43
responsible growth 34
responsible profit 34
responsible production 92, 121
responsible radar 38–9
reuse 50, 66–7, 81, 84–7
Rhodes, Carl 120, 140
Richer, Julian 23
Richer Sounds 23
risk(s)
    non-disclosure of 47–8
    precautionary approach 55
    social boomerang effect 83
    in supply chains 38–9
    triage 134
    unsustainable 157
roadmap 154–9
Romanov, Vladimir 116, 118
Rosling, Hans 56–7, 68
Roundtable for Sustainable Palm Oil
    (RSPO) 98
Rowntree 20
rubber production 88–9
Rumsfeld, Donald 55

S

Samsung 84
satellite data 45
Save the Children 117
Schwartz, Shalom H. 104–6
Science Based Targets Initiative 80
Scotland 44
Seafood Business for Ocean Stewardship
    (SeaBOS) 75–6
Sedex 39
selective reporting 45–9
self-validation theory 103–4, 125
service model 85
shareholder primacy 22
Shell 31, 52–3
sideism 127
SIMPLE measures 43, 44

single-issue campaigns 66–8
single perspective instinct 68
single-use plastics 66–7, 87
six thinking hats technique 136
size instinct 56–7
Sky TV 85, 112
slavery 11, 20, 23, 38, 38–9, 130
small and medium-sized enterprises (SMEs)
    146
SMART measures 36, 42–4
smog 73–4
social boomerang effect 78, 83
social contracts 20, 30, 118, 119, 180,
    182n18
social enterprises 23, 49–50, 99, 112, 113,
    142
social media 121, 141
social movement, business as 111–14
social practice 106–8
social value 14–15, 29–30, 35, 113, 119–20,
    151, 180
socially responsible investing (SRI) 21, 22,
    46, 180
societal goals (UN Global Goals) 167
socio-ecological system
    and accounting 55–6, 58–9
    complex adaptive systems theory (CAS)
        73–5
    definition 180
    Doughnut Economics 72–3
    resilience 74–8
solution aversion 127
Sony 84
staff see employees
stakeholders
    and accounting 49, 52–3, 64–5
    circular economy 85–6, 111
    definition 180
    diversity and inclusion 144, 152–3
    engaging with 30, 65, 132, 138,
        153
    environmental, social and governance
        (ESG) 22
    football supporters 115–19
    and leadership 128, 130, 138, 146–7,
        150
    pressure from 2, 21, 81, 164
    responsible governance 35
    roadmap 156

stakeholder capitalism 28
    trust 146–7
    see also consumers; employees
Stansfield, Nigel 16
Starace, Francesco 137–8
state intervention 110–11
statistics 56–7
stewardship 76, 92, 118
Sullivan, Sian 42
supply chains 29
    blockchain 61, 99–100
    circularising of 135
    fishing industry 75–6
    interrogating 38–9
    process-driven decision-making
        134–5
    and trust 147
    worker conditions 24, 31, 38–9, 111,
        130
supporter-led businesses 115–20
Sustainability Accounting Standards Board
    (SASB) 46
sustainability, definition 180
Sustainable Development Goals (UN) see
    Global Goals (UN)
sustainable mindset 150–1, 153
Sustainable Scotland 44
Syngenta 69–70
System 1 and System 2 thinking 101, 102,
    103, 104, 106, 107, 126, 133
System of Environmental-Economic
    Accounting (SEEA) 41–2
system traps dilemma 78–9
systemic agency 92
systems thinking 151

T

Task Force on Climate- Related Financial
    Disclosures 46
task-related affect 104
Taylor, Alison 141
TCO Certified scheme 62
team leadership 136–8
technology, responsible use of 144–5
temperature rise 45, 58, 68, 80
Tesla 45
third party certification 62, 96–100
thresholds 57–60

Thunberg, Greta 18
tipping points 56, 59–60
tobacco industry 48
Townsend, Solitaire 94
Toyota 89, 149
trade-off fallacy 17
traffic light labelling 96
transparency 146, 147
    open reporting 47, 52, 64–5
Trehan, Kiran 144
Trigema 129–30
triple bottom line 22
trust
    business as trusted institution 139–40
    of consumers 97, 99–100, 119–20, 122,
        123, 146–7
    of employees 143, 146–7
    Global Goals (UN) 153
    importance of 146
    restoring 29–30
    small businesses 146
    trust audits 146–7
Trust Barometer 139–40, 146

U
UCL Institute for Innovation and Public
        Purpose 54–5
Unilever 21, 74–5, 112, 164
United Nations
    Global Compact 26, 129, 131, 134,
        138, 150
    Global Compass 46
    Global Sustainability Index Institute
        (UNGSII) 31, 45–6
    System of Environmental-Economic
        Accounting (SEEA) 41–2
    see also Global Goals (UN)

V
value chain
    carbon emissions 173
    circular economy 84–7
    definition 180
    digital sources of information 99–100
    importance of examining 79, 80, 123

Value Foundation 46
values 14–15, 20, 157
    consumers 104–6, 122
vanity metrics 51, 56–7
Vietnam War 48
Viridor 84
Volkswagen 29, 31, 108

W
wages 32, 88, 117, 156
Waitrose 112
Walmart 108
Warde, Alan 107, 109, 111–12
waste management 8–9
    circular economy 84–7
water companies 30, 89
water supply 32, 109
water treatment plants 89
We Mean Business 77
white supremacy 76
Wildhearts 49–50
Willard, Bob 77–8
woke capitalism 120, 140
woke-washing 113–14, 120
women 145
    empowering 49–50
    leadership roles 137, 143
    water collecting 32
Wonga 117
workforce see employees
working culture 141–4
World Benchmarking Alliance 43
World Business Council for Sustainable
        Development (WBCSD) 62–3
World Economic Forum 22, 28
World Health Organization 133
World Wide Generation 47
WWF 98

Y
Yankelovich, Daniel 48–9

Z
zero growth 18